Principles of Natural Language Processing

PRINCIPLES OF NATURAL LANGUAGE PROCESSING

SUSAN MCROY

Susan McRoy

Milwaukee

Principles of Natural Language Processing by Susan McRoy is licensed under a Creative Commons Attribution-NonCommercial 4.0 International License, except where otherwise noted.

Print ISBN 978-1-7376595-0-1

EPub ISBN 978-1-7376595-1-8

CONTENTS

	Acknowledgements	vii
	Preface	viii
1.	Natural Language Processing as a Discipline	1
2.	Data Structures and Processing Paradigms	25
3.	Overview of English Syntax	54
4.	Grammars and Syntactic Processing	81
5.	Semantics and Semantic Interpretation	126
6.	Benchmark Tasks for Language Modelling	164
7.	Discourse and Dialog	182
8.	Question Answering, Text Retrieval, Information Extraction, & Argumentation Mining	214
9.	Natural Language Generation, Summarization, & Translation	235
	Appendix: Top Down Chart Parsing	251

ACKNOWLEDGEMENTS

The cover image was created by Claire Ali, a mechanical engineer and amateur artist, who provided a custom digital version of an earlier work she created with paint on paper.

The book was created from camera-ready copy provided by the author, and although any errors contained are her own, the work has benefited from the contributions of many others. Along the way copy editing feedback was provided by Syed S. Ali, Mike Castillo, and students at the University of Wisconsin-Milwaukee. Advice on content and publishing was provided by Graeme Hirst and Ronnie Smith.

PREFACE

"I am putting myself to the fullest possible use, which is all I think that any conscious entity can ever hope to do."
As spoken by HAL 9000,
2001: A Space Odyssey (Kubrick, 1968)[1]

Creating computers that are as fluent in human language as people has long been a goal for scientists and the general public. Human language communication both represents and challenges an intelligence, because while languages appear to follow some unseen rules of spelling and grammar, we have never been certain about what they are. Even when one expert seems to have proof of a "universal" theory, another expert may be just as certain to have found an exception to it[2]. And yet, spoken or written language is still seen as the ideal for communicating with both people and complex devices. Systems that understand or use language, which we call "Natural Language Processing" (NLP) systems, have been created by specifying algorithms for computers based on the observable regularities of language noted by experts. There is even enough statistical regularity to language that, with enough examples of the right type, one can create highly accurate systems using methods that "learn" or "program themselves". The time has come when it may not always be clear whether the entity we are communicating with is another person or a "bot".

Read this book to learn the principles and methods of NLP to understand what it is, where it is useful, how to use it, and how it might be used people. The book includes the core topics of modern NLP, including an overview of the syntax and semantics of English, benchmark tasks for computational language modelling, and higher level tasks and applications that analyze or generate language, using both rule-based search and machine learning approaches. It takes the perspective of a computer scientist. The primary themes are abstraction, data, algorithms, applications and impacts. It also includes some history and trends that are important for understanding why things have been done in a certain way.

The book presumes basic proficiency in programming and discusses topics at that level. It does not attempt to teach the underlying mathematics, to reduce the overall length of the book. The book does not focus or depend on any particular programming language or software library, as there are now many options, for a variety of languages including Python, Java, and C++. Examples from the most widely used tools are provided.

This book will be appropriate for anyone who understands computing with data structures and wishes to get an overview of the field of natural language processing and recently developed methods. While background in artificial intelligence, linear algebra, linguistics, probability, or statistics would be helpful, this background is not essential for using this book. To use the software that is discussed, skill prerequisites include programming with arrays, tables, trees, graphs, graph search algorithms (e.g., breadth first and depth first) and installing open source software tools or libraries, such as Anaconda, the Natural Language Toolkit (NLTK) or spaCy. Readers with less programming background can often use online demonstration systems to learn about the capabilities of the different components of modern NLP systems. The book includes URLs to many of these systems that were active at the time the book was written, but the reader should be aware that some may disappear over time.

Notes

1. Kubrick, S. (1968). 2001: A Space Odyssey.
2. Everett, D. L. (2016). An Evaluation of Universal Grammar and the Phonological Mind. *Frontiers in Psychology*, 7, 15.

CHAPTER 1.

NATURAL LANGUAGE PROCESSING AS A DISCIPLINE

Natural language processing (NLP) is the discipline of designing and using computer programs to analyze or generate human language. Human language is an essential tool for expressing ideas, but it is also very diverse. On top of the differences in words and sentence structure of different groups, there are also differences that depend on how language is being used. Language can be formal or informal, technical or nontechnical, and occurs in a growing variety of forms from brief messages (like "tweets") to entire books. Another distinction is between **structured data** and **unstructured data**, sometimes called "free text". Structured text is where the fields of a table or record contain only a single phrase and the range of possible values is determined by the type of record. An example of structured text would be the fields of a database, which might include things like the name of the author, title, subject headings, and the publisher. An example of structured speech would be the phrase-level responses collected by an Interactive Voice Recognition system as it tries to route your call. Unstructured text is where the text contains one or more complete phrases or sentences, without an explicit indication about their intended use or interpretation. Examples of unstructured text are newspaper articles or a physicians' clinical notes. Examples of unstructured speech would be audio recordings of conversations or speeches.

Many documents contain both structured and unstructured text. Figure 1.1. shows examples of both types taken from the website of a gaming platform, *Steam*[1]. The text on the left contains structured data provided by the organizers, while the text on the right is the first sentence of a review posted by a website user.

Figure 1.1 Examples of structured and unstructured content from the Steam webpage for the game Dota 2

Some structured text	Some unstructured text
Title: Dota 2 Genre: Action, Free to Play, Strategy Developer: Valve Publisher: Valve Release Date: Jul 9, 2013 RECENT REVIEWS: Mostly Positive (6,921) ALL REVIEWS: Very Positive (1,004,927)	I started playing this game back when it was a mod on warcraft 3, it was great then, the community was ayy ok, not so bad, a little toxic but not too toxic...as the years went by I moved out from my parents house and had less time to play the game I had become addicted to, the game I would spend my Friday and Saturday night doing whilst the normal kids were out getting drunk on there 18th birthday.

Unstructured text can give valuable insights; for example, NLP can be used to automatically decide if opinions like these are negative or positive. Analyzing structured text can be useful for statistical analysis tasks, such as deciding which game genres are most popular or for building search applications for retrieving games or reviews. These differing degrees of structure will impact the methods needed to make sense of the data: the more structure, the less processing involved.

NLP is both a mature discipline going back to the 1950's[2] and a rapidly evolving discipline, exploiting some of the most recent advances in Artificial Intelligence, such as **Deep Learning**. While the structures and meaning of natural language have not changed much, new applications and implementation strategies have emerged to exploit the growing availability of large amounts of natural language data. Early approaches to NLP were based on researchers' own knowledge, or that of other experts, with limited amounts of evidence to validate the approach. Modern NLP often follows the following general pattern: Identify a real-world concern, obtain samples of relevant data, pre-process and mine data to suggest patterns and research questions, and then answer research questions or solve technical problems by finding functions that capture complex correlations among different aspects of the data and validating these models with statistical measures. For example, Figure 1.2 shows an example conceptualization of an important problem: discovering whether patients have experienced side effects while taking a medication that may not have been discovered during clinical testing when the drug was approved (and may not even have been yet reported to their medical provider).

Figure 1.2 Conceptualization of a typical NLP problem

Conceptualization	Example
Concern	New medications may have negative consequences that emerge after initial testing.
Data	Postings to social media by patients.
Patterns	Certain words reflect positive or negative opinions.
Question	What negative side effects (adverse drug events) are being mentioned most often?

NLP methods combine ideas from computer science and artificial intelligence with descriptive accounts of language and behavior, as provided by the humanities and the social and natural sciences. Human languages most differ from programming languages because of the possibility of **ambiguity**. Ambiguity arises because individual words can have different senses (such as "duck" as a water fowl and "duck" as the action of moving away from something). Words can also have unrelated, nonliteral meanings when they occur together with other words, such as "to duck a question". Ambiguity can also occur at the level of a sentence, as in "We saw a duck in the park", where it is unclear whether the viewer or the viewed was in the park. We do not tend to notice ambiguities like these when we communicate, because usually the context makes the intended meaning clear. An exception are puns, which are humorous exactly because we notice both meanings at once. Figure 1.3 includes an example pun.

Figure 1.3 Example of a pun

Pun	Multiple meanings
Our pet duck keeps biting everyone, so I bought a cheap muzzle for it. Nothing flashy, **but it fits the bill.**	"fits the bill" as an idiom (i.e., "suitable for the purpose") "fits the bill" as a compositional expression ("the right size for the beak of a duck")

Another source of complexity is that language exists at multiple levels of abstraction at the same time. Language produced in context has a literal form (what was said or written) and an intended meaning, which can be explicit or can involve inference to obtain implicitly expressed meanings[3]. An example of this literal/non-literal ambiguity occurs with "Can you pass the duck?," which has the literal form of a yes-no question, but is also used as a request.

To help address these multiple levels of meaning, the discipline of natural language processing draws upon insights from many disciplines including linguistics, mathematics, philosophy, sociology, and computer science. These disciplines have a long history of trying to explain linguistic phenomena or to provide an analysis of human behavior, based on text. (The first concordance of the Bible was created in 1230[4].) Today, insights from these earlier analyses have been used to specify properties of words and methods for identifying legal sequences of words. These insights have also helped us to identify some core tasks for language models such as determining whether a given sequence of words can be derived from the rules of a language, selecting among multiple possible derivations for a sequence, extracting semantic information from sequences, and determining whether accepting the truth of one expression of natural language requires accepting the truth of some other.

1.1 APPLICATIONS OF NLP

Natural language processing is both a method of science and of practical applications. Analyzing human language can help us learn about people who are the target of a product or service or to extract information from user-generated content, to inform the design of new products and services. Information extraction identifies concepts useful for other programs, such as looking for mentions of symptoms in a doctor's notes to aid in decision support or to map what had been expressed as unstructured, free text into relations in a database (structured data). Language analysis can be a part of assessing the writing or the writer, such as to improve the grammar of a document or to measure a writer's skill or knowledge. Generating human language can be a way of presenting structured information in a more understandable or personalized form.

NLP can also be a mechanism for qualitative research. Qualitative research is a method of gaining information from a target population typically by asking a sample to complete a carefully crafted survey and then looking for emergent themes. However, survey bias is always a risk; it is very hard to write questions to test a hypothesis without survey subjects being able to detect what the hypothesis is, which might easily affect their response. An alternative is to look for instances where people have expressed their views on a topic publicly. Social scientists, market researchers, and healthcare providers have been investigating what people have said in their posted reviews of products, services, and medicines through websites like Amazon.com, Yelp.com, and Drugs.com. In the next few sections, we will overview some specific examples and potential opportunities in three broad areas: applications to support social good, applications to support public health or health care, and applications to support business.

1.1.1 Applications for Social Good

There are many dangers in our world, including terrorists, bullies, and even ourselves (when our concerns become depression or anxiety.) The internet has become a place where many of these dangers first appear. In March 2019, there was a mass shooting in New Zealand in which at least 49 people died. According to investigations by journalists, the shooter had been posting to online message boards associated with violence as many as three years before the tragedy[5]. NLP has also been used to identify reports of natural disasters posted to Twitter.[6] We also face some smaller dangers such as poor hygiene in restaurants or intentional misinformation posted to reviews of consumer products and services. In each of these scenarios, NLP could play a role in early detection of such dangers by processing articles created by news services or the postings of the general public in online social media like Twitter, Facebook, and Reddit, much faster than people could. Research on the detection of fake reviews, hate speech and cyberbullying, and depression has been ongoing since 2009, and are now accurate more than three-quarters of the time[7].

In addition to helping keep people safe, NLP also has applications that can help people improve the quality of their lives. For example, there are efforts to help people with visual impairments by automatically translating visual information on the Web into non-visual information, such as a spoken description. There has also been an increasing interest in the creation of chatbots to support humanitarian causes. For example, in 2018, the Computer-Human Interaction (CHI) conference organized a Special Interest Group (SIG) meeting dedicated entirely to creating chatbots for social good. Examples of social good that were discussed include helping find donors to support worthy causes and helping promote social justice by allowing people to document and share their experiences with the police.

1.1.2 Applications for Public Health and Health Care

Public Health involves preventing illness; healthcare involves diagnosing and treating illness. Natural language processing applications related to these topics can help in the dissemination of knowledge about how to stay healthy and the development of new treatments by helping to find associations between diseases and treatments that span multiple published articles. NLP can call attention to consumer-reported problems with medications, treatments, or contaminated food – reports which might appear in social media before formal reports are submitted to government agencies, such as the FDA or the USDA in the United States. NLP is being used to improve health care quality by giving providers quantitative evidence of which treatments are most effective for particular populations of patients. It is still the case that there are clinically documented features and risk factors (such as smoking status or social determinants) that only appear in unstructured clinical notes in electronic health records, rather than in more easily processed data from structured checklists. There are some health conditions where the best treatment option is also dependent on the values or preferences of a patient, but to play a role in more shared decision-making, patients also need to have a good understanding of their condition and options. NLP methods can help assure that they have this understanding and that their concerns are being addressed, by providing descriptions in appropriate language or giving them more opportunities to obtain health information outside a clinical encounter.

In the future NLP may be able to improve the communication between providers and patients by allowing providers to "talk" to their medical records software and their patient at the same time – rather than appearing to remove their focus from the patient. Major health care providers and U.S. government research institutes (including the Mayo Clinic, Harvard Medical School and Massachusetts General Hospital, and the National Library of Medicine) have longstanding research units dedicated to NLP and have been leaders in the dissemination of software and data sets to advance the discipline. There have also been commercial enterprises dedicated to NLP in healthcare, such as TriNetX.

1.1.3 Applications for Business and Commercial Enterprises

Applications of NLP can be used to meet commercial objectives. A company might provide language services such as machine translation, abstraction, summarization or some type of document delivery. For example, starting in the 1970's both LexisNexis and Westlaw began to provide computer-assisted legal research services for professionals; and now these companies provide access to more than 40,000 databases of case law, state and federal statutes, administrative codes, newspaper and magazine articles, public records, law journals, law reviews, treatises, legal forms, and other information resources. Banks and providers of financial services technology are using NLP to help detect fraud. (Ironically, this work has been helped by the availability of datasets derived from Enron employee email[8], following one of the most notorious cases of investment fraud in American history.) Or, a company might be interested in using NLP for keeping their customers engaged or providing them solutions targeted towards their expressed needs or buying habits. (Tasks such as these, as well as customer relationship management (CRM) and customer support, can be found in online job advertisements.) By using NLP, employers hope to automate tedious data entry tasks that require extracting data from unstructured sources such as email, customer support requests, social media profiles, service logs, and automatically populate contact record with individual and company names, email, and physical addresses. They might also want to more easily use data that has been collected in unstructured form, such as website text boxes or telephone calls recorded for quality assurance. Sometimes the goal is to improve customer engagement by answering common customer questions more quickly by deploying a chatbot, rather than making people wait for a human to respond.

Businesses want to know whether customers like their products and why. Very accurate techniques have been developed to recognize whether people are positive or negative about a product based on the words they use in their reviews (called sentiment analysis or opinion mining). A similar strategy can be used for other classification tasks. For example, marketing expert Anne Gherini, has observed that (her) "customers use different words, phrases, and sentence structures at different stages of the buying cycle. Whereas, they tend to use interrogatives such as "who", "what", and "why" in the early stages, they tend to use verbs such as "purchase", "become", "guarantee", and "discuss" in later stages"[9]. These insights suggest that it would be useful to have automatic methods for processing email and other customer communications to predict that customer's stage of the buying cycle (and hence how ready they might be to make a purchase) and even to help generate a reply correctly targeted to the stage. Using data from a variety of existing sources, one can use NLP tools to count the frequency of co-occurring words, phrases, or statistically related words to count potentially emergent themes, one of the fundamental methods of qualitative research[10].

1.2 MAIN ABSTRACTIONS OF NATURAL LANGUAGES

As just discussed, human language can be used to help solve a variety of problems. While human languages are very diverse, there are also many commonalities among languages that enable us to develop many generalizable models and tools. According to classical linguistics, the main levels of abstraction for language are syntax, semantics, and pragmatics[11]:

- ***Syntax*** comprises the rules, principles, and processes that appear to govern the structure of sentences, especially rules that might be common across human languages.

- **Semantics** comprises the interpretation of sequences of words into an expression or set of expressions that captures the entities, relations, propositions, and events in the "real world" they describe or to elements of some "world" created by humans (such as queries to a database). Semantics is what we talk about as "the meaning" of a sentence.

- **Pragmatics** comprises an understanding or representation of how language is used by people to do things, such as make requests or ask questions, or what language reveals about the knowledge or preferences of the people who use it. For example, the sentence "Can you pass the salt?" is not typically a yes-no question, it is a request.

Where language is compositional, smaller units (such as words and phrases) have well-formed meanings that combine in a systematic way to form the meanings of the larger sequences they comprise. An example of a compositional semantics might map each word or phrase onto a relation in a logic. So, "Anu ate a small apple" might be represented as: [person(p1) and name(p1,"Anu") and small(o1) and apple(o1) and event(e1,eat) and agent(e1,p1) and object(e1,o1)]. By contrast, some expressions are idiomatic, forming what are sometimes called collocations or multiword expressions. These expressions are relatively fixed sequences of words that function together as a single word. Examples in English include "see the light at the end of the tunnel" which means to "see a future time that is better than the current one" or "bite off more than one can chew" which means to "have taken on a task one cannot achieve". Another type of non-compositionality arises when we use sequences of common words to give names to organizations or events, such as "Educational Testing Service" or "The Fourth of July".

Philosophers of language classify language along lines similar to linguists' notions of syntax, semantics, and pragmatics. For example, J. L. Austin describes language in terms of a hierarchy of actions, beginning with the **locution**, which is what was said and meant, and corresponds to the physical act of uttering a specific word or sequence of words (the "phone"), as well as its intended interpretation as a sentence (the "pheme") and its referring to specific objects and relations (the "rheme"). The interpretation of the locutions form the **illocution** which includes the intended interpretation of what was done (e.g. making a statement or asking a question). The final level comprises the **perlocution**, which is what happened as a result – (e.g. eliciting an answer). Both approaches begin with the word as the smallest unit of analysis, although new words can be formed from existing ones by adding prefixes and suffixes, a process that is known as **derivational morphology**. Morphology is also used to change the grammatical properties of a word, a process known as **inflectional morphology**.

The specific categories and properties that describe the syntax of a language form its grammar. Evidence for the existence of specific categories comes from the patterns of usage that native speakers find acceptable. Early work involved field studies – asking native speakers to classify sentences as good or not. Today we have additional resources: we can used published documents and datasets of sentences annotated with grammatical features as positive examples – and treat anything not covered by these resources as ungrammatical. Another source of grammaticality information are the papers written by linguists themselves which often have included examples of ungrammatical sentences marked with an asterisk (*)[12].

Unacceptability may be due to any of the levels of abstraction. Figure 1.4 includes some examples and the level where the inappropriateness occurs.

Figure 1.4 Examples of acceptability judgements.

Level of abstraction	Acceptable	Unacceptable
Morphology	Maryann should leave	*Maryann should leaving
Syntax	What did Bill buy	*What did Bill buy potatoes
Semantics	Kim wanted it to rain.	*Kim persuaded it to rain.
Pragmatics	Saying: "What time is it?" as a question; when the hearer does not think the speaker already knows the time.	*Saying: "What time is it?" as a question; when the hearer thinks the speaker already knows the time.

Most of these judgements would be clear to someone who is fluent in English, except perhaps the example for pragmatics. Pragmatics relies on background information not contained in the sentence itself, so multiple scenarios are provided. The underlying background for the example is that it is only appropriate to ask a real question when it is likely that the person asking does not know the answer, because the intended effect of a normal question is to solicit new information. Questions can be used appropriately to do other things however, such as make complaints or indirectly solicit an explanation. A collection of sentences including both acceptable and unacceptable examples, including morphology, syntax, and semantics, is found in the Corpus of Linguistic Acceptability (CoLA). (Chapter 3 will describe the grammar for English as accepted by most modern work in NLP, which was derived from work in computational linguistics.)

1.2.1 Abstractions at the Word Level

Words have a syntax and a semantics, and may also be categorized based on some aspect of their use. One very commonly used aspect is sentiment. Sentiment is the overall polarity of opinion expressed by the speaker, which might be positive, negative, or neutral. Sentiment is expressed through the choice of words that are conventionally associated with that polarity, which might differ for a specific domain. For example, a book might be "fascinating" (positive) or "predictable". (We will consider sentiment analysis in greater detail in Chapter 3.) The syntax of a word includes its main part of speech (such as noun or verb) and subtypes of these categories, based on their properties, such as a plural noun, or a past tense verb. As mentioned above, there is no one standard set of categories, although there are sets of categories that have become standardized. Standardized sets of category labels are known as tagsets, and a specific example will be provided when we discuss English grammar. One can also describe categories as collections of features. In addition to properties like number and tense, a word type is characterized by the constraints or preferences it has for words or phrases that precede or follow it. For example, some nouns, like "bag" must be preceded by an article and are often followed by a modifier that says what holds, as in "a bag of rice". (We will discuss word syntax in greater detail in Chapter 4). The semantics of a word is the concept or relation that the word would correspond to in the real world. Because of the existence of homonyms, the mapping from a word to semantics (or even syntax) requires information from the context (either surrounding sentences or a representation of the visible context) to determine the intended analysis. Figure 1.5 shows the entries for duck found in Wordnet 3.1[13], which contains four distinct noun senses and four verb senses for duck.

Figure 1.5 Senses of duck found in WordNet 3.1 online (http://wordnetweb.princeton.edu/perl/webwn)

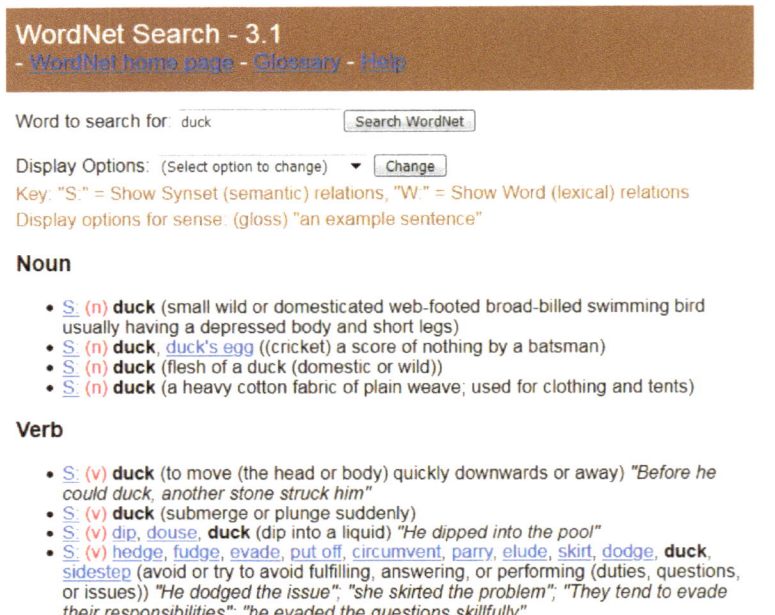

1.2.2 Abstractions at the Phrase and Sentence Level

Words in sequences form phrases and sentences. The difference between a phrase and a sentence is that a phrase must describe a complete entity or property-value pair, but it does not fully describe an event or state of affairs. A sentence by contrast, will have a main predicate, typically a verb, and some number of arguments and modifiers. A simple example would be the declarative sentence: "The cat sat on the mat." Regardless of whether it is true, it is complete because it says who did the sitting and where it sat. In English, we can also have passive sentences, such as "The mat was sat upon" which are also complete, even though who did the sitting is unknown. The phrase and sentence types of a language are determined in much the same way as its word level categories. Linguists may ask native speakers to judge the acceptability of combinations of words. They may also try replacing a whole sequence of words with some other sequence and ask about its acceptability, as a way of testing whether those sequences correspond to the same type of phrase.

Phrases and sentences have a syntax, semantics, and a pragmatic interpretation. They can also be labelled with general categories. One commonly used classification is by sentiment, which was discussed above as a word-level abstraction. The syntax of a phrase or sentence specifies the acceptable linear order of words, and the hierarchical structure of groups of words, which is called constituency. Both order and constituency constraints can be described by a grammar, using either a set of production rules, such as Context Free Grammar, or as a set of dependency relations among words. (We will discuss examples of grammars for English phrases and sentences in Chapter 4.) A parse tree represents a trace of a derivation of a sentence from a given grammar.

The semantics of a phrase can be shallow or deep. A shallow representation involves labeling the phrases of a sentence with semantic roles with respect to a target word, typically the main verb.

For example, the following sentence

> The doctor gave the child a sticker.

would have roles labeled as follows:

> [AGENT The doctor] **gave** [RECEPIENT the child] [THEME a sticker].

A deep semantics of a phrase or a sentence is an expression in some formal logic or structured computational framework that maps the words onto the units of that framework. In a logic that would include terms and well-formed formulas, whereas a computational approach might use an ad hoc slot and filler structure (such as a record in Java or an object in Python or C).

The pragmatics of a phrase or a sentence captures how it is being used in context. We will discuss these in Chapter 6.

1.2.3 Abstractions above the Sentence Level

We can also consider language forming units larger than a single sentence. The larger units include paragraphs and documents, but also include structures derived from interactive communication, such as dialog or multi-party interaction. Unstructured representations include sets of discrete words or continuous (weighted) vectors of words, which ignore the order or syntactic structure within the original units. These representations are used for information retrieval where the goal is to facilitate matching rather than to extract information. Structured representations include ad hoc slot and filler representations, similar to what is done for single sentences, but meant to capture complex events described in say, a news article. Structured representations can also include tree or graph-like structures, where phrases or sentences combine to form higher order relations, such as question-answer, or cause-effect that can be represented as hierarchical structures based on semantics or rhetorical relations (e.g., justification or concession). Collections of such structures are contained in the Penn Discourse Treebank and Rhetorical Structure Theory Discourse Treebank, respectively.

1.3 SUBTASKS OF NATURAL LANGUAGE PROCESSING

In computer science, qualitative insights have been expressed as both declarative representations (sets of facts) and processing models (procedures and functions). Early work relied on representations created entirely by hand, by highly trained experts, and used search algorithms to derive a solution. Now, one can often use input representations and processing models that have been created by algorithms whose parameters have been adjusted automatically using raw (or lightly processed) data. Moreover, this data is often made available for use by anyone and the algorithms also exist in open source libraries.

Pipelines for processing unstructured natural language start with the text (possibly including metadata, such as HTML tags) and convert it into a form that is usable by a software application before applying a sequence of algorithms that each perform a different automated analysis and create outputs, in stages. These stages may be defined independently or as a single networked architecture with layers that address specific tasks. Figure 1.6 illustrates the default pipeline used in spaCy, a widely used NLP software library [14]. First there is a process, called **tokenization**, where the boundaries between words are identified (usually when there is a space) and punctuation is removed. Tokenization typically also includes identifying the root form of a word (also called its type, or lexeme). The next steps enrich the input representation, such as by labelling individual words with their syntactic category (e.g. "noun"), a process called **part of speech tagging** which is performed by a tagger. This process is normally followed by **lemmatization** (not shown) which involves identifying the root form of a word and syntactic attributes (such as past or plural). Then sequences of words from the text are labelled with their syntactic function (e.g., subject or object). This process is called parsing and is performed by a parser. Processing might stop here, or it might continue by recognizing and labelling specific expressions with a general semantic type, such as names of people, locations or times, by a process called **named entity recognition** (NER). Sometimes words, phrases, or sentences will also be annotated with a representation of their meaning.

Figure 1.6 Typical NLP pipeline. (Image by spaCy.io)

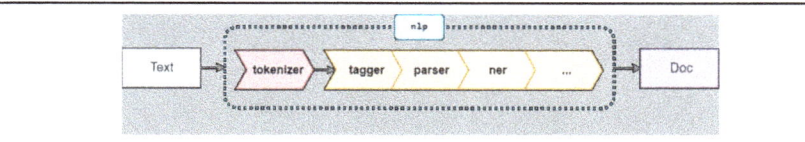

After the input sequence is suitably enriched, the result is a complex data structure that is represented in the figure as "Doc". This structure can be used to form a descriptive analysis of a text (or set of texts), fed into another processes for automated categorization or used as input to a software application, such as a text summarization system. An NLP pipeline might also be extended to integrate the results with the results from previously processed sentences, such as to identify the overall rhetorical structure (e.g., one text might explain or elaborate upon another), or to identify when entities mentioned in multiple sentences are in fact talking about the same entity (a process called reference resolution). These latter steps are not standardized and are topics for current research and development.

Although many natural language tasks can be accomplished using existing software libraries, using them effectively still involves human judgement and skill. Only human judgement can determine what problems or opportunities are both worthy and feasible. The first task for many is to identify and obtain suitable data. If the data does not yet exist, one can plan a method for creating new data, such as through web-scraping or conducting a survey study. The difficulty of these tasks will vary across domains. Obtaining "personal information" such as health or financial records is the most difficult, because there are typically laws to protect the privacy of patients (e.g. HIPAA)[15] and safeguards must be put in place to prevent unintended breeches of security. Instead, one may need to develop methods using older data (the records of the dead are not protected) or data that has been de-identified and made public. After one has data, the next task is to select (or develop) methods for processing it that are appropriate to the amount of data. If there is only a small amount, then one might hand-craft the structures or rules for processing. Voice applications, such as chat bots, are often developed this way.

When there is a moderate amount of un-annotated data for a task, one can develop a phased strategy beginning with hand-annotation or data labelled with hand-written rules and then use the labelled data to train an algorithm to do the rest of the task. For problems with large quantities of existing data, there may be a way to interpret part of the data as a label for a task, such as the number of stars in a product review. Then one can train an algorithm to label other similar examples. Algorithms that learn strategies for labelling (or assigning a probability distribution to a set of possible labels) are what is meant by machine learning and the models they create include both statistical classifiers and neural networks. It is usually necessary to experiment with a variety of alternative learning strategies to see what works best, including reusing models from existing systems, or coding a moderate amount of data by hand and then using it to train a model to code a larger set. Classification-based approaches often treat the structures produced by NLP as input features, but classifiers can also be used to perform many of the tasks in the NLP pipeline. Open source data science workbench tools, such as Weka, allow one to compare different strategies easily, by providing most of the algorithms and configuration alternatives that one might want, without installing any additional software. Workbenches allow one to select data, algorithms, and parameter settings using simple menus and check boxes, and provide functions for analyzing or visualizing the results.

1.4 RESOURCES FOR NLP: TOOLKITS, DATASETS, AND BOOKS

The availability of resources for NLP has been increasing, to serve a wide range of needs. A recent search of software tool kits for NLP with updates with in the past 5 years yielded at least 11 different systems, spanning several programming languages and architecture (see Figure 1.7). A few organizations (AllenAI, Google, Microsoft, and Stanford) have created online demos that have helped people to understand some of the terminology of NLP (by providing concrete examples). Figure 1.8 lists some notable demos that provide word and sentence level analysis in real-time for examples submitted by visitors to the website, without creating an account or downloading any software.

Publicly available datasets are also propelling the field forward. Datasets have been collected from a variety of genres. The oldest collection of freely available text, spanning multiple genres, is the Brown Corpus. The largest public collection of cultural works is distributed by Project Gutenberg, which contains over 60,000 complete literary works in electronic form. The most widely used annotated data resource for NLP has been the Penn Treebank. The Linguistic Data Consortium distributes many NLP specific datasets, some openly and some for a licensing fee. Totally free datasets can be obtained from the Stanford Natural Language Processing Group, the Apache Software Foundation, the Amazon Open Data Registry, and Kaggle.com, to name a few. There are also online discussion groups devoted to the discussion of datasets themselves, e.g the Reddit forum, r/datasets.

In addition to the documentation for the software frameworks mentioned above, there are some notable books that include examples of NLP programming using specific programming languages. The book "Natural Language Processing with Python: Analyzing Text with the Natural Language Toolkit[16]" is freely available online under a Creative Commons License (CC-BY-NC-ND), in addition to its printed version. Other books (e.g. for Java or a tool like PyTorch) are offered as part of a monthly subscription service that often includes a free trial. One of them might be a good companion to this book.

Figure 1.7 Software libraries and tool kits for NLP

Name of Project	What it is
AllenNLP	PyTorch-based toolkit for most medium and high level NLP tasks; includes Elmo word vectors
ClearTK	UIMA wrappers for NL tools (Snowball stemmer, OpenNLP tools, MaltParser dependency parser, and Stanford CoreNLP) and UIMA corpus readers
FRED	Machine reading produces RDF/OWL ontologies and linked data from natural language sentences, includes Named Entity Resolution and Word-Sense Disambiguation, as a REST service or Python library
GATE	Java framework for most symbolic NLP tasks
Gensim	Python software library for topic modelling and similarity detection, with an embedded word2vec implementation
Natural language Tool Kit (NLTK)	Python software library for most symbolic and statistical NLP tasks with access to many corpora for many languages (widely used in education)
Scikit-learn	General Python toolkit for ML, but also has functions for text analytics (e.g., tokenization, classification)
spaCy	Industrial strength libraries for NLP, loadable via Conda or pip, but has only a dependency parser
Stanford CoreNLP	Java software library (with Python wrappers) for most symbolic NLP tasks; maintained by Stanford researchers (used in education and production systems)
SyntaxNet	Tensorflow-based toolkit for dependency parsing; created by Google
Textblob	Python libraries for most common NLP tasks; built from NLTK but somewhat easier to use, by Steven Loria
Tweet NLP	Python software for most NLP task, trained on Twitter data; older versions for Java 6 also available (now maintained by CMU researchers)
Weka	Java datamining software including many NLP tasks with GUI/API; maintained by researchers at the University if Waikato, NZ. Also has WekaDeeplearning4j

Figure 1.8 Examples of online demos for NLP tool kits with unrestricted access

Software Demo	Location on the web
AllenNLP demos of semantic labelling, sentence labelling in several formats, reading comprehension, and semantic parsing	https://demo.allennlp.org/
FRED demos of machine reading	http://wit.istc.cnr.it/stlab-tools/fred/demo/
Google Parsey McParseface demo of dependency parsing	https://deepai.org/machine-learning-model/parseymcparseface
Stanford CoreNLP demos of word, phrase, and sentence level annotation in several formats	corenlp.run

1.5 OUTLINE OF THE REST OF THIS BOOK

This chapter presented an overview of the discipline of natural language processing. The goal was to convey both the scope of the discipline and some of the key application areas and knowledge-level abstractions. Chapter 2 will consider abstractions at the data and processing level, to overview the types of methods used to solve the subtasks of NLP. Chapter 3 presents an overview of English Syntax. Chapter 4 discusses grammars and parsing. Chapter 5 covers semantics and semantic interpretation. Chapter 6 presents modern benchmark tasks for language modelling, including grammaticality analysis and sentiment analysis. Chapter 7 covers the analysis of multi-sentential texts, including discourse and dialog. Chapter 8 covers various applications of, and methods for, text content analysis, including question answering and information extraction. Chapter 9 covers applications of, and methods for, text generation, including machine translation and summarization.

1.6 SUMMARY

Natural language processing is a discipline that allows us to tap into one of the richest resources of human experience. It is hard to even imagine an area of social or commercial interest that does not result in artifacts containing natural language. Although natural languages and the purposes for which we use it are diverse, there are essential abstractions that are essential to all of them: words, sentences, syntax, semantics, and pragmatics that create an opportunity for creating generalizable methods for analyzing language. While the first NLP methods relied on small sets of examples and a high level of human expertise, there are now large sets of digitized data that have been made available for public use that makes methods based on large data sets and the latest advances in artificial intelligence feasible. Additionally, today there are many highly accurate, freely available software tools for analyzing natural language.

Notes

1. Steam (2021) Dota 2 URL https://store.steampowered.com/app/570/Dota_2/ (Accessed June 2021).
2. Hutchins, J. (1998). Milestones in Machine Translation. No.4: The First Machine Translation Conference, June 1952 *Language Today* (13), 12–13
3. Austin, J. L. (1962). *How to Do Things with Words.* Cambridge: Harvard University Press.
4. Fenlon, J.F. (1908). Concordances of the Bible. In *The Catholic Encyclopedia.* New York: Robert Appleton Company. Retrieved April 19, 2020 from New Advent: http://www.newadvent.org/cathen/04195a.htm
5. Mann, A., Nguyen, K. Gregory, K. (2019). Christchurch shooting accused Brenton Tarrant supports Australian far-right figure Blair Cottrell. Australian Broadcasting Corporation. Archived from the original on 23 March 2019. URL:https://web.archive.org/web/20190323014001/https://www.abc.net.au/news/2019-03-23/christchurch-shooting-accused-praised-blair-cottrell/10930632.
6. Maldonado, M., Alulema, D., Morocho, D. and Proaño, M. (2016). System for Monitoring Natural Disasters using Natural Language Processing in the Social Network Twitter. In *Proceedings of the 2016 IEEE International Carnahan Conference on Security Technology*

(ICCST), pp. 1-6.

7. Zhang, Z., Robinson, D. and Tepper, J. (2018). Hate Speech Detection Using a Convolution-LSTM Based Deep Neural Network. In *Proceedings of the 2018 World Wide Web Conference* (WWW '18).

8. There are many datasets based on the Enron email data. One of the more recent and well-docmented versions is distributed by researchers at the University of British Columbia from their project website. URL: https://www.cs.ubc.ca/cs-research/lci/research-groups/natural-language-processing/bc3.html (Accessed June 2021)

9. Gherini, A. (2018). Natural Language Processing is Revolutionizing CRM. Published online August 14, 2018. URL: https://aithority.com/guest-authors/natural-language-processing-is-revolutionizing-crm/ Accessed January 2021.

10. Austin, Z., and Sutton, J. (2014). Qualitative Research: Getting Started. *The Canadian Journal of Hospital Pharmacy*, 67(6), 436–440. https://doi.org/10.4212/cjhp.v67i6.1406.

11. Silverstein, M. (1972). Linguistic Theory: Syntax, Semantics, Pragmatics. *Annual Review of Anthropology*, 1, 349-382. Retrieved April 19, 2020, from www.jstor.org/stable/2949248

12. Warstadt, A., Singh, A. and Bowman, S. R. (2018). Neural Network Acceptability Judgments, arXiv preprint arXiv:1805.12471.

13. Princeton University (2020). WordNet: A Lexical Database for English.

14. spaCy.io, 2019. Language Processing Pipelines (Image) URL: https://spacy.io/usage/processing-pipelines Accessed April 2019.

15. Moore, W. and Frye, S. (2019). Review of HIPAA, Part 1: History, Protected Health Information, and Privacy and Security Rules. *The Journal of Nuclear Medicine Technology* 47: 269 - 272.

16. Bird, S., Klein, E., and Loper, E. (2021). *Natural Language Processing with Python*. URL:https://www.nltk.org/book/ Accessed January 2021.

CHAPTER 2.

DATA STRUCTURES AND PROCESSING PARADIGMS

This chapter discusses the most commonly used data structures and general problem solving strategies for natural language processing (NLP). Many data structures of NLP reflect the structure of language itself. Language in use has both a sequential order and a hierarchical structure. Thus, data structures such as strings, lists, trees, and graphs are commonly used. Other essential data structures for NLP reflect the processes of statistical machine learning and data science, where vectors and their generalizations, called tensors, are used for representing associations between entities and values, such as probability distributions over categories.

The main processing paradigms for NLP are search and classification. The search methods all derive from techniques for searching graphs that are common across computing, such as breadth-first and depth-first search. NLP also makes use of AI-specific techniques that aim to make the search more efficient by modifying the order of the traversal. As an abstract process, search is a method for addressing questions, where we do not have a set of candidate answers, such as finding out *how* a sentence can be derived from a set of rules. By contrast, classification is a method for addressing questions, where we do have a set of candidate answers. We call the systems that select or rank the answers "classifiers". There is a search process, but it usually only occurs when we build the classifier, rather than when it is used. However, some implementations of classifiers first create a probability distribution over the candidate answers and then use search as a final step to find the best one.

The construction of modern classifiers uses machine learning. Machine learning systems take minimally processed data as input and iteratively adjust the values of internal parameters, to build models that optimize some function, such as minimizing the error over some set where the answer for each is known. This phase is called training. It is a type of search where each step involves increasing or decreasing the value of numeric variables and evaluating the impact on the error measure. Training often takes a long time, (and a large amount of data) to create an accurate model, but during use classifiers are very fast – and robust because they always provide an answer. However, when a problem is new, training data may not yet exist, so we may start with a search-based method.

We will start by discussing data structures and then two processing paradigms and their application to NLP. We will also take a more in-depth look at machine learning, since it plays such an important role in current implementations of NLP.

2.1 THE DATA STRUCTURES FOR NATURAL LANGUAGE PROCESSING

The data structures most common to NLP are strings, lists, vectors, trees, and graphs. All of these are types of sequences, which are ordered collections of elements. Unprocessed data is usually input as string data which are processed into lists or vectors, representing individual words, before subsequent processing in the NLP pipeline. This processed data is usually not just a list or vector of strings, but sequences of complex objects that keep track of various attributes associated with each token, such as part of speech. Later stages may add additional annotations, such as marking the beginnings and endings of important sequences within a sentence, such as the names of entities. This section will overview the most commonly used data types along with examples of their application in NLP.

2.1.1 Strings

Strings are sequences of characters. They are the primary way that unprocessed text data is represented in NLP systems. One string may be used to hold an entire document, a line of a text file, a sentence, or a single word. Important operations for strings include concatenation (creating a string by sequentially combining two input strings into one), matching substrings (e.g., to check for a prefix or suffix), and finding the length of a string (e.g., strings that are very short might be abbreviations). Specifying patterns within strings, such as punctuation or word endings, is usually done by means of strings of text that allow one to name specific characters, possible ranges of characters (such as [a-z]), and how often they occur (e.g., once, zero or more, or one or more times). These formatted strings are called **regular expressions** and have been in use since the 1940's but have become more standardized over time, such as the POSIX Basic Regular Expression (BRE) format.[12]

Today, most programming languages (e.g. C++, Python, and Java) have functions for handling regular expressions[3]. They also have mechanisms for specifying substrings (slicing) or particular ranges of characters within a string. When input to an NLP system is provided as a string, the first thing the system will need to do is separate the string into separate words and sentences. This step is called tokenization. The general idea is to use whitespace as a delimiter, but the task must also consider special cases, such as contractions and quoted speech. Software libraries for NLP, such as spaCy and the Natural Language Toolkit (NLTK), include prebuilt functions for tokenizing sentences. NLTK includes five different options, each of which provides slightly different results.[4] Sometimes, getting tokenization right requires using hand-built patterns, because people will differ in punctuation habits, such as placing quote marks or parentheses inside or outside end-of-sentence punctuation.

2.1.2 Lists

Lists and vectors are both ordered collection of elements. Lists are used to hold sequences where the sizes of elements might vary, such as sequences of words. Lists can also have more or less elements over time. (Lists that are immutable during the execution of a program are sometimes called tuples.) Some programming languages allow direct access to elements of a list using an index, while some may only allow iterating through them sequentially from the front. Lists (and more generally sequences) are often used as the representation format for sharing results between different stages of an NLP pipeline; for example each element corresponds to all the information about a particular token in the order in which it occurred in the original input.

Important operations over lists include being able to find individual elements or patterns of elements within the list. Patterns over elements of a list can make use of regular expressions for looking within a single token or a list of tokens. For example, the spaCy toolkit has a function called "matcher" that finds sequences that match a user defined pattern[5]. These patterns can match a variety of word attributes, including the word type (lemma) or the part of speech. Figure 2.1 shows some example patterns for spaCy and phrases they would match. Addition examples can be tested using an online pattern tester provided by Explosion.ai[6]

Figure 2.1 Examples of patterns to use with the spaCy matcher function

Pattern	Example of matching phrase

`[{"TEXT": {"REGEX": "^[Uu](\.?|nited)$"}},`
`{"TEXT": {"REGEX": "^[Ss](\.?|tates)$"}},`
`{"LOWER": "president"}]`
	United States president

`[{"ORTH": "("}, {"SHAPE": "ddd"}, {"ORTH": ")"},`
`{"SHAPE": "ddd"},{"ORTH": "-", "OP": "?"},`
`{"SHAPE": "dddd"}]`
	(414) 229-5000

`[{'LIKE_NUM': True, 'OP': '?'},`
`{'POS': 'ADJ', 'OP': '?'},`
`{'LEMMA': 'duck', 'POS': 'NOUN'}]`
	three yellow ducks

Note that the most common sequences of language will be determined by the syntax, or grammar, for that language. Deriving the syntactic structure of a sentence for a particular grammar using an algorithm is called parsing. Syntax for English will be discussed in detail in Chapter 3 of this book. Parsing will be discussed in Chapter 4.

2.1.3 Vectors

Vectors hold elements of the same size, such as numbers, and are of fixed size. They are one-dimensional, which means elements can be accessed using a single integer index. Similar representations of higher dimension are given special names; a matrix is a two-dimensional, rectangular structure arranged in rows and columns. The term tensor is used to describe generalizations of matrices to N-dimensional space.[7] Important operations for vectors include accessing the value of an element of the vector, finding the length of a vector, calculating the similarity between two vectors, and taking the average of multiple vectors.

For much of data science, including modern NLP, vectors are used as a representation format for a variety of tasks. For example, vectors can represent subsets of words or labels from a fixed vocabulary. To do this, each element corresponds to a single word in the vocabulary and the value is either one or zero to indicate whether or not the word is included in the set. Vectors where only a single element can be zero[8] are often used as an output format (to indicate the selected class label or type of word in context– e.g. to discriminate between a noun versus verb sense.) Vector elements can also capture a probability distribution over a set, where the value of each element corresponds to the probability of that element, a value between 0 and 1, and the sum across all such values is 1. Calculating such a probability distribution is often done using a "softmax" function, which is a mapping from a vector of real numbers, onto a probability distribution with the same number of elements, where the probabilities are proportional to the exponentials of the input values. Two applications of vectors are of special note here: the use of vectors to represent documents for information retrieval (which has been termed the "Vector Space Model") and the use of vectors for word embeddings which are a representation of the meaning of words, which can also be generalized to represent longer phrases and sentences.

2.1.3.1 The Vector Space Model for Information Retrieval

The Vector Space Model (VSM) [9] was introduced for automated information retrieval. In the VSM, the elements of the vector correspond to words in a vocabulary and the value is a weighted measure that combines the frequency of a term (word type) within a document with a measure of its frequency across a set of documents. The VSM draws on the insight that the importance of a word in a document is directly proportional to the number of times it appears in a document, but inversely proportional to the number of documents in which it appears[10]. The combined measure is called "term frequency-inverse document frequency" (tf-idf). In this context, term frequency is the raw count of the term in a document divided by the total number of words in the document. Inverse document frequency is most commonly calculated as the log of the quotient of the total number of documents in the corpus divided by the number of documents that contain the term. The log is used to prevent calculation errors caused by numbers that are too small (called underflow). Variations of these measures are sometimes used to address data sparsity (called smoothing) or to prevent bias towards longer documents (normalization).

Using this model, the similarity between documents (or between a query and a document) can be determined using cosine distance, which measures the angle between two vectors. Figure 2.2 shows the formula for cosine distance, a graph of it as a function, and a visualization of the angle measured[11]. What makes cosine good for measuring similarity is that this function ranges between zero and one, reaching it maximum only when the two vectors line up exactly. Cosine similarity is also used to assess semantic similarity in other applications including when vectors are used to represent the meaning of words, phrases or sentences, where they are called "embeddings". Embeddings are the topic of the next subsection.

Figure 2.2 Calculation and visualization of cosine similarity of two vectors

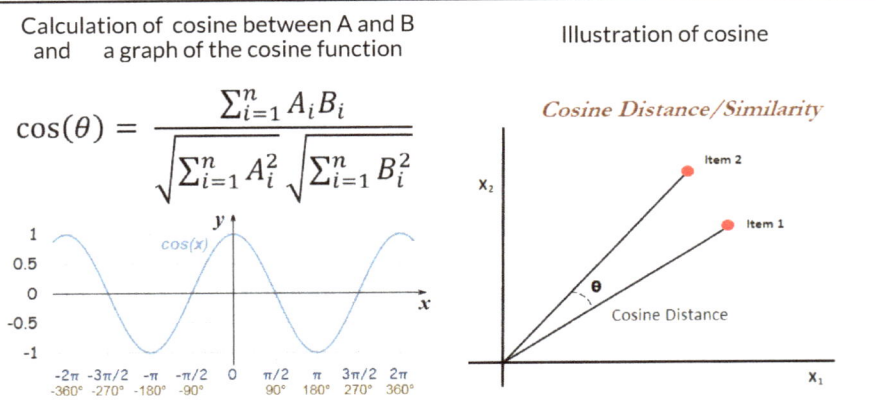

2.1.3.2 Word Embeddings

Vectors are commonly used to represent meanings of words. These vector representations are called word embeddings. Embeddings differ from document vectors in that the components of word embeddings might not correspond to anything in the real world. Instead, these vectors organize words into a kind of continuous thesaurus or hash table, giving each word type a unique vector of numbers that allows us to tell words apart and also to measure their similarity (such as by the cosine measure discussed in the previous section). This idea has been explored most directly in an approach called hash embeddings[12].

Vectors are created through an optimization process where the objective is to minimize the error for some measurable task or set of tasks. The optimal value is found by searching; the method used is typically a stochastic approximation of gradient descent. (We will discuss gradient descent in a later section of this chapter). When pretrained embeddings are used it is important to use the embeddings that were trained on data most like what is anticipated in the target application. Well-known approaches to creating word embeddings include: Word2vec, GloVe, and Elmo, which we overview here.

Word2vec[13] converts a corpus of words into numerical vectors using local statistics; it can either use context (e.g., a fixed number of words on either side) to predict a target word (a method known as continuous bag of words), or use a word to predict a target context, which is called a skip-gram. Two variations of Word2vec are available: one that works better on high frequency words and one that works better on low frequency words. For high frequency words, an approach called "negative sampling" is used to maximize the probability of a word and context being in the corpus data if it is, and maximize the probability of a word and context not being in the corpus data, if it is not. Finding these optimal values can take a very long time. For low frequency words, which require higher dimensionality vectors, a more efficient approach called hierarchical softmax can be selected. It uses a binary tree representation that reduces the computational complexity to $O(\log_2 |V|)$ instead of $O(|V|)$, where $|V|$ is the size of the vocabulary.

GloVe vectors[14][15] use global statistics to predict the probability of word j appearing in the context of word i with a least-squares objective. The general idea is to first count for all pairs of words their co-occurrence, then find values such that for each pair of word vectors, their dot product equals the logarithm of the words' probability of co-occurrence.

Elmo (Embeddings from Language Models) vectors[16] contain values that have been learned from a neural network with a particular architecture known as a bidirectional Long Short Term Memory (biLSTM or biLM) network. These networks have multiple internal layers, some of which provide feedback to each other. Bidirectionality refers to training on both the original sentences and its reverse to captures certain syntactic dependencies on the semantics of a word. In addition, unlike the other types of vectors discussed here, the representation of a word using an Elmo vector is a function of the *entire sentence* in which it occurs, rather than just a small number of nearby words.

For a particular application, the method of training is likely to not be as important as the data that was used to create the vectors, which should be as similar to the target domain as possible. There are pretrained vectors available for several common domains. A common source of pretrained embeddings is the Stanford Natural Language Group[17]. There are also programs (with detailed instructions) that are available to train new vectors from a corpus. Software for training on new data can be found within open source and commercial (but free) software libraries, including Rehurek's Gensim[18] and Fast Text[19]. The spaCy library [20] also includes pretrained embeddings within the larger versions of their language models. The domains commonly used for pretraining are: Wikipedia (a web-based encyclopedia), Gigaword (newspaper text, including Associated Press and New York Times), Common Crawl (web page text), Twitter (online news and social networking text), Google News (aggregated newspaper text), and the "1 Billion Word Benchmark", approximately 800M tokens of news crawl data first distributed at a machine translation conference (WMT) in 2011. These pretrained vectors cover vocabularies of 400K to 2.2M words, with vectors of dimension from 50 to 300.

2.1.4 Trees and Graphs

When one considers the organization of an entire sentence, or processing architectures for finding such organization, NLP algorithms rely on the datatypes of trees and graphs. Graphs are specified by a set of nodes and connections between pairs of nodes, called edges. Trees are a special case of graphs where edges are directed edges and each node has a unique predecessor (the parent) and multiple possible successors (the children). By convention the root (a node with no predecessor in the tree) is drawn at the top. For NLP, data is most likely to be represented as a tree. Graphs are used as a processing model as a way of representing the state of a search or the architecture used to train a classifier.

Trees are used to represent the syntactic structure of sentences, because sentence structure includes relations among words and phrases that may be nested, and each sentence has a unique head. (The head of a sentence is usually given as the main verb of the main clause.) Consider the sentence, "The dog ate the beef." In this sentence (S), "ate" is the main verb (VBD). The sentence has two noun phrases (NP) nested inside it: "the dog" and "the beef". These noun phrases (NP) both contain a determiner (DT) and a noun (NN). Figure 2.3 shows what this would look like drawn as a tree, using the symbols from a typical grammar.

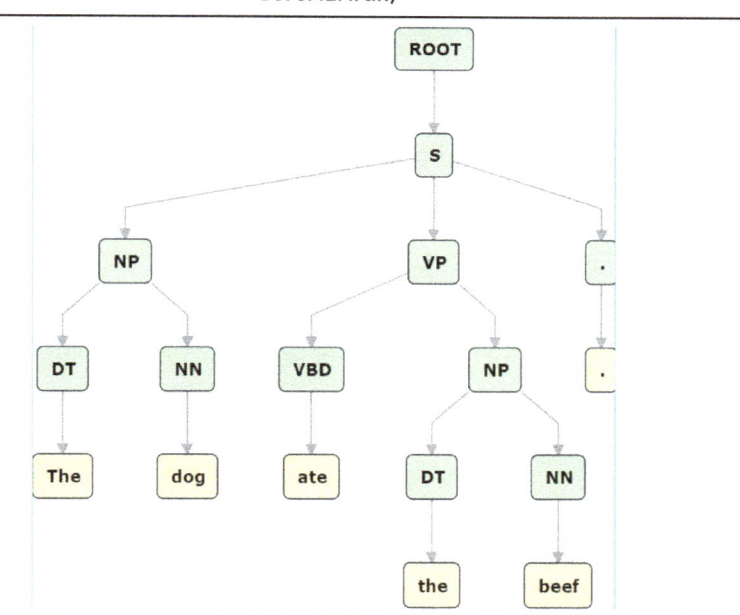

Figure 2.3 Example phrase structure parse tree (Image from Stanford CoreNLP.run)

There is a direct correspondence between nested lists and trees, so both can be used to represent syntactic structures of sentence. The structure for the sentence shown in Figure 2.3 is the same as the following nested list:

```
(S (NP (DT the)  (NN dog))
(VP (VBD ate)  (NP (DT the)  (NN beef))))
```

We can also capture this information as a list of subsequences (called spans), as in the following:

[(DT, the, 0, 1), (NN, dog, 1, 2), (VBD, ate, 2,3),(DT, the, 3, 4), (NN, beef, 4, 5), (NP, 0, 2), (NP, 3,5), (VP, 2, 5), (S, 0, 5)]

The type of grammar in this example is called a phrase structure grammar. Other approaches to syntax focus on binary relations, or dependencies among the words in a sentence. Figure 2.4 shows a dependency parse of the sentence "I saw three ducks" (which has been analyzed to include four dependencies: I is the nominal subject of saw; three is a number modifier of ducks; ducks is a direct object of saw; and the period is a punctuation mark).

Figure 2.4 Example dependency structure parse tree (Image from Stanford Corenlp.run)

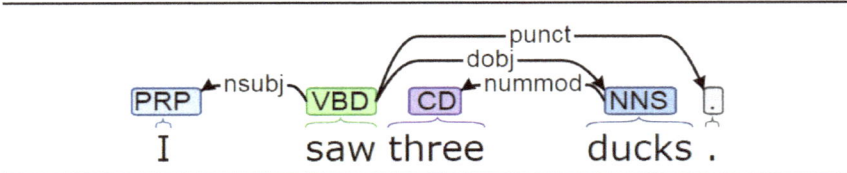

Graphs are more general that trees, because they allow nodes to have multiple incoming edges. While they are not needed to represent sentence structure, they are helpful in describing how language is processed. Graphs form the basis of the processing architectures for both search based parsing and analysis using neural networks. In a search, the nodes of the graph correspond to a machine state and possible alternative next states. In a neural network, the nodes of a graph correspond to operations or functions, which can have any number of inputs and outputs. The edges of a neural network, which represent the data that flows from the output of one node to the input of another are tensors, as they may be scalars, vectors, matrices, or higher-dimensionality structures. In both search graphs and neural network, the nodes and edges represent models of process rather than data.

This concludes our introduction to the data structures of NLP. We will next consider the two primary processing paradigms: search and classification.

2.2 PROCESSING PARADIGMS FOR NATURAL LANGUAGE PROCESSING

NLP is an instance of Artificial Intelligence (AI) problem solving. AI methods for NLP include search and classification. Search is used when we do not have a ready set of answers or we are interested in the derivation of a solution, that is, the steps involved in reaching it. Search has a variety of uses for NLP, but has been most closely associated with rule-based parsing. In a search, at each step, what happens next, is determined from a combination of stored knowledge and current inputs. Often, there may be more than one rule or function that applies with different outcomes depending on which one is applied. When this happens, different alternatives are considered as part of a search process, with the search terminating when either the desired outcomes are achieved or it is determined that a solution is not possible. Classification involves labeling observations with one of a known set of categories. This labeling can be done by either rule-based matching or by applying a classifier that has been created using statistical machine learning. This section will consider both general paradigms. In the next section we will overview how statistical classifiers are created.

2.2.1 The Paradigm of Search

The general type of search used in AI is called **state space search**. Such searches are specified by providing a specification of the initial conditions, a specification of the termination condition, and a specification of methods that manifest a transition from a given set of conditions (or "state") to another. An AI search space may be only implicit; nodes may be generated incrementally. States may be explored immediately or stored in a data structure for future exploration. After being explored, states may be discarded, if they are not part of the solution itself. Sometimes the solution is the goal state – to answer a "yes-no" or "what" question – but sometimes the solution is the path – to answer a "how" question, such as "how is a sentence derivable from a given set of rules that constitute a grammar".

State space search is a generalization of algorithms for traversing tree and graph data structures, including breadth-first search, which expands all nodes adjacent to the current node before exploring further nodes, and depth-first search, which expands one node adjacent to the current node and then makes that node the current one, expanding along a single path from the root. Another type of search is known as best-first search. A best-first search chooses what node to expand on the basis of a scoring function. For example, a scoring function might favor nodes believed closest to the goal, which is known as a "greedy" search. Or, the function might try to balance the accumulated cost of getting to a node with the estimated distance to the goal, as in A* search. Another useful best-first search is **beam search**, where the number of states kept for future consideration is bounded by a fixed number, called the "width" of the beam. (This list of search strategies is not exhaustive, but covers the primary ones that have been used for NLP.)

Search algorithms are used in NLP for identifying sequences of characters within words, such as prefixes or suffixes. They have also been used for parsing, to find sequences of words that correspond to different types of phrases, where these patterns have been described using rules. These rules can specify simple linear sequences of types that are mandatory, optional or can have specified number of occurrences (e.g. zero, zero or more, one, one or more), or can specify arbitrarily nested sequences, as with a context free grammar. For parsing, Beam search has been used to limit the number of alternatives that are kept for consideration when there are a large number of rules that might be applicable. Beam search has also been used as a way of finding the best possible sequence given the results of a machine learning algorithm designed to provide a probability distribution over each word in the vocabulary for each word in an output sequence. This type of algorithm, known as an encoder-decoder, is now commonly used for generating text, such as for creating captions or brief summaries.

Hill-climbing search and its variants use a function to rank the children of a current node to find a node that is better than the current one, and then transitions to that state, without keeping any representation of the overall search path. **Gradient descent** is a variant of hill climbing that searches for the child with minimum value of its ranking function. For machine learning, this type of search is used to adjust parameters to find the minimum amount of error or **loss** in comparison to the goal by making changes proportional to the negative gradient, which is the multivariate generalization of a derivative (akin to the slope of a line). Hill-climbing and gradient searching do not backtrack, and hence do not require any memory to track previously visited states.

2.2.2 The Paradigm of Classification

A classifier is a function that takes an object represented as a set of features and selects a label for that object (or provides a ranking among possible labels). The first classifiers were given as a set of rules. These rules were hand-written patterns (e.g., regular expressions) for assigning a label to an object. Rules for NLP often name specific tokens, their attributes, or their syntactic types. Examples of patterns are shown in Figure 2.1, in the section that discusses lists. Statistical classifiers select or rank classes using an algorithmically generated function called a language model that provides a probability estimate for sequences of items from a given vocabulary. Language models can contain varying amounts of information. A small, simple model might only have information about short sequences of words and the correlation between those sequences and sequences of labels (such as parts of speech or entity types), while a more complex model might also include meaning representations, called embeddings, that were discussed as an example of vectors.

Statistical classifiers can be designed to either pick the single best class or to provide a ranked list of possible classes along with a score of their certainty or estimated probability of being the correct class. One example of a single-best classifier is a Perceptron Classifier, which represents both the input features and model weights as vectors, computes their dot product (which is a sum of the products of the corresponding entries of the two vectors) and returns the one with highest value. Figure 2.5 shows the pseudocode for a perceptron classifier. (The training of a perceptron will determine the value of the weights.)

Figure: 2.5 Pseudocode for a Perceptron classifier

```
def predict(self, features):
"Dot-product of features and current weights and return best class."

    scores = defaultdict(float)
    for feat in features:
        if feat not in self.weights:
            continue
        weights = self.weights[feat]

    for clas, weight in weights.items():
        scores[clas] = weight
    return max(self.classes, key=lambda clas: (scores[clas], clas))
```

Today, most classifiers are created via supervised machine learning. Supervised Machine Learning (SML) is a method of creating a function for combining the contributions of different features of the input to select an output class that will best match the output classification given to similar examples from the training data. SML models are trained using data sets of instances where the correct class has been provided, either by asking people to annotate the data based on a guideline, or by using some aspect of the data itself, such as a star rating, as the class.

Classification as an approach has become increasingly important as many NLP tasks can be mapped to classification tasks, given the right representation. For example, the task of recognizing named entities within a sentence and labelling them with their type, such as PERSON (PER) or LOCATION (LOC) can be cast as a classification task using an encoding called IOB, which stands for "inside" "outside" "beginning", to classify each word in the entity sequence. Words marked with tags with the prefix "B" are the first word in the sequence. Words marked with tags with the prefix "I" are "inside" the sequence. All other words are "outside" which means that they are not part of any recognized entity. After a named entity classifier is used, another process can traverse the classified tokens to merge the tokens into objects for each entity. Figure 2.6 includes an example of IOB encoding for named entity recognition.

Figure: 2.6 IOB encoding for the sentence "Ruth Bader Ginsberg went to New York"

Ruth/B_PER Bader/I_PER Ginsberg/I_PER went/O to/O New/B_LOC York/I_LOC

The same approach can be used for the task of marking the noun phrases within a sentence. Figure 2.7 shows an example of an IOB encoding for bracketing noun phrases[21].

Figure 2.7 IOB encoding for the sentence "The bull chased the big red ball around the yard."

The/B_NP bull/I_NP chased/O the/B_NP big/I_NP red/I_NP ball/I_NP around/O the/B_NP yard/I_NP

Classification can be applied to units of different sizes (e.g. words or complete sentences) and can be applied either to each input unit independently, or performed to optimize over a sequence of units (called sequence modelling). For example, we might want to classify all elements of a sequence of words in a phrase at the same time. Examples of methods used for sequence modelling include Conditional Random Fields, Hidden Markov Models, and neural networks. A simple neural model that has been used effectively for some NLP tasks is the Averaged Perceptron. Another alternative is to classify sequences using a structured output label (such as a parse tree) rather than a discrete symbol or an unordered set of symbols. Structured modelling can be more accurate than either word-level modelling or sequence modeling, however obtaining training data with structured labels is harder, and would require a much more complex type of neural network, involving multiple layers. More information about machine learning, and its use in training classifiers, will be discussed in the next section.

2.3 OVERVIEW OF MACHINE LEARNING

Approaches for learning models based on machine learning have their origins in search, where the goal of the search is to find a function that will optimize the performance of the system. The term "machine learning" was first coined by Arthur Samuel in the 1950's to describe his method for developing a program to play the board game of checkers. His game player selected the correct move for each turn based on a function that combined the contributions from features such as piece position and material advantage. This function was trained by adjusting the coefficients of a linear polynomial to favor "book moves" (a type of supervised learning) and moves that increased the average number of wins over repeated games against itself. Today we would call such an approach reinforcement learning or semi-supervised machine learning. Thus, although ML classifiers do not search during the classification process itself – it is more like table lookup or hashing – the training algorithms for machine learning do use search to create the functions that combine the contributions of different features. A common type of search used in machine learning algorithms is gradient descent, as they try to minimize the amount of error or "loss" between the output value of the system and the true value, based on the data.

Samuel's approach introduced several ideas that are still used among all machine learning methods today: algorithms learn models for making a decision about what to do (or how to label something) based on a set of observations, each of which is represented as a finite number of attributes (also called features). These features may correspond to an unordered set, or they may represent a sequence. The algorithms all have some training objective which can be internal (e.g., minimize the amount of error on training data) or external (e.g., maximize the number of games to be won when the model used in simulated play). The algorithms "train" by changing the values of internal parameters, such as coefficients of scoring functions over several iterations until they converge at an optimal configuration (or some fixed maximum determined externally).

A machine learning approach that has a long history, and is still used today, is decision tree learning (such as ID3, C4.5, J48, Random Forest, etc.). A decision tree is a tree where each node represents a test on one of a fixed set attributes of the input. Each edge out of a node represents one possible outcome for the test, like the different branches in a case statement (or switch) in a programming language. For example, a binary test has two branches one for true and one for false. Figure 2.8 shows a decision about whether the weather is comfortable for being outside, which can be yes or no. The tree considers three attributes of the input: the wind (which can be strong or weak), humidity (which can be high or normal), and weather (which can be sunny, cloudy, or rainy). The paths through a tree correspond to rules that can be used to classify examples, with the leaves indicating the value of the class variable. Thus, any input whose value for weather is cloudy would be classified as yes (a comfortable day to be outside).

Figure 2.8 Example of a decision tree

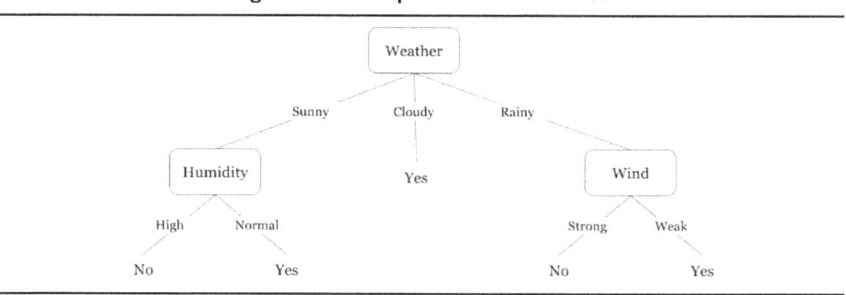

Over a set of attributes, many different decision trees are possible, but there are a small number of optimal trees that minimize the number of tests that must be performed. The trees can be learned from labelled examples by searching through the space of all possible trees by doing a greedy best-first search that picks the best attribute at each step and terminates when either all remaining examples fall within a single branch or all attributes have been tested. It has been shown that the "best" attribute to test at a given node in the tree is the one that best splits subset of examples that match a particular path in a decision tree. The best split is determined by some function, such as information gain[22]. One advantage of decision tree learning is that it provides easily extractable information about the importance of each attribute in how examples are classified.

Today, there are many algorithms for training classifiers with labelled data. The goal of all of them is to find decision boundaries between classes that will work well on both the training data and the future test data. For some problems, a linear boundary is sufficient (see Figure 2.9A) but for others, a nonlinear boundary is needed (see Figure 2.9B). Linear methods include decision tree learning algorithms, statistical approaches, like Naïve Bayes or Support Vector Machines, and shallow neural networks, such as Perceptrons. Nonlinear boundaries can be found for clustering methods (such as K-nearest neighbors) and for neural networks that include multiple internal layers (Deep Learning). Workbench tools such as Weka and WekaDeepLearning4J allow one to experiment with a variety of algorithms and visualize the results.

Figure 2.9 Examples of linearly and non-linearly separable data (images from Wikipedia)

A: Data that is linearly separable	B: Data that is non-linearly separable

In general, employing machine learning approaches is an iterative process of training and testing. Training means running a learning algorithm on a data set where the correct class is provided to the algorithm so it can use the information to find values for internal parameters. Testing means applying the trained classifier to a subset of the data that was not used for training, but where the correct class is known. The performance of the classifier is then assessed. The most common measures to use are precision, recall, and F1. Precision is the proportion of correctly classified items of a given category among the total number of items it classified as the category. Recall is the proportion of correctly classified items among the total number of items that should have been classified as the category. F1 is their harmonic mean (which is calculated as two times the product of precision and recall divided by their sum).

Training and test sets can be created through a manual or automated selection process. Manual selection, while less common, is sometimes done to assure consistency across training and testing over time. Manual selection risks biasing the results however. Instead, experimenters will use N-fold cross-validation, which is an iterative process where the data set is first partitioned into N equal subparts (the "folds") and then training is repeated N times, each time with a different one of the subparts held out as a test set. Afterward, the performance measures are averaged over all test sets.

The success of training classifiers (of all types) depends primarily on the data set available to train the model. (There can also be differences due to the training algorithm, so several are usually tried and compared.) The data used for training should always be as similar as possible to the target test data and have enough positive and negative examples for each category, to minimize the impact of small differences in placement of boundaries. It is also important to choose an appropriate internal representation of the data as features. A simple approach might consider each of the individual words – but this can be both too much and too little. The set of unique word types in any natural language is in the hundreds of thousands. One can reduce the number of features by using only the most important words for a corpus (e.g., using a tf-idf measure) or the most discriminative words for a classification problem (e.g., using a mutual information measure). On the other hand, just using individual words may fail to discriminate among different senses of a word, so one may add bigrams (pairs of words) or part of speech bigrams (words with part of speech tags) or pretrained word embeddings for each word in the input as features.

Training classifiers using neural networks requires additional manual intervention. All versions of these algorithms are run repeatedly for a preset number of iterations (set by the experimenter) and make adjustments to the model of a fixed size, called the learning rate (also set by the experimenter) in the direction indicated by the objective function. Values set by the experimenter are called hyperparameters and generally they are set by a process of generate and test. For example, the experimenter tries different numbers of iterations to see what value provides the best performance. More is not always better, because running for too many iterations eventually leads to a problem called overfitting, which means that the model will not perform well on unseen examples. One approach to overfitting in neural networks is dropout[23], which is where the inputs of some units are disabled randomly. Whether or not to use dropout is another user-settable parameter.

Neural networks also have a variety of architectures that can be configured. So-called "deep" neural networks are organized with several layers of different types of nodes. See Figure 2.10 from Ruder(2018)[24].

Figure 2.10 Example Deep Network architecture for NLP (Image credit: Ruder, 2018)

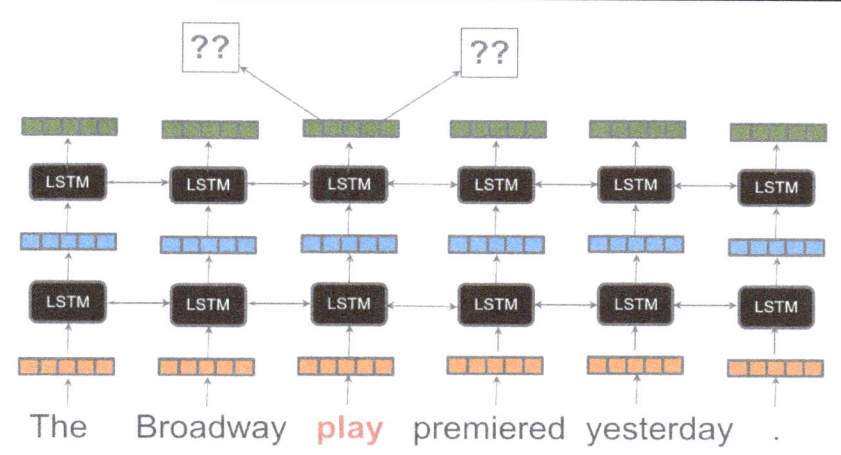

Typically, as in the figure, the initial (bottom) layers are used to create a representation (encoding) of the input or to control the order in which the network will process an input that comprises sequence (such as a sentence or pair of sentences). Interior layers (called "hidden layers") are used to change the dimensionality of the data (e.g., to match the input expected by the next layer) or to learn different substructures or dependencies among features of the input. The last (top) layers are used to create an output of the proper type. For example, a softmax layer takes a vector of real-valued inputs and maps it onto a probability distribution, which is a value between 0 and 1. The types of optimization functions used to update the nodes can vary; common examples include Stochastic Gradient Descent and AdaDelta.

The first systems to use deep learning were built from separately trained, pipelined models of tasks such as labelling words with a part of speech (such as noun or verb) or labelling phrases with a semantic type, or a syntactic type or function (such as person, noun-phrase or noun-subject). However, the focus has been shifting towards creating networks that learn general models of language and work well for a variety of tasks, from discriminating word senses to selecting the best answer to a question. These general networks often are built as so-called "transformer" models, such as BERT, GPT-2 and XLNet, which are good for classification problems involving pairs of sequences. Transformers pair two general purpose subnetworks, an "encoder", and a "decoder". (See Figure 2.11 for an illustration.) The encoder is trained to model input sequences. A decoder is trained to model output sequences.

An encoder may be trained to learn dependencies within the sequences by including layers of "self-attention" that take inputs from different positions within the sequence[25]. A unidirectional model of attention uses the initial words in a sequence to predict later ones; a bidirectional model[26], uses the words on either side to predict a left-out word, using an approach called "masking", resembling the technique of cloze tests used for assessing reading comprehension[27] or the assessment of age-related loss of hearing[28] Decoders are trained to include attention to both the output of the encoder, sometimes called the "context vector", and to dependencies within the output sequences.

Figure 2.11 Attention within Encoder and Decoder of a Transformer (Image credit: Vaswani et al, 2017)

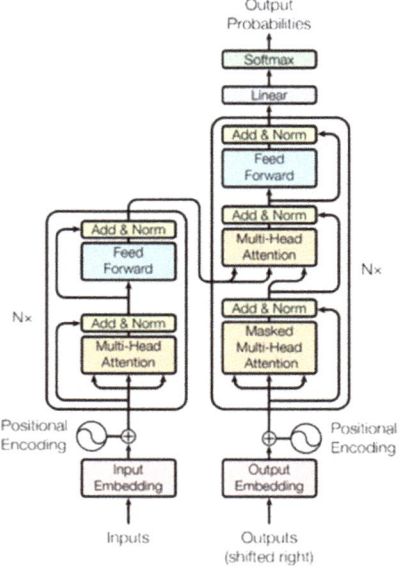

Newer architectures for encoders, developed by Lee-Thorp et al (2021), replace multiple layers of self-attention with a single layer of linear transformations that "mixes" different input tokens, to create faster processing models; the group report that a "standard, unparameterized Fourier Transform achieves 92% of the accuracy of BERT on the GLUE benchmark, but pre-trains and runs up to seven times faster on GPUs and twice as fast on TPUs"[29]. Other versions mix a single self-attention layer with Fourier transforms to get better accuracy, at a somewhat less performance benefit. Exploring such tradeoff is likely going to remain an active area of research for awhile.

Both encoder and decoders are trained on large collections of text, such as Gigaword[30], which includes text from several international news services. Transformers for dialog must be trained on data collected from interactions between people, which can be gathered either by scraping portals where people interact (e.g., for language learners to practice conversation skills) or by creating tasks for pairs of crowd-workers. These datasets have then been annotated by researchers at universities or large companies, such as Google. Facebook research has assembled one of the most comprehensive collections of openly available datasets and software tools, which they make available through its ParlAI project[31].

For specific sequence to sequence classification tasks, the pre-trained models are fine-tuned or updated with additional data from the target domain, such as pairs of questions and answers[32]. The pairs of sequences can be given as two separate inputs, {S1, S2} or, more commonly, they are given as one concatenated input, by adding special tokens to indicate the start, separation, and end of each part of the pair, e.g., [Start]-[S1]-[Separator]-[S2]-[End]. These models have been shown to work fairly well for question answering, sentiment analysis, textual entailment and parsing[33]. One limitation is that these models are big and slow in production – and thus cannot yet be used for real-time systems – however they could be used to create training data for simpler models. Another concern has been that retraining such models consumes a huge amount of power; the carbon equivalent of BERT has been estimated to be around the same a transatlantic flight[34].

Workbench tools for deep learning include a growing number of preconfigured architectures and also support changing the values of the control parameters to assess their impact. Finding the best approach is an experimental process. When trying to solve a particular problem with these tools, a good way to start is to learn what algorithms and parameter values have been used most effectively in the past for similar problems and then try to replicate the setup for one's own data using a workbench tool. There are also software libraries specifically for performing NLP using Deep Learning, some organized as notebooks, that can be used to perform experiments or build applications. Software from the start-up Hugging Face is most available, as currently it can be run either directly, within Google's "Colaboratory", which includes notebooks for transformer-based NLP libraries using either TensorFlow 2 or PyTorch[35], or from within spaCy, as "spacy-transformers".

2.4 SUMMARY

This chapter considered the most used data types and problem-solving strategies for natural language processing. The data types include strings, lists, vectors, trees, and graphs. Most of these are meant to capture sequences (e.g., of letters or words) and the hierarchical structures that emerge because of grammar. Feature structures or objects are needed to associate various attributes with tokens or types (as a way to keep the number of unique types of a manageable number). The processing paradigms of natural language processing include search, classification, and more generally, machine learning, where the development of a language model (including classifiers) using machine learning represents a complex combination of manual and automated search to find an optimal model for performing a given task. Many steps for these processing paradigms have been implemented in the form of software libraries and workbench style tools, however no tool exists that can predict the optimal approach or identify the most relevant data or the internal representation to use. For these tasks, understanding of language, including levels of abstraction, benchmark tasks, and important end-to-end applications, will be discussed in the remainder of this book.

Notes

1. Fitzgerald, M. (2019) Introducing Regular Expressions, O'Reilly Press, URL: https://www.oreilly.com/library/view/introducing-regular-expressions/9781449338879/ch01.html
2. An online tester for regular expressions is provided by Regexpal.com at URL: https://www.regexpal.com/
3. The Python function for handling regular expressions is "re". These two webpages are helpful: https://docs.python.org/3/howto/regex.html and https://docs.python.org/3/library/re.html. The Java package for regular expression is java.util.regex. A helpful page is: https://docs.oracle.com/javase/tutorial/essential/regex/
4. A demo by Jacob Perkins can be used to compare results for the different tokenizers. URL: https://text-processing.com/demo/tokenize/
5. spaCy. (2020). Rule-based matching. URL: https://spacy.io/usage/rule-based-matching Accessed April 2020.
6. Explosion.ai Rule-based Matcher Explorer. URL https://explosion.ai/demos/matcher Accessed April 2020
7. Thus, a vector is also a one-dimensional tensor.
8. Vectors where only one element is a "1" are called "one-hot" vectors.
9. Salton, G., Wong, A. and Yang, C. S. (1975). A Vector Space Model for Automatic Indexing. *Communications of the ACM*, 18(11), pp 613–620.
10. Spärck Jones, K. (1972). A Statistical Interpretation of Term Specificity and Its Application in Retrieval. *Journal of Documentation*. 28: 11–21.
11. The formula for the cosine of two vectors computes their dot product, divided by their magnitudes., so that the vector lengths do not

matter.

12. Svenstrup, D.T., Hansen, J., and Winther, O. (2017). Hash Embeddings for Efficient Word Representations. In *Advances in Neural Information Processing Systems* (pp. 4928-4936).

13. Mikolov, T., Sutskever, I., Chen, K., Corrado, G. S., and Dean, J. (2013). Distributed Representations of Words and Phrases and Their Compositionality. In *Advances in Neural Information Processing Systems*, pages 3111–3119.

14. Pennington, J., Socher, R., and Manning, C.D. (2014). GloVe: Global Vectors for Word Representation. In *Proceedings of the 2014 Conference on Empirical Methods in Natural Language Processing* (EMNLP) (pp. 1532-1543).

15. GloVe Project Website: URL https://nlp.stanford.edu/projects/glove/

16. Peters, M.E., Neumann, M., Iyyer, M., Gardner, M., Clark, C., Lee, K. and Zettlemoyer, L. (2018). Deep Contextualized Word Representations. arXiv preprint arXiv:1802.05365.

17. Stanford NLP Group main website URL: https://nlp.stanford.edu/

18. Gensim URL: https://radimrehurek.com/gensim/

19. Facebook FastText URL https://fasttext.cc/

20. The main spaCy website URL: https://spacy.io/

21. This example was inxpired by this youtube video: https://www.youtube.com/watch?v=l_sxJtiR4fc

22. Information gain is the difference in "information" between a set and subsets created by a partition of the set on the basis of some feature. It is calculated as a function of another measure called entropy, that measures the uniformity of a probability distribution. A distribution where events have equal probability has a larger entropy than a distribution where the probability of events are very different from each other. The formulas for information gain and entropy are not essential for understanding decision trees and thus are not included here; however, they can be found in any introductory AI textbook.

23. The technique of dropout was patented by Google (see https://patents.google.com/patent/US9406017B2/en) but is widely available in open source toolkits for neural networks. The patent specifies "(f)or each training case, the switch randomly selectively disables each of the feature detectors in accordance with a preconfigured probability. The weights from each training case are then normalized for applying the neural network to test data."

24. Ruder, S. (2018) NLP's ImageNet moment has arrived. URL

https://ruder.io/nlp-imagenet/, Accessed February 2021.

25. Vaswani, A., Shazeer, N., Parmar, N., Uszkoreit, J., Jones, L., Gomez, A.N., Kaiser, L. and Polosukhin, I. (2017). Attention is All you Need. In NIPS.

26. Devlin, J., Chang, M. W., Lee, K., & Toutanova, K. (2018). BERT: Pre-training of Deep Bidirectional Transformers for Language Understanding. arXiv e-prints, arXiv-1810.

27. Alderson, J. C. (1979). The Cloze Procedure and Proficiency in English as a Foreign Language. TESOL Quarterly, 219-227.

28. Bologna WJ, Vaden KI Jr, Ahlstrom JB, Dubno JR. (2018) Age Effects on Perceptual Organization of Speech: Contributions of Glimpsing, Phonemic Restoration, and Speech Segregation. *Journal of the Acoustical Society of America* 144(1):267. doi: 10.1121/1.5044397. PMID: 30075693; PMCID: PMC6047943.

29. Lee-Thorp, J., Ainslie, J., Eckstein, I., and Ontanon, S. (2021). FNet: Mixing Tokens with Fourier Transforms. arXiv preprint arXiv:2105.03824.

30. Graff, D. (2003). English Gigaword. Technical Report LDC2003T05, Linguistic Data Consortium, Philadelphia, PA USA

31. Facebook Research (2021) "ParlAI" github site. URL: https://github.com/facebookresearch/ParlAI (Accessed May 2021).

32. Wang, A., Pruksachatkun, Y., Nangia, N., Singh, A., Michael, J., Hill, F., Levy, O. and Bowman, S. R. (2019). SuperGLUE: A Stickier Benchmark for General-Purpose Language Understanding Systems. *Proceedings of Advances in Neural Information Processing Systems 32* (NeurIPS 2019). Also available as: arXiv preprint arXiv:1905.00537.

33. Kitaev, N., Cao, S., & Klein, D. (2019, July). Multilingual Constituency Parsing with Self-Attention and Pre-Training. In Proceedings of the 57th Annual Meeting of the Association for Computational Linguistics (pp. 3499-3505).

34. Strubell, E., Ganesh, A., & McCallum, A. (2019, July). Energy and Policy Considerations for Deep Learning in NLP. In *Proceedings of the 57th Annual Meeting of the Association for Computational Linguistics* (pp. 3645-3650).

35. Hugging Face Team (2020) Transformers Notebooks URL https://huggingface.co/transformers/notebooks.html Accessed May 2021.

CHAPTER 3.

OVERVIEW OF ENGLISH SYNTAX

The order in which words and phrases occur matters. Syntax is the set of conventions of language that specify whether a given sequence of words is well-formed and what functional relations, if any, pertain to them. For example, in English, the sequence "cat the mat on" is not well-formed. To keep the set conventions manageable, and to reflect how native speakers use their language, syntax is defined hierarchically and recursively. The structures include words (which are the smallest well-formed units), phrases (which are legal sequences of words), clauses and sentences (which are both legal sequences of phrases). Sentences can be combined into compound sentences using conjunctions, such as "and".

The categories of words used for NLP are mostly similar to those used in other contexts, but in some cases they may be different from how you were taught when you were learning the grammar of English. One of the challenges faced in NLP work is that terminology for describing syntax has evolved over time and differs somewhat across disciplines. If one were to ask how many categories of words are there, the writing center at a university might say there are eight different types of parts of speech in the English language: noun, pronoun, verb, adjective, adverb, preposition, conjunction, and interjection[1]. The folks who watched Schoolhouse Rock also were taught there were eight, but a slightly different set[2]. By contrast, the first published guideline for annotating part of speech created by linguists used eighty different categories[3]. Most current NLP work uses around 35 labels for different parts of speech, with additional labels for punctuation.

The conventions for describing syntax arise from two disciplines: studies by linguists, going back as far as 8th century BCE by the first Sanskrit grammarians, and work by computational scientists, who have standardized and revised the labeling of syntactic units to better meet the needs of automated processing. What forms a legal constituent in a given language was once determined qualitatively and empirically: early linguists would review written documents, or interview native speakers of language, to find out what phrases native speakers find acceptable and what phrases or words can be substituted for one another and still be considered grammatical. This technique is still useful today as a means of verifying the syntactic labels of rarely seen expressions. For example, in the sentence "I would rather deal with the side effects of my medication", one might wonder if "with" is part of a complex verb "deal with" or it acts as a preposition, which is a function word more associated with the noun phrase "the side effects". The fact that we can substitute the verb "tolerate" for "deal with" is evidence that "deal with" is a single entity.

There is always some risk of experimental bias when we depend on the judgements of untrained native speakers to define the legal structures of a language. As an alternative, there have been attempts to use evidence of language structure obtained directly from physical monitoring of people's eyes (via eye tracking) or brains (via event-related potentials measured by electroencephalograms) while they process language. Although such physiological evidence is less subject to bias, the cost of the equipment and the difficulty of using it has limited the scale of such studies. Moreover, both of these physiological approaches rely on experts to hypothesize about the structure of language, conduct experiments to elicit human behavior, and then generalize from a relatively small set of observations.

3.1 THE ROLE OF CORPORA IN UNDERSTANDING SYNTAX

Today, best practice for many subtasks of natural language processing involves working with large collections of text, each of which comprises "a corpus". Early on in the advent of computers, some researchers surmised the importance of collecting unsolicited examples of naturally occurring text and performing quantitative analyses to inform our understanding. In the 1960's, linguists from Brown University created the first "large" collection of text[4]. This collection is known as the Brown Corpus. It includes 500 samples of English-language text, totaling roughly one million words, compiled from works published in the United States in 1961. The words of the corpus were then annotated with part-of-speech labels, using a combination of automated labeling and laborious hand correction[5]. Although this corpus is no longer considered large, it still provides a useful benchmark for many studies and is available for use within popular NLP tools such as NLTK (with updated part-of-speech tags). Also, the technique of combining automated processing and manual correction is still often necessary.

The second large-scale collection and annotation of natural language data began in the early 1990's with a project conducted by a team at the University of Pennsylvania, led by a Computer Scientist, Mitchell Marcus, an expert in automated sentence processing. This data set is called "the Penn Treebank" (PTB), and is the most widely used resource for NLP. This work benefited from a donation of three years of Wall Street Journal (WSJ) text (containing 98,732 news stories representing over 1.2 million word-level tokens), along with past efforts to annotate the words of the Brown Corpus with part-of-speech tags. Today, the PTB also includes annotations for the "Switchboard" corpus of transcribed spoken conversation. Switchboard includes about 2,400 two-sided telephone conversations, previously collected by Texas Instruments in the early 1990's[6]. However, the WSJ subset of the Penn treebank corpus is still among the largest and most widely used data sets for NLP work. The word-level categories used in the PTB are very similar to those previously used by linguists, but with changes to suit the task at hand: labels were chosen to be short, but also easy for annotators to remember. Special categories were added for proper nouns, numbers, auxiliaries, pronouns, and three subtypes of wh-words, along with common variants for tense and number.

Another important English language resource is the English Web Treebank[7], completed in 2012. It has 254,830 word-level tokens (16,624 sentences) of web text that has been manually annotated with part-of-speech tags and constituency structure in the same style as the PTB. The corpus spans five types of web text: blog posts, newsgroup threads, emails, product reviews, and answers from question-answer websites. It has also been annotated with dependency structures, in the style used in the Stanford dependency parser[8].

The most recent widely used English language corpus is OntoNotes Release 5.0, completed in 2013. It is a collection of about 2.9 million words of text spread across three languages (Arabic, Chinese, and English)[9]. The text spans the domains of news, conversational telephone speech, weblogs, Usenet newsgroups, broadcast, and talk shows. It follow the same labelling conventions used in the Penn Treebank, and also adds annotations based on PropBank, which describe the semantic arguments associated with verbs. OntoNotes has been used to pretrain language models included in the spaCy NLP software libraries[10]. It includes words that did not exist when the Penn Treebank was created such as "Google"[11]. Another large, but less well known corpus, is the Open American National Corpus (OANC) which is a collection of 15 million words of American English, including texts spanning a variety of genres and transcripts of spoken data produced from 1990 through 2015. The

OANC data and annotations are fully open and unrestricted for any use.[12]. Another well-known, large annotated collection of newswire next is Gigaword[13].

Terminology for describing language has become more standardized with the availability of larger corpora and more accurate tools for automated processing. Today, nearly every form of human communication is available in digital form, which allows us to to analyze large sets of sentences, spanning a wide variety of genres, including professional writing in newspapers and journal articles, informal writing posted to social media, and transcripts of spoken conversations and government proceedings. Large subsets of these texts have been annotated with grammatical information. With this data, the existence of linguistic structures and their distribution has been measured with statistical methods. This annotated data also makes it possible to create algorithms to analyze many sentences automatically and (mostly accurately) without hand-crafting a grammar.

For NLP analysis, there are four aspects of syntax that are most important: the syntactic categories and features of individual words, which we also call their parts of speech; the well-formed sequences of words into phrases and sentences, which we call constituency; the requirements that some words have for other co-occurring constituents, which we call subcategorization; and binary relations between words that are the lexical heads (main word) of a constituent, which we call lexical dependency, or just "dependency". In this chapter, we will discuss each of these four aspects. Along with our discussion of the parts of speech, we will consider part-of-speech tags, which are the labels that NLP systems use to designate combinations of the syntactic category of a word and its syntactic features. (Some systems also use a record structure with separate fields for each feature, as an internal structure, but specialized tags are more compact for use in annotated datasets.)

3.2 WORD TYPES AND FEATURES

In English, we typically think of the word as the smallest unit. However, trained linguists make some finer grained distinctions. For example, linguists use the term lemma, or root, or base form to describe the canonical form of a word that has several variations for forming the plural or a particular tense. For common nouns, like "apple", this would be the singular form. For verbs, it is the untensed form (that is the one that would follow the word "to" in an infinitive, such as "to eat", "to be", or "to go"). Linguists use the term lexeme to describe a word type – which includes the set of the lemma and all its variants. The term morpheme is used to describe strings that carry meaning but may be smaller than a word, such as prefixes (which are substrings at the front of a word) and suffixes (which are substrings at the end of a word). Both can add either syntactic or semantic information to a word. Analyzing a word into morphemes is called "morphology". Finding the root is called lemmatization. NLP work sometimes uses the notion of "stems" instead of roots. Stems are substrings of a word, which can depend on an implementation, as there is no standard form. They are useful for specifying patterns to match all members of a lexeme. NLP work also uses the term "token", which is an instance of a word as it occurs in use. So, if a sentence includes the same word twice, there will be two separate tokens created for it.

Now we will consider broad syntactic categories of words and the syntactic attributes that occur as variants of spelling. We will consider these ten types: nouns, pronouns, proper nouns, determiners, verbs, prepositions, adverbs, adjectives, conjunctions, and wh-words. Most syntactic attributes are indicated by a specific characters associated with the features involved (e.g., plurals are usually formed by adding "s" and past tense is usually formed by adding "ed"), but sometimes these forms exist as an entirely different word, that we refer to as "irregular", such as "was" being the "first person past tense" form of the verb "to be".

3.2.1 Nouns, Pronouns, and Proper Nouns

Nouns are used to name or describe entities, which might be physical (such as "cat" or "rock") or abstract (such as "freedom" or "laughter") or both (such as "city" or "company"). Nouns can be singular or plural. The plural form is usually marked with the suffix "s" or "es", as in "cats"; if a word ends in "y", it is changed to "i" before adding the suffix. Figure 3.1 includes several examples. Some plurals are irregular, as in "children" or "knives". Figure 3.2 includes examples of irregular nouns. Some nouns (called "count" nouns), unless they are plural, require a determiner or cardinal number to specify the denoted set, e.g. "the boy" or "three boys". Nouns occur in the subjects of sentences and as objects following a verb or preposition. Figure 3.3 shows the typical placement of nouns within a simple sentence.

Figure 3.1 Example of nouns with a plural formed with -s or -es suffix

Singular form	Regular plural form
frog	frogs
idea	ideas
fly	flies
fox	foxes
class	classes

Figure 3.2 Example of nouns with an irregular plural

Singular form	Irregular plural form
child	children
sheep	sheep
goose	geese
knife	knives

Figure 3.3 Typical placement of nouns

Noun in the subject	Main verb	Noun in an object	Noun in a prepositional phrase
The boy	put	his towel	in his locker

There are some subtypes of nouns, namely proper nouns and pronouns, that are so different from common nouns that annotation for NLP treats them as separate categories, although they occur in similar contexts.

Proper nouns are the names of people, places, and things and are capitalized wherever they occur, as in "My name is Susan". Proper nouns rarely appear as plurals, but since they sometimes do, as in "We visited the Smiths", NLP systems include a category for plural proper nouns.

Pronouns are used to refer to people and things that have been mentioned before or presupposed to exist. They have different forms to specify whether they are singular or plural and their syntactic role (subject or object). In a grammatical sentence, the form should agree with the properties of the verb, although current NLP systems often ignore these features and only use only one category. One subclass of pronouns that is distinguished are those that express possession, and can be used in place of a determiner, e.g., "my book" or "your house," and this subclass may also be assigned a separate part of speech. Also, some pronouns are used to form a question and thus also merit their own labels. They include both regular wh-pronouns, including "what", "who", and "whom," and possessive wh-pronouns, such as "whose".

Common nouns and proper nouns are considered an **open class** of words, which means people may invent new ones to describe new objects or names. By contrast, pronouns are considered a **closed class** of words. With open-class words, algorithms must address that new items might occur that will be outside of the known vocabulary.

PRINCIPLES OF NATURAL LANGUAGE PROCESSING 61

3.2.2 Determiners

Determiners include "the", "a", "an", "that", "these", "this", and "those". There are also determiners that are used in questions, such as "what" and "which". Determiners only occur in noun phrases, before any adjectives or nouns. Some common nouns, when they express a mass quantity, like "water" or "rice", or when they are plural like "cats", do not require a determiner. Proper nouns generally do not allow a determiner, except when they are plural, e.g., "The Smiths" or when it is part of the name itself, e.g., "The Ohio State University". Possessive phrases, which are marked with an apostrophe and the suffix "-s", can take the place of a determiner, as in the phrase "my mother's house". Pronouns, regular or possessive, are *never* preceded by determiners. Determiners are considered a closed class of words.

3.2.3 Verbs and Auxiliary Verbs

Verbs are usually tensed (past, present, future). They include both verbs where the tensed forms are regular (see Figure 3.4) or irregular (see Figure 3.5). Also, in some contexts, verbs can appear untensed, such as after an auxiliary or after the word "to". Verbs are also marked for number (singular or plural), and for person. First person is "I"; second person is "you"; and third person is "he", "she", or "it". The third-person singular form is marked with "-s"; the non-3rd person singular present looks the same as the root form. Verbs also have participle forms for past (eg., "broken" or "thought") and present (e.g., "thinking").

Some verbs require a particle which is similar to a preposition except that it forms an essential part of the meaning of the verb that can be moved either before or after another argument, as in "she took off her hat" or "she took her hat off".

Verbs that can be main verbs are an open class. Verbs that are modals or auxiliary verbs (also called helping verbs) are a **closed class**. They are used along with a main verb to express ability ("can", "could"), possibility ("may", "might"), necessity ("shall", "should", "ought"), certainty ("do", "did"), future ("will", "would"), past ("has", "had", "have", "was", "were"). NLP systems treat modals and auxiliaries as a separate part of speech. They are also all irregular in the forms that they take for different combinations of features, such as past, plural, etc. For example, the modal "can" uses the form "can" for any value for number and "could" for any value for "past".

Figure 3.4 Example of a regular verb and some suffixes

Example	Regular Forms	Suffix	Features
walk	walks; walked; walking	-s; -ed; -ing	3rd person singular, present; past; participle

Figure 3.5 Some irregular verb forms

Example	Irregular forms	Features
break	broke; broken	past; past participle
eat	ate; eaten	past; past participle
sit	sat; seated	past; past participle

3.2.4 Prepositions

Prepositions, such as "with", "of", "for", and "from" are words that relate two nouns or a noun and a verb. Prepositions require a noun phrase argument (to form a prepositional phrase). It is estimated that there about 150 different prepositions (including 94 one-word prepositions and 56 complex prepositions, such as "out of")[14]. Prepositions are generally considered a closed class, but the possibility of complex combinations suggests that algorithms might be better off allowing for out of vocabulary examples.

3.2.5 Adjectives and Adverbs

Adjectives normally modify nouns, as in "the big red book", but may also be an argument of a verb (including forms of "be", "feel", "appear", and "become"). Adjectives can also be marked as comparative (meaning "more than typical", using the suffix "-er") or superlative (meaning "more than any others", using the suffix "-est"). Adverbs modify verbs, adjectives, or other adverbs. They express manner or intensity. They may be comparative (e.g., "better") or superlative (e.g., "best"). Adverbs that end in the suffix "-ly" have been derived from a related adjective (e.g., "quickly" is derived from "quick").

3.2.6 Conjunctions

Conjunctions, such as "and", "although", "because", "but", "however", "or", "nor", "so", "unless", "when", "where", "while", etc. are words that join words, phrases, clauses, or sentences. They can be discontinuous, e.g,. "either … or", "neither … nor", "both … and", "not only … but also", "on the one hand … on the other (hand)", "not just … but", and "not only … but". They can take modifiers, such as "particularly", as in Figure 3.6.

Figure 3.6 Example of a modified conjunction

These have been among the country's leading imports, particularly last year when there were shortages that led many traders to buy heavily and pay dearly. [wsj 1469]

There are three major types of conjunctions: coordinating conjunctions, subordinating conjunctions, and correlative conjunctions. A coordinating conjunction (e.g., "and", "but", "or", and "so") joins two structures that have the same type. Their purpose is to express that two entities did something together, or two events happened at the same time. A subordinating conjunction (e.g., "after", "although", "because", "before", "if", "how", "however", "since", "once", "until", "when", "where", "while", "whenever", "as soon as", "even if", "no matter how", etc) join a subordinate (dependent) and a main (independent) clause. The main clause can be understood on its own. The dependent clause can only be fully understood in the context of the main clause, as its purpose is to provide background, explanation, justification, or possible exceptions to what is said in the main clause. Thus, they express what is known as *rhetorical structure* or *discourse relations* among clauses, which can occur either within the same sentence or between adjacent sentences. When they link adjacent sentences at the sentence level, these words function as adverbs, so subordinating conjunctions are often labelled as adverbs, wherever they occur, and some experts refer to them as conjunctive adverbs. Sometimes subordinating conjunctions are labelled as prepositions, as in the Penn Treebank II. Discourse relations can exist without any explicit conjunction, but by using hand-annotated data, such as the Penn Discourse Treebank or the Biomedical Discourse Relation Bank, they can be identified using automated discourse parsing. A correlative conjunction is a discontinuous conjunction that joins words, phrases, or clauses that have a complementary relationship. Because they are discontinuous, they are harder to learn, and so automated systems do not always label them consistently. Figure 3.7 includes some sentences illustrating different types of conjunctions and how they are labelled using the default Stanford CoreNLP part-of-speech tagger.

Figure 3.7 Examples of conjunctions

Example sentences	Type of expression with labels given by CoreNLP
You can walk but you cannot run.	Coordinating conjunction, labelled as conjunction
You can read at home or in the library.	Coordinating conjunction, labelled as conjunction
My daughter and her friends like to climb.	Coordinating conjunction, labelled as conjunction
My cat purrs when **you pet her**.	Subordinating conjunction, labelled as adverb
If *you study hard*, **you will do well**.	Subordinating conjunction, labelled as preposition
You can either walk or take the bus.	Correlative conjunction, labelled as adverb, conjunction
The car not only is quiet but also handles well.	Correlative conjunction, labelled adverb, adverb, conjunction, adverb
Embryonic Stem cells have a high mitotic index and form colonies. So, *experiments can be completed rapidly and easily*.	Discourse adverbial, labelled as adverb
Obese cats have higher levels of inflammatory chemicals in their bloodstream. However, *rapid shifts in fat tissue further increase this inflammation*.	Discourse adverbial, labelled as adverb

3.2.8 Wh-Words

Wh-words that begin with the letters "wh-" like "who", "what", "when", "where", "which", "whose", and "why" and their close cousins "how", "how much", "how many", etc. They are used for posing questions and are thus sometimes called interrogatives. Unlike the word types mentioned so far, they can be determiners, adverbs, or pronouns (both regular and possessive), and so it is typical to see them marked as a special subtype of each. Identifying phrases that include wh-words is important, because they usually occur near the front in written text and fill an argument role that has been left empty in its normal position, as in "Which book did you like best?" In informal speech one might say "You left your book where?" or "You said what?", but the unusual syntax also suggests a problem (like mishearing, shock, or criticism). The semantics of the wh-expression specify what sort of answer the speaker is expecting (e.g., a person, a description, a time, a place, etc) and thus are essential to question-answering systems.

3.3 PART-OF-SPEECH TAGS

The general syntactic category of a word is also known as its part of speech (POS) whereas "tag" refers to labels for specifying the category and syntactic features (such as singular or plural). Today, the use of "tag" is often synonymous with the labels given in the Penn Treebank II (PT2) tagset[15,16]. There was no process of agreement for adopting this tagset as a standard. Instead, a group of linguistic experts, with resources to support the work, developed them and disseminated them widely. Along the way, refinements have been made so that human annotation is more reliable and the sets of words in each category are not too sparse; early versions had about 80 tags, while the current only has only about 35. The tag set and associated guidelines for English have been stable since 2015. (The word tags have been stable since 1999). Figure 3.8 includes the complete English tagset for words, excluding punctuation.

Figure 3.8 Penn Treebank tags for words (excluding punctuation)

Tag	Description	Example
CC	conjunction, coordinating	and, or, but
CD	cardinal number	five, three, 13%
DT	determiner	the, a, these
EX	existential there	there were six boys
FW	foreign word	mais
IN	conjunction, subordinating or preposition	that, of, on, before, unless
JJ	adjective	nice, easy
JJR	adjective, comparative	nicer, easier
JJS	adjective, superlative	nicest, easiest
LS	list item marker	1), 2), etc
MD	verb, modal auxiliary	may, should
NN	noun, singular or mass	tiger, chair, laughter
NNS	noun, plural	tigers, chairs, insects
NNP	noun, proper singular	Milwaukee, Rex, Claire
NNPS	noun, proper plural	I go out on Fridays, We go to the Smiths'
PDT	predeterminer	both his children
POS	possessive ending	's
PRP	pronoun, personal	me, you, it, him, her
PRP$	pronoun, possessive	my, your, our
RB	adverb	extremely, loudly, hard
RBR	adverb, comparative	better
RBS	adverb, superlative	best
RP	adverb, particle	about, off, up
SYM	symbol	%, #
TO	infinitival to	what to do, I want to sleep

UH	interjection	oh, oops, gosh
VB	verb, base form	think, eat
VBZ	verb, 3rd person singular present	she thinks, she eats
VBP	verb, non-3rd person singular present	I think
VBD	verb, past tense	they thought
VBN	verb, past participle	a sunken ship
VBG	verb, gerund or present participle	thinking is fun
WDT	wh-determiner	which, whatever, whichever
WP	wh-pronoun, personal	what, who, whom
WP$	wh-pronoun, possessive	whose, whosever
WRB	wh-adverb	where, when

3.4 MULTI-WORD CONSTITUENTS

For each of the primary types of words, there is a corresponding phrase type that includes the main word (called the "head"), along with any modifiers (optional words or phrases that enhance the meaning), or arguments (words or phrases that are required to be present). These phrases can also be combined recursively to form more complex phrases, clauses, or sentences. Below we will overview the major types of phrases and some of the conventions that define them. A complete discussion of English grammar fills a book of over 1800 pages[17]. This complexity is one reason that modern grammars are learned from large collections of text, rather than written by hand.

3.4.1 Noun Phrases and Prepositional Phrases

Noun phrases are the most used type of phrase but also have the most variation. Noun phrases can be simply a pronoun or proper noun, or include a determiner, some premodifiers (such as adjectives), the head noun, and some postmodifiers at the end.

The determiner might be a single word or a complex expression such as a complete noun phrase that includes a possessive marker ("-'s" or "-s' ") at the end. Gerunds are noun phrases where a verb that ends in "-ing" (tagged as VBG) acts as a head noun, as in the sentence "Walking is good exercise".

It is common to describe noun phrases as a combination of a determiner and a nominal, where the nominal is an ordered sequence of optional premodifiers, the head, and the postmodifiers. The premodifiers can include a cardinal (such as "third"), an ordinal (such as "three"), a quantifier (such as "all" or "most"), other common nouns, an adjective, or an adjective phrase (such as "very green and slimy"). English only permits three types of postmodifiers: relative clauses (such as "the dog *that found a bone*" or "the dog *that I got at the humane society*"), non-finite clauses (such as "I had something *to eat*"), and prepositional phrases. Relative clauses following the head of a noun often begin with a relative pronoun, such as "that", "which", "who", "whose", "whom", or "whomever" and sometimes also "when" or "where"[18]. Sometimes these words can be omitted. So, instead of saying "The meal that I ate was yummy" we might say "The meal I ate was yummy". When the relative pronoun is omitted, this is sometimes described as being a reduced relative clause. Also, the head noun will always fill some syntactic role within the relative clause (either a subject or object), so a grammatical relative clause cannot also include a filler for this same role. So, one cannot say "The meal that I ate the meal was yummy.", as it overfills the object role of "ate".

Prepositional phrases comprise a preposition followed by a noun phrase. Semantically, we use them to add locations, times, or generic modifiers to a noun or to a sentence. They can follow a head noun or verb in a noun phrase or verb phrase, respectively. They can also modify an entire clause, where they typically occur either at the very beginning or the very end.

3.4.2 Verb Phrases

Verb phrases (VP) comprise a sequence of auxiliaries or modals, a main verb, the arguments of the main verb, and optional prepositional phrases as modifiers. Adverbs can appear almost anywhere within the VP. The arguments of a verb will depend on the verb, some take no arguments, some take one or two. An argument may also be restricted to be a particular syntactic structure such as a noun phrase or a clause, or it may be a semantic requirement, such as being a description of a location. Linguists have used case grammars[19] or slot grammars[20] to describe the argument structures of verbs. For NLP several resources have been created that are available as part of the **Unified Verb Index**[21]. These resources include VerbNet, FrameNet and OntoNotes. For example, VerbNet is the largest verb lexicon for English. It groups together verbs with identical sets of syntactic frames and semantic predicate structures and provides information about those structures. Syntactic frames are sometimes also called "thematic roles". Figure 3.9 shows some of the syntactic structures associated with "cut21.1". OntoNotes is a corpus of text that includes annotation of a wide variety of text (telephone conversations, newswire, newsgroups, broadcast news, broadcast conversation, and weblogs) with syntax, argument structure, and shallow semantics.

Figure 3.9 Example of syntactic argument patterns for cut (sense cut21.1) from VerbNet 3.3

Verb Pattern	Example with syntactic frame	
NP V NP	example	"Carol cut the bread."
	frame	Agent V Patient
NP V PP	example	"Carol cut through the bread."
	frame	Agent V {through|into} Patient
NP V NP ADJP	example	"Carol cut the envelope open."
	frame	Agent V Patient Result
NP V NP PP.instrument	example	"Carol cut the bread with a knife."
	frame	Agent V Patient {with} Instrument

3.4.3 Clauses and Sentences

Clauses and sentences are structures that include a verb with a complete set of arguments. Sentences can either be statements (declaratives), questions (interrogatives), or commands (imperatives). Questions can either be yes-no questions (constructed by putting the auxiliary in front of the subject noun phrase) or wh-questions which include a question word at the front ("who", "what", "when", "where", "why", "how"), and sometimes also an auxiliary before the subject noun phrase. In wh-questions the question word takes the place of some other constituent in the sentence (either a subject or an object of a verb or preposition) that is an unknown, such as the type of something. A passive sentence is one where the semantic object appears as the syntactic subject (the one before the VP) as in "The apple was eaten".

Some examples of different types of sentences are shown in Figure 3.10.

Figure 3.10 Example sentences and their types

Example sentence	Sentence type
The cat sat.	Statement
The cat chased a mouse.	Statement
The mouse was chased	Passive statement
The girl gave her cat a toy	Statement
The cat slept in the bed.	Statement
What did the cat do?	Wh – question
What did the cat chase?	Wh – question
Who gave the cat a toy?	Wh – question
Who did she give the toy to?	Wh – question
What did she give the cat?	Wh – question
Where did the cat sleep?	Wh – question
Did the cat catch the mouse?	Yes – no question
Is it time to put the cat outside?	Yes – no question
Wake up the cat.	Command
Wash the bed when she is done sleeping.	Command

Clauses in English include complete declarative sentences (comprising a subject main verb and its required objects), dependent relative clauses introduced by a subordinating conjunction (e.g., "that", "before"), interrogative sentences (i.e., questions) marked by a wh-word or by inverting the subject and the main verb or a modal, or a combination. When the wh-word at the front refers to one of the objects of the main verb or a prepositional phrase, then the normal position for that object will be empty in a grammatical sentence. Linguists refer to this phenomenon as *movement* and the location of the missing object is a *gap* or *trace*. In the treebank data this information is not tracked, except to note that the sentence is a question introduced by a wh-word (i.e.,

SBARQ). Lastly, adverbs, adjectives, and interjections can also occur as sequences of several adjacent words. Figure 3.11 shows some examples of these constructions and the category labels that are used in the Penn Treebank, and thus have become the standard for automatic processing as well.

Figure 3.11 Examples of some common Penn Treebank Constituent tags

Tag	Description	Examples
NP	Noun phrase	**The strange bird** in the tree sang.
PP	Prepositional phrase	I walked **in the park**
VP	Verb phrase	I **was looking around.**
S	Sentence, declarative	**The cat slept.**
SQ	Inverted yes/no question	**Did the cat sleep?**
SBAR	Relative clause	A cat **that sleeps** is happy. The cat slept **before she ate.**
SBARQ	Direct questions, introduced by a wh-word	**Who slept on the floor?**
SINV	Inverted declarative sentence (subject follows tensed verb or modal)	**Never has she been so happy.**
ADVP	Adverb phrase	I am **also very** happy.
ADJP	Adjective phrase	The bed is **warm and cozy.**
QP	Quantifier phrase	She had **no more than 100.**
INTJ	Interjection with several words	**Hello in there,** I did not see you.

3.5 SUBCATEGORIZATION

Subcategorization is when one lexical category constrains the categories of its arguments. So, a verb like "give" takes two NP as internal arguments (the object and the recipient). Verbs also often occur with an external argument, which would be its subject. All verbs constrain their arguments; but other words can too, e.g., adjectives and nouns[22]. Figure 3.12 shows some examples of subcategorization. The pattern of subcategorization of a word is sometimes referred to as its "subcategorization frame" or just "frame". An extensive collection of verbs and their expected arguments can be found in the **Unified Verb Index**.

Figure 3.12 Examples of subcategorization

Example	Subcategorization
She was happy to get a puppy.	"happy" requires a VP in the infinitive form
The front of the bus was empty.	"front" requires a PP that starts with "of"
She said she wanted to be president.	"said" requires a complete S (any form)

3.6 LEXICAL DEPENDENCY

An alternative to constituency for describing the legal sequences of words, is to describe sequences in terms of binary syntactic relations between a head word and an argument. These relations are called lexical dependencies or just "dependencies". These dependencies include the categories of subject, direct object, and indirect object, and categories for different types of modifiers. Which of these arguments is required depends on the subcategorization constraints of the head word. When both a direct and an indirect object are required, the indirect object occurs first, unless it is contained inside a prepositional phrase that begins with "to". Figure 3.13 shows examples where the main part of the dependency is marked in bold and the dependent part is marked in italics.

Figure 3.13 Example dependency relations

Name	Description	Example
nsubj	nominal subject	The *cat* **chased** the mouse.
dobj	direct object	The cat **chased** the *mouse*.
iobj	indirect object	The bird **fed** her *babies* a worm.
iobj	indirect object	The bird **fed** a worm to her *babies*.
pobj	prepositional object	The **bird** in the *tree* was sleeping.
amod	adjective modifier	The *happy* **bird** sang.

Both constituency and dependency induce a tree structure over legal sequences of words. The main difference between dependency trees and constituency trees is that dependency trees store words at every node, whereas in constituency trees only store words in the leaves, and the nodes are marked with part-of-speech tags. Figure 3.14 includes an example of the representation for the sentence, "The cat slept in her warm bed". The dependencies include that "cat" is the noun subject of the verb "slept", "bed" is a noun modifier of "slept", "her" is a possessive noun modifier of "bed", and "warm" as an adjective modifier of "bed". (The relations "det" and "case" are the labels used for the corresponding function words.)

Figure 3.14 Example dependency parse (Image from CoreNLP.run)

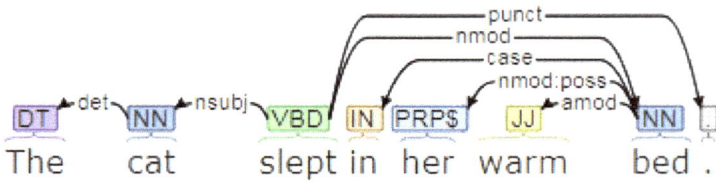

There are currently 37 universal syntactic relations defined by the Universal Dependencies organization (See Figure 3.15).

Figure 3.15 Universal Dependency Relations defined in UDv2

Universal dependency and description	Universal dependency and description
acl: clausal modifier of noun (adjectival clause)	fixed: fixed multiword expression
advcl: adverbial clause modifier	flat: flat multiword expression
amod: adjectival modifier	goeswith: goes with
appos: appositional modifier	iobj: indirect object
aux: auxiliary	list: list
case: case marking	mark: marker
cc: coordinating conjunction	nmod: nominal modifier
ccomp: clausal complement	nsubj: nominal subject
clf: classifier	nummod: numeric modifier
compound: compound	obj: object
conj: conjunct	obl: oblique nominal
cop: copula	orphan: orphan
csubj: clausal subject	parataxis: parataxis
dep: unspecified dependency	punct: punctuation
det: determiner	reparandum: overridden disfluency
discourse: discourse element	root: root
dislocated: dislocated elements	vocative: vocative
expl: expletive	xcomp: open clausal complement

3.7 SUMMARY

The syntax of a natural language can be described in terms of:

- The types and features of words,
- The constituency of legal sequences of words, or
- Dependency relations that hold between pairs of words, and

- The subcategorization constraints that some words impose on sequences of words.

At one time, all these aspects required coding from scratch using manually created dictionaries and grammar rules. Today, large annotated data sets exist that allow one to either extract most vocabulary items and grammar rules or to train statistical language models for automated processing. However, there are types of text that are not well covered by such corpora, including social media and text within proprietary data warehouses (e.g., user and repair manuals for devices). Some of this data is important as it includes the notes of medical providers and records created by marketing and service departments of enterprises. In this chapter, we have discussed the basis for computational methods of language analysis. In the next chapters, we will consider computational descriptions of language syntax and processing models for identifying syntactic structure and meaning.

Notes

1. Butte College 2020. The Eight Parts of Speech. URL: http://www.butte.edu/departments/cas/tipsheets/grammar/parts_of_speech.html Accessed May 2020.
2. The videos can be found online. Here is one place to find them: https://www.teachertube.com/collections/school-house-rock-grammar-4728
3. Francis, W. N. and Kučera, H. (1964). *Manual of Information to accompany A Standard Corpus of Present-Day Edited American English, for use with Digital Computers*. Providence, Rhode Island: Department of Linguistics, Brown University. Revised 1971. Revised and amplified 1979. Available online at: http://icame.uib.no/brown/bcm.html
4. Kučera, H. and Francis, W.N. (1967). *Computational Analysis of Present-Day American English*. Dartmouth Publishing Group.
5. Greene, B. B., and Rubin, G. M. (1971). Automatic Grammatical Tagging of English. Technical Report, Department of Linguistics, Brown University, Providence, Rhode Island.
6. Godfrey, J. and Holliman, E. (1993) Switchboard-1 Release 2

LDC97S62. Web Download. Philadelphia: Linguistic Data Consortium.

7. Beis, A., Mott, J., Warner, C., and Kulick, S. (2012). English Web Treebank LDC2012T13. Web Download. Philadelphia: Linguistic Data Consortium, 2012. URL: https://catalog.ldc.upenn.edu/LDC2012T13

8. Silveira, N., Dozat, T., De Marneffe, M.C., Bowman, S.R., Connor, M., Bauer, J., and Manning, C.D. (2014). A Gold Standard Dependency Corpus for English. *Proceedings of the Ninth International Conference on Language Resources and Evaluation* (LREC'14), pp. 2897-2904.

9. Weischedel, R., Palmer, M., Marcus, M., Hovy, E., Pradhan, S., Ramshaw, L., Xue, N., Taylor, A., Kaufman, J., Franchini, M., El-Bachouti, M., Belvin, R., and Houston, A. (2013). *OntoNotes Release 5.0* LDC2013T19. Linguistic Data Consortium, Philadelphia.

10. spacy.io (2020). spaCy English Available Pretrained Statistical Models for English. URL: https://spacy.io/models/en

11. Li, S. (2018). Named Entity Recognition with NLTK and spaCy URL: https://towardsdatascience.com/named-entity-recognition-with-nltk-and-spacy-8c4a7d88e7da

12. ANC.org (2015) Open American National Corpus URL: http://www.anc.org/

13. Napoles, C., Gormley, M. R., & Van Durme, B. (2012, June). Annotated Gigaword. In Proceedings of the Joint Workshop on Automatic Knowledge Base Construction and Web-scale Knowledge Extraction (AKBC-WEKEX) (pp. 95-100).

14. Essberger, J. (2012). *English Preposition List*. Ebook Online: http://www.englishclub.com/download/PDF/EnglishClub-English-Prepositions-List.pdf

15. Bies, A., Ferguson, M., Katz, K., and MacIntyre, R. (1995). *Bracketing Guidelines For Treebank II Style Penn Treebank Project*. URL https://web.archive.org/web/20191212003907/http://languagelog.ldc.upenn.edu/myl/PennTreebank1995.pdf

16. Warner, C., Bies, A., Brisson, and C. Mott, J. (2004). *Addendum to the Penn Treebank II Style Bracketing Guidelines: BioMedical Treebank Annotation,* University of Pennsylvania, Linguistic Data Consortium.

17. Huddleston, R. D. and Pullum, G. K. (2002)*The Cambridge Grammar of the English Language.* Cambridge, UK: Cambridge University Press.

18. Grammars for NLP use a variety of categories for these words including wh-determiner (which, that, who, whom), wh-possessive

pronoun (whose), and wh-adverb (when, where).
19. Fillmore, C. J., and Fillmore, S. (1968). Case Grammar. Universals in Linguistic Theory. Holt, Rinehart, and Winston: New York, pp. 1-88.
20. McCord, M. C. (1990). Slot Grammar. In *Natural Language and Logic.* pp. 118-145. Springer, Berlin, Heidelberg.
21. Kipper, K., Korhonen, A., Ryant, N., and Palmer, M. (2008) A Large-scale Classification of English Verbs. *Language Resources and Evaluation Journal*,42(1). Springer Netherland. pp. 21-40.
22. Yallop, J., Korhonen, A., and Briscoe, T. (2005). Automatic Acquisition of Adjectival Subcategorization from Corpora. 10.3115/1219840.1219916.

CHAPTER 4.

GRAMMARS AND SYNTACTIC PROCESSING

If one wants to build systems that communicate with people in human language or that analyze people's beliefs and behavior it is useful to perform a syntactic analysis of the text into either phrase or dependency structures first. The correct structures are specified using a grammar. Identifying the structure involves a variety of steps, that can be performed independently, in a sequence (which is known as a pipeline architecture) or can be learned as part of a complete language model trained using Deep Learning. Both NLP pipelines and Deep Learning models input unstructured text, as a file or stream of characters, and output either a single best analysis or a ranked set of alternatives. In between, they may include steps that assign part of speech tags to individual words, that group words into segments and provide labels to sequences of tagged segments.

Figure 4.1 shows a modern natural language processing pipeline. This pipeline is the one implemented in the NLP software library spaCy.

Figure 4.1 NLP pipeline implemented in spaCy (figure adapted from https://course.spacy.io/chapter3)

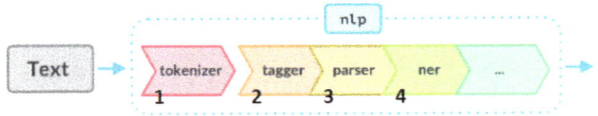

The steps associated with syntactic processing include tokenizing documents into individual sentences and words (1), followed by labelling words with syntactic categories (2), and identifying the syntactic structure that spans sequences of words, which is called parsing (3). These steps might be followed by a shallow analysis of meaning, such as named entity recognition (4), sentiment (not shown), or by a deeper analysis of semantic relations (not shown), which we will discuss in later chapters.

The pipeline processes of Figure 4.1 may be implemented as either search or classification (the processing paradigms we discussed in Chapter 2). Search-based parsing requires a computer-readable lexicon and grammar. The lexicon specifies the vocabulary, while the grammar describes constraints on the linear order of words and the sequences that correspond to well-formed constituents (phrases and clauses). Grammars and lexicons can be provided in a formal language, to be processed by a separate interpreter, or provided as functions in a programming language, that can be executed directly. Classification-based approaches require datasets annotated with the target structure that can be used for training. Widely used datasets for English include the Penn Treebank and OntoNotes for phrase-based annotations and the English Web Treebank (en-EWT)[1] for dependencies. These datasets have been used to create pretrained functions in software libraries such as NLTK, spaCy, Stanza, and UDPipe.

The remainder of this chapter will discuss pipeline processes 1 to 3 from Figure 4.1 (tokenization, tagging, and parsing).

4.1 TOKENIZATION

Tokenization divides a string into substrings and returns a set of tokens that represent the individual substrings. Simple tokenizers spit strings at whitespace (typically tabs and spaces) and create separate substrings for each punctuation symbol. More complex versions also find the root form (lemma) for each word, as shown in Figure 4.2, which shows how the tokenizer of Stanford's CoreNLP system would split the string "I sold my book for $80.00."

Figure 4.2 The tokenization of "I sold my book for $80.00.". (Image by Stanford CoreNLP.run (2020)

| I | sell | my | book | for | $ | 80.00 | . |

I sold my book for $ 80.00 .

NLP software libraries include predefined tokenizers and mechanisms for defining new ones. Figure 4.3 shows how tokenization can be called from NLTK and SpaCy in just a few lines of code. (The example is for processing the phrase "My pet cat.") In some programming languages (e.g., Python) tokenizers can be implemented from scratch using built-in functions for splitting strings and regular expressions to find punctuation symbols or other characters, like "$", in the spans between whitespace. More sophisticated tokenizers also create separate tokens for parts of a contraction (e.g., don't is tokenized as {"do", "not"}). Another system, the Wordpiece tokenizer (used by the BERT to create word vector representations[23]), splits unknown (out of vocabulary) words into substrings; for example "kindle" is split into ['kind', '##le'] and "recourse" is split into ['rec', '##ours', '##e']. The most sophisticated tokenizers (such as nltk.tokenize.punkt) have been trained on annotated data, such as the Penn Treebank, to identify strings that correspond to abbreviations, words that are at the start of a sentence (and hence can be safely changed to lower case), and collocations (or multiword expressions). Depending on the implementation, the result of tokenization may be just a list of strings or a list of objects with features set to capture the syntactic features and the canonical or dictionary form of the word (lemma) for spans that corresponds to words in a known vocabulary.

Figure 4.3 Code for performing tokenization and part-of-speech tagging in NLTK and spaCy

Tagging in NLTK

```
import nltk
from nltk.tokenize import word_tokenize
from nltk.tag import pos_tag def preprocess(sent):
sent = nltk.word_tokenize(sent)
sent = nltk.pos_tag(sent)
return sent s= preprocess('My pet cat.') print(s[0])
```

Tagging in spaCy

```
import spacy nlp = spacy.load("en_core_web_sm")
text = "My pet cat." #Tokenize, tag, NER,  and parse
doc = nlp(text) #word and its tag
print(doc[0].text, doc[0].pos_)
```

4.2 PART-OF-SPEECH TAGGING

Part-of-speech tagging takes a tokenized text and provides syntactic label for each token. Today, tags refers to either labels from the Penn Treebank II tagset (which is what NLTK uses) or tags from the Universal Dependencies tagset (which is what spaCy uses)[4]. Implementations of tagging use either hand-crafted rules, statistical modelling, or language modelling implemented with neural networks. Because part-of-speech tagging is such a common NLP task, prebuilt functions for tagging exist in major NLP software libraries, and can either be called individually (as in NLTK) or will be invoked as part of the standard NLP processing pipeline (as in spaCy). Figure 4.3 (in Section 4.1), shows example code for invoking the tagger within these two libraries, after sentences are tokenized.

The earliest successful taggers were rule-based or combined a rule-based approach with simple statistical modelling. Statistical taggers were first introduced by Marshall in 1983[5], but were not very accurate until larger and better datasets, such as the Penn Treebank, became available, so that more advanced modelling was feasible. The most successful taggers combine a wide range of information including the possible syntactic categories of nearby words, the overall probability associated with words being used a particular way (e.g., "eats" can be a noun or a verb, but it is more typically a verb), the probability of suffixes and prefixes being associated with different parts of speech (e.g., words that end in "-ly" are usually adverbs), and the capitalization of a word (e.g., words that begin with a capital letter are usually proper nouns). Rules for tagging can capture these known linguistic generalizations.

The simplest statistical models just use the most frequent category for each word. Sequence-based modelling (a type of sequence classification) involves finding the best sequence of tags for an entire sentence (rather than just a single word). These approaches can combine information about the most common category of a single word with those of nearby words, which is the approach taken by Hidden Markov Models. More advanced approaches, such as Maximum Entropy Markov Models (used by the Stanford CoreNLP tagger) and Averaged Perceptrons (a neural approach used in NLTK), consider the frequency of subsequences, as well as the other linguistic features, but adjust their impact by measuring the association between each feature and tag in a training corpus. Thus, sequence classification requires a data set of sentences where each word has been correctly tagged. Also, the corpus must be large enough so that the algorithm can find enough examples within the training corpus for the estimates to be meaningful. A third factor in the success of taggers trained from data is the similarity between the genre used for training and the genre of the target. Treebanks exist for newspaper text, as part of the Penn Treebank, and a variety of Web texts, such as blogs, as part of the English Web Tree Bank (a treebank created from Twitter posts as part of the CMU TweetNLP corpus), and a treebank created from GENIA, a collection of abstracts from the medical literature (which can be obtained from the Stanford NLP group[6]).

In sections that follow, we will consider rule-based, statistical, and neural approaches to tagging.

4.2.1 Rule-based tagging

A basic rule-based part-of-speech tagger can be created by using regular expressions to specify a list of patterns and their corresponding tag. Figure 4.4 contains an example set of patterns suitable for working with the regular expression tagger of NLTK. It would provide PTB tags similar to what you might see if you tagged a sentence like "I wanted to find 12.5 percent of the oldest words." This approach can work for small domains, but requires effort and expertise to create a broad set of rules and will sometimes err on words that have more than one part of speech (such as "her", which can be either a personal pronoun, when used as an object, as in "given to her", or a possessive pronoun, as in "her cat").

Figure 4.4 Example of a tagger created using regular expressions in NLTK

```
>>> regexp_tagger = RegexpTagger(
...     [(r'^-?[0-9]+(.[0-9]+)?$', 'CD'),
...     (r'(The|the|A|a|An|an)', 'DT'),
...     (r'(I|We|we|You|you|They|them)', 'PRP'),
...     (r'(I|He|he|Him|him|She|she|Her|her|It|it)', 'PRP'),
...     (r'to', 'TO'),
...     (r'.*able$', 'JJ'),
...     (r'.*est$', 'JJS'),
...     (r'.*ness$', 'NN'),
...     (r'.*ly$', 'RB'),
...     (r'.*s$', 'NNS'),
...     (r'.*ing$', 'VBG'),
...     (r'.*ed$', 'VBD'),
...     (r'.*', 'NN')
...     ])
```

The most successful rule-based POS tagger was created as part of a Constraint Grammar Parser for English (ENGCG). Its accuracy has been consistently reported as 99.7%, which is better than comparable purely statistical approaches, but does not use either of the most the widely accepted tagsets (e.g., the Penn Treebank or Universal Dependencies)[7]. (It would also be difficult to update to handle corpora, such as weblogs and social media.) This rule-based tagger used an approach based on an AI problem solving technique known as constraint satisfaction. This is a type of search that tries to find an assignment of values to variables such that bindings to variables satisfy any constraints that mention those variables, which can be performed either as depth-first search or as optimization (gradient descent). At each step of the search, remaining values are compared to the constraints and values that conflict are removed from consideration. The tagging algorithm uses a large hand-crafted dictionary, ENGT-WOL, that includes a list of all possible part-of-speech categories for each word and a set of rules that specify various constraints between the category labels for different words in the same sentence. ENGTWOL had about 1100 rules that were based on their syntactic grammar and another 200 or so that were just "heuristic". The number of rules was so large because the dictionary used 139 different tags for words (whereas modern tagsets have only 36 tags for words).

The ENGCG algorithm starts by retrieving all possible tags for each word and then applies the constraints that match, eliminating tags that violate constraints until each word has a unique tag. An example of a constraint is "A past participle cannot immediately follow a pronoun at the start of a sentence." (This is true because, in the grammar, a past participle requires a preceding auxiliary verb.) A more complex example of a constraint is shown in Figure 4.5. Note that, in the rule shown, "1" means the next word, "2" means the second word to the right of the current word. This rule expresses the constraints associated with selecting the adverbial (ADV) sense of "that" which is a synonym for "very" (as in the sentence *"I wasn't that drunk."* which is a sentence that is not tagged correctly by the default taggers within either NLTK or spaCy, which have been trained on data that likely never saw an example of this construction).

Figure 4.5 ENGTWOL/ENGCG tagging rule for "that" as ADV

```
Given input "that"

If
      (1 A/ADV/QUANT)   ; if next is adjective, adverb, or quantifier
      (2 SENT-LOM)      ; and the end of sentence follows next
      (NOT -1 SVOC/A)   ; and the prior cannot have ADJ complement

Then eliminate non-ADV tags
Else eliminate ADV
```

Later versions of the analyzer added information from the XEROX statistical tagger (XT) to remove ambiguities that remained *after* the applicable rules were applied, eventually reaching an accuracy of over 99.7% compared to the rate of 97% for XT alone. This approach worked better than either using the statistical tagger alone, or using the statistical tagger first. When the errors were reviewed, it was revealed that the hand-written rules tended to solve all but the "hardest" cases of ambiguity, while the statistical model made about 80% of its errors on "easy" cases, but sometimes did better on cases that people think would be "hard", but were correctly tagged in its training data. (Statistical tagging only got better than rule-based tagging when enough high-quality annotated data was available, e.g., after the competion of the Penn Treebank.)

4.2.2 Brill Tagger

The Brill Tagger, first described in 1993, uses a hybrid of a rule-based and a statistical approach, which can be useful when there is only a limited amount of training data. In this tagger, a simple statistical model is used first and then rules are used to correct specific types of errors observed by experts. Correction rules can be hand-crafted, or learned from an annotated corpus. The algorithm begins by selecting the most frequent category for the word, based on the training data. This is known as a "unigram" model, because it only looks at one word at a time. The rules test for specific suffixes of a word, the surrounding words, and the categories of surrounding words and suggests replacement tags. For example, there is a specific rule for an error in tagging the word "while" in sentences like "She/PRP was/VBD gone/VBN for/IN a/DT while/IN" that occur because "while" is most often a preposition (IN), but in context should be a common noun (NN).

Hybrid tagging addresses the insight that statistical taggers do not always resolve ambiguity correctly, however their errors are generally understandable enough (by experts) to correct by hand using a fixed set of rules. Even when statistical taggers consider more context, and are trained over more data, there will be examples that have not been seen or may not be resolvable without reference to common sense knowledge[8]. A Brill-style tagger, if trained on suitable data, can address the errors seen for a target domain task. A trained instance of Brill's tagger also requires relatively little space, as it only creates a unigram model. Implementations for versions of the Brill tagger and software for using a corpus to learn rules can be found in the NLTK software library (e.g., nltk.tag.brill and nltk.tag.brill_trainer).

4.2.3 Statistical Classification-Based Tagging

Today, the most accurate POS taggers use sequence classification. The earliest examples used straightforward statistical modelling; more recent ones create models by training neural networks, which allow them to discover novel statistical relationships. The general idea of a sequence-based classifier is to find the ordered list of tags that maximizes the estimated probability of being the correct sequence of tags. This generally involves enumerating and scoring all possible combinations, while keeping track of the best one. Efficiencies can be made by pursuing a greedy strategy that prunes all but the best choice for each word as it moves across a sentence from left to right. Implementations exist that use different statistical models (e.g., Hidden Markov Models, Maximum-Entropy Markov Models, and Conditional Random Fields), which can be implemented by dynamic programming (e.g., the Viterbi algorithm[9]). The newest approaches use various types of neural networks. We will start by discussing the general idea behind sequence classification. Later in Section 4.3.5 we will overview some neural network approaches.

The general idea behind most statistical approaches to language modelling is a two-step process. The first step involves counting the frequency of words and tags within a suitable corpus for subsequences of the original sequence. The second step involves calculating several types of estimated probabilities for each word-tag pair and then selecting the best combination of pairs for the entire sentence. We estimate probabilities when there is no way to get a true probability. The estimates are relatively easy to do by counting. For example, the probability of a single word having a tag can be estimated as the simple proportion of times the word occurs with the tag and to build a bigram model, which is a bit more accurate, we look at words two at a time. To do this we traverse a corpus tagged with part of speech to count and store three things: 1) The number of times that each word occurs with each tag (i.e., $C(w_i, t_j)$); 2) the total number of times that each tag occurs (i.e., $C(t)$); and 3) the number of times that each pair of tags occurs (i.e., $C(t_i,t_{i+1})$). Figure 4.6 shows how these counts are used to estimate probabilities, where the real probabilities are on the left, along with the expression used to estimate the value on the right. In line a, we estimate the lexical generation probability because the expression we really want to use ($P(t|w)$) can be simplified by first using Bayes Rule and then ignoring the $P(w)$ term, since it will be the same for all tags we are considering. In line b, to estimate the probability that tag t_i follows tag t_{i-1}, we count the number of occurrences of (t_{i-1}, t_i), divided by the total number of occurrences of t_{i-1}. In line d, we justify combining the estimates for the different parts of the joint probability using simple multiplication by making an assumption that the events can be treated as independent (even though in real life they are not). This is called a *Markov Assumption*. For real data, where the proportions of counts are very small, we convert the expression in line d to log scale and use addition instead of multiplication to combine the terms. (This conversion is both more efficient and avoids rounding errors.)

Figure 4.6 Estimated probabilities used in a bigram model for part of speech tagging

Probability value	Counting-based estimate
a) $P(w\|t)$, "the lexical generation probability"	$C(t,w) \div C(t)$
b) $P(t_i\|t_{i-1})$, "the probability a tag follows a given one"	$C(t_{i-1},t_i) \div C(t_{i-1})$
c) $P(t_i\|t_{i+1})$, "the probability a tag precedes a given one"	$C(t_i,t_{i+1}) \div C(t_{i+1})$
d) $P(t_i\|w_i, t_{i-1}, t_{i+1})$, probability of a tag for a word	$(C(t_{i-1},t_i) \div C(t_{i-1})) * (C(t_i,t_{i+1}) \div C(t_{i+1})) * (C(t_i,w_i) \div C(t_i))$ – that is, take the product of the three estimates

This idea can be extended to longer sequences such as trigrams, or in general ngrams. There is a practical tradeoff between the length of the subsequences used to model a sentence and the number of instances available to train the model. A bigram-based tagger only uses the category of the one immediately preceding word to predict the current one; a trigram-based tagger will use the categories of the two previous words to predict the third. Thus a bigram model will likely include more examples of any given pair. A dataset might have very few of all but the most common triples. When there are insufficient examples of sequences, tagging algorithms can use a backoff strategy, where it applies a sequence of different tagging functions in a fixed order, so that if it does not have enough data to count sequences of length three it will "back off" and use sequences of length two, and so on, or it might default to a rule-based tagger. Another way of avoiding zeros in the calculations for estimated probability is to use a technique called smoothing. Smoothing techniques add very small quantities to the numerator and denominator, just big enough to prevent a zero, without affecting the overall ordering. Examples of smoothing techniques include Laplace smoothing, which adds one to the counts in both the numerator and the denominator and Good-Turing smoothing, which estimates the probability of examples missing in the training corpus by the estimated probability of examples that occur once[10]. One can also build a more complex, and potentially more accurate model, using Conditional Random Fields (CRF). CRFs do not require that one assume independence and also provide a certainty value for different possible sequences. Maximum Entropy Markov Models (MEMM), such as the Stanford CoreNLP tagger, and CRF models do not assume independence so they allow one to use ad hoc features, including suffixes and capitalization, but as a result, they are much slower, and rarely used for relatively simple tasks, such as part-of-speech tagging.

4.2.4 Sequence Classification-Based Tagging with Neural Networks

Statistical taggers are not completely accurate and require a large amount of space to build tables, which can range into the hundreds of millions of entries, in addition to the time they need to compute and compare the estimated probability values. Thus, there has been an interest in alternative methods using neural networks, which compare quite favorably for both accuracy and efficiency, especially for domains which are less standard than newspaper texts, such as micro-blogs[11]. The simplest neural approach uses an Averaged Perceptron, which is a single-layer network (discussed in Chapter 2) that is both accurate and efficient. An implementation of an Averaged Perceptron based tagger became the default tagger for NLTK 3.1 starting in 2017. In that implementation, (originally created by Matthew Hannibal for Textblob[12]), thirteen input features were used, capturing things like the suffixes on the current word and the two preceding words, and the tags on the preceding words (both separately and as a bigram).

The most recent neural network-based implementations use variants of a Deep Learning Architecture, which learn their features rather than depending on experts to select them, making them more adaptable to new domains. This aspect is especially helpful for domains, like microblogs and other types of social media, where nonstandard spelling and out-of-vocabulary words are common. Figure 4.7 shows an example from Twitter and the corresponding tags. (In the figure, UH is the tag for "interjection", USR is a new tag for "user name").

Figure 4.7 Example of Twitter text and tags from Gui et al 2017

Untagged sequence	@DORSEY33 lol aw i thought u was talkin bout another time . nd i dnt see u either !
Tags as labelled in Gui et al 2017.	USR UH UH PRP VBD PRP VBD VBG IN DT NN . CC PRP VBP VB PRP RB

Deep neural network architectures can address nonstandard spellings by using an input representation that maps the word sequence onto vectors or matrices that combine dense word-level representations to capture the general meaning of a word (i.e., a word embedding) with a dense character-level representation of each word (i.e., a character embedding), created using another, previously trained neural network[13]. The number of dimensions for these embeddings can be relatively small (e.g., 32 for the word embeddings and 2 for the character embeddings), compared to the overall size of a vocabulary, which might span hundreds of thousands of words. This combined input structure is then passed to layers that account for sequences (such as a bidirectional Long Short Term Memory layer or a Gate Recurrent Unit layer), followed by some additional layers (e.g., feed-forward or fully-connected) to select the best tags. Figure 4.8 is an illustration of this sort of architecture[14].

Figure 4.8 Example neural network architecture for part of speech tagging (Image from Meftah and Semmar (2018)

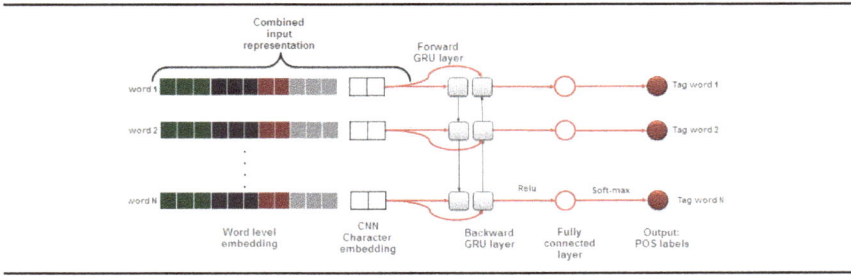

An emerging approach that has been proposed for dealing with novel domains is to combine the input with embeddings trained from a domain that is large and more conventional to enrich information from the smaller target domain, an approach known as transfer learning, which has been applied to Twitter text[15]. The tradeoff for these newer models is in the time needed for training. Thus a reasonable approach might start with a pre-trained tagger and then address errors with some domain-specific correction rules, if necessary. (One can also provide synthetic training data, meant to teach the model how to handle the erroneous cases.) We will now move to the next stage of syntactic processing which is to identify the syntactic structure over entire sequences of words.

4.2.5 Summary of Part of Speech Tagging

We have just overviewed the four main approaches to word-level tagging: rule-based, hybrid, statistical and heural network based approaches. The task is to which assign to each word a part of speech tag, now generally from the Penn Treebank II tagset, although early approaches, like ENGTWOL used other tagsets. Tagging can be performed separately or included as part of a pipeline.

Now we will consider how structures above the level of an individual word are described and identified computationally.

4.3 GRAMMARS

The assignment of an appropriate syntactic structure to a sequence of words depends on their being some pre-existing notion of what is the correct structure. In NLP syntactic correctness is specified by a grammar. Grammars describe the linear order in which words can occur and, ideally, do so in a way that is generalizable. There are sequences of words that correspond to well-formed constituents and thus longer structures can be specified recursively in terms of these constituents. For NLP work, two general types of grammars are most commonly used, context free grammars (CFG) and dependency grammars. CFGs are used to specify grammars in terms of linguistic categories such as NP and VP are thus are also called "phrase structure grammars" or "constituency grammars". In a dependency grammar, syntactic structure consists of binary asymmetrical relations (the dependency relations) that hold between words. Information about possible relations is given by the lexical entry for each word, as part of the lexicon that defines the vocabulary of the language. One of the earliest examples was McCord's Slot Grammar[16]. Figure 4.9 shows the lexical entry associated with the word "given" in a McCord's lexicon. The entry says that given is a past participle and has three relations: subject (subj), direct object (obj), and indirect object (iobj). Formally, a lexical entry can also be given as a combination of the word and a pair of finite state automata that define what relations exist to the right and to the left of the word, respectively [17].

Figure 4.9 Lexical entry for "given" in the Slot Grammar lexicon of McCord (1990)

```
wframe (3, s (give, i), verb(pastpar ta),
slot (subj (n) ,op,X).
slot (obj ,op,Y).
slot (iobj, op,g) .nil).
```

Parsing is the computational process of determining the correct structure for a given sequence of words, given the specification provided by the grammar. Parsing can use search or classification. A search-based parser traverses either the words of the sentence or the rules of the grammar to find a match between subsequences of the words and the rules of a grammar. Grammars for language tend to overgeneralize, resulting in thousands of possible parses, so the best approaches rely on mechanisms for ranking and pruning, so that only the most likely structures are considered. Like machine learning-based approaches, the algorithms for determining the most likely structures make use of information from a dataset of previously parsed sentences to estimate probabilities.

A classification-based parser takes a model that has been

learned from sentences previously annotated with the correct parse in the target format and applies it to an unparsed sentence to determine which of its previously seen structures (or equivalently, previously seen sequences of parser actions) is best according to that model. The coverage and accuracy of a classification-based parser thus depends on a combination of the quality of the training set and the sensitivity and specificity of the modelling algorithm.

4.3.1 Context Free Grammars

Context Free Grammars (CFGs) are a formalism for describing both the syntactic structure of human language and of programming languages. The formalism was developed in the 1950's and applied to describe natural language syntax by Noam Chomsky[18]. A CFG consists of a set of re-write rules, A -> B_1 B_2 ... B_n, where symbols that appear on the left-hand side (LHS) are called "nonterminals" and the symbols on the right-hand side (RHS) can be either nonterminals or terminals. The terminal symbols are those that do not appear on the left-hand side of any rule, because they are "atomic" for the language in question. In a grammar for a human language the terminals are the words and the nonterminals are phrase categories such as NP, VP, and S. Every CFG also has a distinguished "root" nonterminal that can serve as a starting place for a top-down search or an ending place for a bottom-up search. CFGs can have any number of symbols on the RHS, but the most efficient algorithms for parsing CFGs require that the rules all be binary (i.e., have exactly two symbols on the RHS. A nonterminal can have more than one RHS, in which case they are defined as separate rules, although parsers also allow an abbreviated notation, where the different RHS are listed together, separated by a vertical bar.

Parse trees are a way of depicting the derivation of a sequence according to the grammar. In trees, the root nodes are the nonterminals of the grammar, the leaf nodes are the words. Figure

4.10 shows an example of a parse tree for a phrase structure analysis of the sentence "The dog ate the beef".

Figure 4.10 Parse tree for the sentence "The dog ate the beef." (parse and image from Stanford CoreNLP.run 2020)

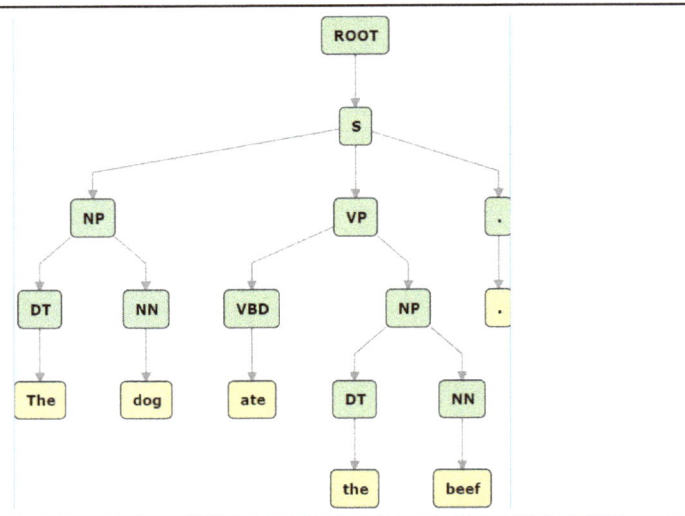

A CFG can be defined explicitly, after a qualitative analysis of a language (such as described in Chapter 3), or it can be induced from a dataset where sentences have been previously annotated with their correct parse, i.e., a treebank. To induce a grammar, a computer algorithm can traverse all the trees starting from the root and for each subtree that has children, create a rule where the root of the subtree is the LHS nonterminal and its children form the RHS. Figure 4.11 shows the rules that might be learned from a parse of the sentence "The dog barked." If the parse trees in the data set had more than two branches, but a binary branching grammar is desired, then the induced rules can be rewritten using additional nonterminals to create binary trees. For example, the rule **NP-> DT NN CC NN PP**, can be rewritten as **NP -> DT N1** and **N1-> N1 PP | N1 CC N1**, where **N1** is a new nonterminal. Terminals are just the words, which can be collected directly from the unannotated text or from the treebank.

Figure 4.11 Example CFG learned from parse of "The dog barked". (parse and image from Stanford CoreNL

Parse tree	Induced rules
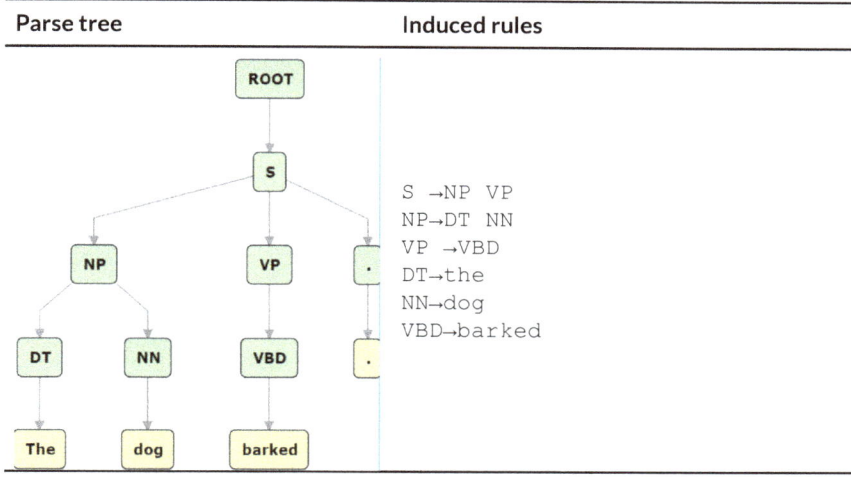	S →NP VP NP→DT NN VP →VBD DT→the NN→dog VBD→barked

4.3.2 Probabilistic Context Free Grammars

Probabilistic Context Free Grammars (PCFG) are a variant of context free grammars where each rule is annotated with a numerical value that expresses the likelihood that the rule will be used when rewriting the terminal on the left-hand side. The numbers follow the conventions of a probabilities where the sum of the values for the same nonterminal must equal 1. Figure 4.12 shows an example of a small PCFG.

Figure 4.12 Example of a PCFG created by hand

Grammar	Probability	Lexicon	Probability
S → NP VP	1.0	NN → talk	0.6
NP → DT NN	.4	NN → money	0.4
NP → NN	.2	NNS → talks	1.0
NP → PRP$ NN	.3	PRP$ → my	0.4
NP → PRP$ NN NNS	.1	PRP$ → your	0.6
VP → VBZ	.6	RB → loudly	1.0
VP → VBZ RB	.4	VBZ → talks	1.0

PCFGs can be created by hand, as in Figure 4.12 but in practice they are usually induced from annotated collections of bracketed sentences or a treebank. Bracketed sentences (also called shallow parses) include only the top-level phrase categories, and are used when full trees are not available or needed. Figure 4.13 shows some sample bracketed data that might be used to induce a PCFG.

Figure 4.13 Example of patterns that might be used to estimate a PCFG

Pattern Type	Count
[S [NP] [VP]]	300
[S [VB] [NP]]	100
[S [S [NP] [VP]] [CC] [S [NP][VP]]]	200

For the example in Figure 4.13, we must also consider the phrase types within a pattern. So in Figure 4.13 there are 700 examples of "**S →NP VP**" (including 400 that appear nested within the third type of pattern). There are 100 examples of "**S → VB NP**" and 200 examples of "**S → S CC S**", resulting in a probability of assignment for the PCFG sentence rule of **S → NP VP [0.7] | VB NP [0.1] | S CC S [0.2]**.

Simple PCFGs provide a way to resolve local syntactic ambiguity, but they are not always very accurate, because many ambiguities depend on relationships between specific words, as in "They ate udon with forks." versus "They ate udon with chicken." Often accuracy can be improved by conditioning the probabilities by the word that is the head of the constituent (such as the main verb in a verb phrase or the main noun in a noun phrase). Figure 4.13 gives an example rule by Collins[19] that might be used for finding the head of a noun phrase.

Figure 4.13 Collins rule for finding the head of a NP

If the rule contains NN, NNS, or NNP:
   Choose the rightmost NN, NNS, or NNP
Else If the rule contains an NP:
   Choose the leftmost NP
Else If the rule contains a JJ:
   Choose the rightmost JJ
Else If the rule contains a CD:
   Choose the rightmost CD
   Else Choose the rightmost child

Collins used rules like this to define a lexicalized context free grammar (LCFG), which includes the head words for each phrase. Figure 4.14 shows an example of a lexicalized CFG (shown without estimated probabilities).

Figure: 4.14 Example of a lexicalized grammar from Collins
$S(\text{questioned}) \rightarrow_2 NP(\text{lawyer}) \ VP(\text{questioned})$ $NP(\text{lawyer}) \rightarrow_2 DT(\text{the}) \ NN(\text{lawyer})$ $DT(\text{the}) \rightarrow \text{the}$ $NN(\text{lawyer}) \rightarrow \text{lawyer}$ $VP(\text{questioned}) \rightarrow_1 Vt(\text{questioned}) \ NP(\text{witness})$ $NP(\text{witness}) \rightarrow_2 DT(\text{the}) \ NN(\text{witness})$ $DT(\text{the}) \rightarrow \text{the}$ $NN(\text{witness}) \rightarrow \text{witness}$

Another way to improve PCFG grammars is to combine the syntactic categories of a PCFG with a neural network that learns vector representations that combine syntactic and semantic information. This approach, called a Compositional Vector Grammar (CVG)[20], uses a neural network to learn weights for each nonterminal. The CVG captures the notion of head words that are needed for ambiguities that require semantic information, such as PP attachments, and also addresses the problem of sparsity, because it generalizes over similar words (e.g., words that had similar neighbors) in the training data.

4.3.3 Dependency Grammars

Dependencies are asymmetric binary relations that express the functional role of the word with respect to another word that is considered the head of the relation. These relations form head-dependent pairs. Researchers have refined and standardized the types of dependency relations, following the work on creating lexicalized context free grammar rules. There are three general types of relations: relations that specify modifiers, relations that specify complements (required arguments), and relations which essentially name the type of word itself, such as determiners, conjuncts, and copula. The most standardized set of dependency relations and their definitions is maintained by the Universal Dependency organization. Figure 4.15 shows an example dependency tree, which groups all the dependencies originating at the same word together at a single node. Note that unlike a constituency tree, the words are root nodes and the dependencies are labels on the edges between them.

Figure 4.15 Example of a dependency tree for *"Bills on ports and immigration were submitted by Senator Brownback."* (Image: Stanford CoreNLP)

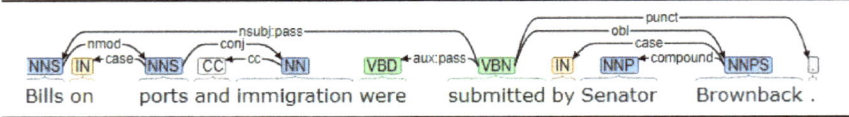

The specifications of dependency grammars can be specified by hand, in the lexicon, as in the original slot grammars described above, or they may be induced from treebanks. It has been shown that dependency grammars and context free grammars are equivalent in expressiveness, and dependency grammars can be learned from either treebanks based on constituency (such as the Penn Treebank) or tree banks created using dependency parsers. Using a treebank, dependency grammars and parsers can be augmented with estimated probabilities (in a manner similar to PCFGs), including creating rules that are conditioned on the specific head-dependent pairs.

In the next sections, we will consider parsing algorithms for both constituency and dependency grammars, considering both search and classification-based approaches to parsing.

4.4 SEARCH-BASED PARSING

The most widely used search-based algorithms for parsing are the CKY algorithm (named for its creators: Cocke, Kasami, and Yonger), and the Shift-Reduce Algorithm. Both CKY and Shift-Reduce are "bottom-up" algorithms, which means they begin the parse with individual words, and work their way "up" towards a structure that spans the entire sentence. (Bottom up algorithms are also useful for traversing a parse tree, for example to compute a semantic representation in a compositional way.) CKY is relatively efficient (for a bottom up algorithm), because it can be implemented as dynamic programming using a matrix to keep track of partial results. An example of a CKY algorithm, is bottom-up chart parsing, which can also make use of rules annotated with probabilities or semantics. It is also used in some neural neural network approaches to build the final result.

Because bottom-up chart parsing has so many applications, we will be doing an in-depth dive into the algorithm.

4.4.1 CHART PARSING

Chart parsers create structures, called edges, to represent both complete constituents and partially complete constituents (of a sentence). The partially complete structures allow them to make predictions about what will be processed next and to use those predictions to guide the parse. Each edge stores the grammar rule that is being used and locations where it begins and ends. By convention, locations begin at 0 (zero) just before the first word, and end just after the last word of the constituent. Figure 4.16 is an example of a sentence, marked with locations, showing all possible spans for the sentence "The cat ate a mouse", listing all spans of length 1, all of length 2, etc. We use the notation [i:j] to describe the span of words from location i to location j and [k:k] to describe the point just before processing the word that begins at location k. For example, in Figure 4.16, [0:2] corresponds to "the cat" and [2:2] is the location before "ate". Chart parsers can be used both for parsing context free grammars, and for dependency parsing. For clarity, we will consider chart parsing only using a simple CFG. (We will consider parsing with dependencies when we discuss transition-based dependency parsing in the next section.)

Figure 4.16 Example of the locations of some individual words and spans of words

	0	1	2	3	4	5
Spans of length 1	The	cat	ate	a	mouse	
Spans of length 2	The	cat		a	mouse	
Spans of length 3			ate	a	mouse	
Spans of length 5	The	cat	ate	a	mouse	

Chart parsing is an exhaustive enumeration of all edges induced by a grammar—any and all grammar rules that can match will result in an edge being added to the chart. The more ambiguity a grammar allows, the more edges will be created. Figure 4.17 shows the edges we would get if we used a context free grammar along with all the parts of speech for each word as found in a typical dictionary, using the tags of the Penn Treebank tagset (e.g., JJ is "adjective" and RB is "adverb"). Here, the word "the" has two parts of speech (DT, IN, RB), "horse" has four (NN, JJ, VB, and VBP), "raced" has two (VBD, VBN), "past" has four (NN, IN, JJ, and RB), "barn" has one, and "fell" has three (NN, JJ, VBD)[21]. To the left, the figure shows all the edges of length 1 that could be created by matching rules from the bottom up.

Figure 4.17 Edges of length 1 for a bottom-up parse with ambiguity

Sentence:
0 The 1 horse 2 raced 3 past 4 the 5 barn 6 fell. 7

Grammar	Edges of length 1
DT -> the	[([0:1], DT), ([0:1], IN), ([0:1], RB]),
NN -> horse | past | barn | fell	([1:2], JJ), ([1:2], NN), ([1:2], VB), ([1:2], VBP),([2:3], VBD),([2:3], VBN),
IN -> past | the	([3:4], JJ), ([3:4], IN), ([3:4], NN), ([3:4], RB), ([4:5], DT), ([4:5], IN), ([4:5], RB),
JJ -> past | fell | horse	([5:6], NN),
RB -> the | past	([6:7], VBD), ([6:7], NN), ([6:7], JJ)]
VB -> horse	
VBD -> raced | fell	
VBN -> raced	
VBP -> horse	

The edges that are created to keep track of the state of a parse before a rule is completely matched are called "active edges". As the sentence is processed from left to right, for each partially matched grammar rule, the algorithm will create an active edge to store what has been matched, and what is still needed. A dot (*) is used to designate the dividing point between what has been matched and what is still needed. (If an edge is created with no parts matched, then the dot will be immediately after the arrow, as in **A → * B1 B2**.) As more parts are matched, new edges are added, with the dot moved over to the right. When the dot reaches the far right end of a rule, then the edge is "complete" (also called "inactive") and it can be used to extend other active rules. Figure 4.18 shows another small grammar and some edges that would be created, midway through the parse.

Figure 4.18 Example of edges created after parsing the first two words of "the cat sat".

Sentence:
0 The 1 cat 2 sat 3

Grammar	Edges for "the cat"
S -> NP VBD	([0:2], "NP-> DT NP *")
DT -> the	([0:2], "S-> NP * VBD")
NP -> DT NP	
NN -> cat | dog	
VBD -> sat | barked	

The steps in a bottom up chart parsing algorithm can be specified by the two parsing rules shown in Figure 4.19. These rules describe how to combine edges to create longer edges.

Figure 4.19 Chart parsing rules used in CKY

Bottom-up rule: When a new category is seen (or nonterminal rule for that category is completed completed), then for any rule where that category is leftmost on the RHS, create a new edge with the dot just to the left of the category.
If (([i:j], X) or [i:j] X -> U V *) and A -> X Y, then add ([i:i], A -> * X Y)
Note: Y can be empty.

Fundamental rule: When a new category is seen or nonterminal created, then for all active rules where the category is leftmost on the RHS of the dot, and the spans are adjacent, create a new edge with the dot moved to the right of that category and combine the spans.
If ([i:j], A -> X * Y Z and [j:k] Y -> U V *, then add ([i:k], A -> X Y * Z)
Note: X and Z can be empty.

In practice, CKY can be most efficiently implemented as dynamic programming using a two dimensional matrix. In dynamic programming, instead of explicitly representing a location [i:j] when we parse a sentence of length N, we create an N by N matrix and store the edges with span [i:j] at row i and column j in the matrix[22]. Then, for any complete parse with topmost rule $S \rightarrow X\ Y$, there would be an edge ([0:N], $S \rightarrow X\ Y$ *). Figure 4.20 shows the pseudocode for the CKY algorithm as dynamic programming. To start, we place the words or unary lexical rules at their corresponding locations. then we iterate over all possible lengths of spans, starting at 2 and ending at the length of the sentence, and for each span length we iterate over all locations in the table. Then we iterate over all possible edges, from all possible starting points, and apply bottom up and fundamental rules wherever they would apply. (The pseudocode does not list the empty edges created by the bottom up prediction rule, but they are shown in the trace shown in Figure 4.21 that follows.)

Figure: 4.20 Pseudocode for a basic CKY algorithm (an exhaustive enumeration over all possible edges)

```
Given a sentence with words a₁,..., aₙ, create the chart as an n by n matrix
where, for each aᵢ, we add an edge to the chart at location [i-1:i]

For w = 2 to N:                        ; the length of an edge
    For i = 0 to N-w:                  ; the start of the edge
        For k = 1 to w-1:              ; each location within an edge
            If (the grammar has A -> B C) and
               (the chart has ([i:i+k], B -> α) and ([i+k: i+w], C -> β)

            Then:                      ; Apply the fundamental rule
                Add ( [i:i+w], A -> B C) to the chart

If ([0:N], S) is in the chart, return the corresponding parse
```

Figure 4.21 shows a bottom up chart parse of the sentence "The dog barked.", along with the corresponding active and inactive edges and their placement within a matrix when using dynamic programming. This trace follows the implementation of the bottom up chart parsing algorithm as implemented in NLTK. (It also follows the convention that when matrices for a chart parse are shown, they are shown with the vertical axis reversed so that the parse appears in the upper right corner.)

Figure 4.21 Trace of a bottom up chart parse of "The dog barked."

Matrix values	Edges in chart	Parser actions

NP -> * DT NN   NP -> DT * NN
DT -> *the   DT -> the *
                            The
                                       dog
                                              barked
0   1   2   3
	[0:0] DT → *the
	[0:1] DT → the *
	[0:0] NP → * DT NN
	[0:1] NP → DT * NN
		Predict *the*, and **apply the fundamental rule** to create a completed edge from 0 to 1. **Predict** bottom up an empty NP (* NP) and **apply the fundamental rule** to get NP -> DT * NN.

S -> * NP VBD
NP -> * DT NN   NP -> DT * NN   S -> NP * VBD
DT -> *the   DT -> the *   NP -> DT NN *
                            The
                            NN -> *dog   NN -> dog*
                                      dog
                                                  barked
0   1   2   3
	[0:0] DT → *the
	[0:1] DT → the *
	[0:0] NP → * DT NN
	[0:1] NP → DT * NN
	[1:1] NN → *dog
	[1:2] NN → dog *
	[0:2] NP → DT NN *
	[0:0] S → * NP VBD
	[0:2] S → NP * VBD
		Predict *dog* and **apply the fundamental rule** to create a completed edge from 1 to 2. **Apply fundamental rule** to complete the NP at [0:2] and extend the S, to get S -> NP * VBD.

S -> * NP VBD
NP -> * DT NN   NP -> DT * NN   S -> NP * VBD   S -> NP VBD *
DT -> *the   DT -> the *   NP -> DT NN *
                            the
                            NN -> *dog   NN -> dog*
                                      dog
                                       VBD -> *barked   VBD-> barked*
                                                       barked
0   1   2   3
	[0:0] DT → * the
	[0:1] DT → the *
	[0:0] NP → * DT NN
	[0:1] NP → DT * NN
	[1:1] NN → * dog
	[1:2] NN → dog *
	[0:2] NP → DT NN *
	[0:0] S → * NP VBD
	[0:2] S → NP * VBD
	[2:2] VBD→* barked
	[2:3] VBD→ barked *
	
	[0:3] S → NP VBD *
		Predict *barked* and **apply the fundamental rule** to complete VBD and **apply the fundamental rule** again to complete the S.

In practice, when using a bottom-up chart parsing algorithm, there will be huge number of possible edges and so some mechanism is needed to prune edges that are not likely to be part of the final parse. This difficulty is the primary reason for using a probabilistic context free grammar (PCFG). When using a PCFG rather than a CFG, the CKY algorithm is adapted to use the probabilities values associated with each rule in the grammar. For simplicity, the probabilities are treated as independent, which means that during parsing they are combined using multiplication. The probability of a parse tree will be calculated as the product of the probability of the rule for the root times the product of the probabilities associated with each of the subtrees (i.e.,, categories on the right-hand side). Thus, for the grammar shown in Figure 4.12, the probability for the sequence *"Your money talks"* as a NP would be calculated as the product "0.1*0.6*0.4*1.0" (0.024), whereas the probability for a S would be the product "1.0*0.3*0.6*0.4*0.6*1.0" (0.0432). When multiple parses for a span [j:k] of text are possible, the CKY algorithm for PCFG will store, for each nonterminal X at location [i:j], the highest probability parses found for X, a variant of beam search, where the beam can be 1, 1000, 10000, or whatever seems suitable. When a PCFG is lexicalized, the process is similar, except that when the product for the entire parse tree is computed, there is an additional multiplicand for the estimated probability (based on the frequency in the source corpus) associated with the top level S having the designated lexical head (e.g., S(talks)); so if "talks" occurs as the main verb for 2 sentences out of 1000, for the sentence above, we would multiply 0.002 with the 0.0432).

4.4.2 Shift-Reduce Parsing

A Shift-Reduce parser, also called a transition-based parser, maintains the state of the current parse and applies transitions that update the parse state, such as combining two inputs or combining an input with a previously built structure. When implemented as a search procedure, the state is usually represented using two data structures: a queue of words to be parsed and a stack of partially completed structures. (In some cases, the parser also maintains an agenda of the best partial parse states.) The initial state has all the words in order on the queue and an empty stack. At each parsing step, the parser selects and applies transitions to the current state until its queue of inputs is empty and the current stack only contains a finished tree.

The two main types of transitions are **shift**, which is where a word moves from the queue onto the stack and **reduce**, which is where nodes on the stack are combined and relabeled. Implemented SR parsers may use additional transitions (such as "accept", "finalize," or "idle") or specialize the reduce action into several subtypes (e.g., based on the lexical head), to control the parsing process or make it more efficient. Shift-reduce parsing can either be used to do constituency parsing for context free grammars or dependency parsing. It has also been used in the implementation of compilers for programming languages. Figure 4.22 below gives an example of a small CFG grammar and a sample parse, for the expression "T and T", where "$" is used to indicate the bottom of a stack or the back of a queue.

Figure 4.22 Example of a shift-reduce parse for "T and T"

Sample grammar	Sample parse			
		Stack	Buffer	Action	Rule
	1	$	T and T$	Shift	NA
	2	$T	and T$	Reduce	S → T
S → T	3	$S	and T$	Shift	NA
S → S and S	4	$S and	T$	Shift	NA
S → S or S	5	$S and T	$	Reduce	S → T
	6	$S and S	$	Reduce	S → S and S
	7	$S	$	Accept	

For constituency parsing, with a grammar rule **A → B C**, a reduce operation might replace two nonterminals B and C by the LHS nonterminal A. For a dependency grammar, if the top two items on the stack could be linked by a dependency relation, the items will be removed and replaced by the one that is considered the head, such as the verb in an nmod relation, and the relation added to another data structure. We will consider another example of shift reduce parsing in the next section, when we discuss Dependency Parsing.

As with probabilistic context free parsing, shift-reduce parsing may be adapted to use a scoring function to choose what type of transition to apply in each state when there are multiple options. These scoring functions are normally learned from data, either as probabilities estimated from a treebank or as values derived from trained neural network models. A shift-reduce parser might be greedy about transitions, always choosing the option that scores best. Or, it might implement a type of beam search (see Chapter 2) where only the a subset of top-scoring partial states are kept on the agenda and continues until the highest scoring state on the agenda is finalized. Beam search can provide better accuracy in less time, but it requires models that were specifically trained to work with beam search. A model not trained for beam search only has features for states reached for the correct parse trees. By contrast, a model trained to use beam search also trains with negative features for incorrect states on the beam, (i.e., features for phrase-level ambiguities that were not part of the final parse) resulting in many more features and therefore a much larger model.

4.4.3 Search-Based Dependency Parsing

First we will consider how dependency parsing can be understood using search; in the next section we will reconsider dependency parsing as classification-based parsing. Dependency parsing involves choosing for each word, what other word it is related to as a dependent. By convention, the top-level node is called the root and the main verb is its dependent. A variety of search-based algorithms have been used to build dependency structures including ones based on: dynamic programming, maximum spanning trees, constraint satisfaction, or greedy algorithms, similar to those already discussed, although some also combine supervised machine learning to get better results[23].

Search-based dependency parsing algorithms all start the

search with the main verb and then try to generate dependents by traversing the different types of edges known to be associated with the root, based on subcategorization information (see Chapter 3) stored in the lexicon. For example, in the sentence: "I baked a cake in the oven." the main verb (root) is "baked". The verb has a noun subject (nsubj) relation to "I". There is a determiner (det) relation between "cake" and "a". There is a determiner object (dobj) between "cake" and "baked" . There is a case relation between "oven" and "in" and a determiner (det) relation between "oven" and "the". There is a noun modifier (nmod) relation between "cake" and "oven".

Naive dependency parsing algorithms based on breadth first search consider and score all possible combinations of head and dependent – which leads to a Big-O complexity of $O(n^5)$, but McDonald et al's (2005) approach is $O(n^2)$. Using a corpus annotated with dependency trees, a classifier is trained to compute a score for each type of edge. The types of features include: the head word, the dependent word, and part of speech (POS), separately; the head word, dependent word and POS, as bigrams (e.g., (the, DT)); the words between head and dependent; and the length and direction of the dependency. The training is based on maximizing the accuracy of the overall tree. The classifier is then used to discriminate among alternative trees, where the score of a tree is calculated as the sum of the score of the dependencies. An alternative classifier-based approach involves training classifiers to optimize the actions of a shift-reduce parser[24,25]. The algorithms extend the traditional operators of a shift-reduce parser to include different types of reduce operators for the different types of edges and directions of the edges, to allow for more accurate scoring. Once actions are scored, then a greedy search algorithm can be used to select the actions that comprise the single best parse or a beam search can be used to select from just a subset of the best scoring ones.

Figure 4.23 shows the start of a shift-reduce dependency parse of the sentence "Happy children like to play with their friends." In the figures, the first column shows the action (where LA and RA designate two types of attachment, left and right respectively). LA attaches the front element of the queue to the top of the stack with the element taken from the queue placed on the left; RA attaches the front element of the queue to the top of the stack with the element on the right. The subscript shows the type of dependency, such as *amod*. The second column shows the symbols that have been shifted from the input buffer onto the stack. The third column shows the queue remaining input; and the last column shows the set of dependency structures that have been created.

Figure 4.23 Example initial set of actions of a shift-reduce dependency parse

		Happy children like to play with their friends .	
	[ROOT]	[Happy, children, ...]	∅
Shift	[ROOT, Happy]	[children, like, ...]	∅
LA_{amod}	[ROOT]	[children, like, ...]	{amod(children, happy)} = A_1
Shift	[ROOT, children]	[like, to, ...]	A_1
LA_{nsubj}	[ROOT]	[like, to, ...]	$A_1 \cup$ {nsubj(like, children)} = A_2
RA_{root}	[ROOT, like]	[to, play, ...]	$A_2 \cup$ {root(ROOT, like) = A_3
Shift	[ROOT, like, to]	[play, with, ...]	A_3
LA_{aux}	[ROOT, like]	[play, with, ...]	$A_3 \cup$ {aux(play, to) = A_4
RA_{xcomp}	[ROOT, like, play]	[with their, ...]	$A_4 \cup$ {xcomp(like, play) = A_5

Figure 4.24 shows the last few steps of the same parse. Note, if one were to draw a tree at the same time, every shift action would create a sibling whereas each LA/RA adds a new edge between a head and a dependent. In Figure 4.24, the "Reduce" actions at the end of the parse remove items from the stack without creating any new dependencies. The parse ends when the queue (column 3) is empty.[26].

Figure 4.24 Final actions of a shift-reduce dependency parse

Happy children like to play with their friends .

RA_{xcomp}	[ROOT, like, play]	[with their, ...]	$A_4 \cup \{xcomp(like, play)\} = A_5$
RA_{prep}	[ROOT, like, play, with]	[their, friends, ...]	$A_5 \cup \{prep(play, with)\} = A_6$
Shift	[ROOT, like, play, with, their]	[friends, .]	A_6
LA_{poss}	[ROOT, like, play, with]	[friends, .]	$A_6 \cup \{poss(friends, their)\} = A_7$
RA_{pobj}	[ROOT, like, play, with, friends]	[.]	$A_7 \cup \{pobj(with, friends)\} = A_8$
Reduce	[ROOT, like, play, with]	[.]	A_8
Reduce	[ROOT, like, play]	[.]	A_8
Reduce	[ROOT, like]	[.]	A_8
RA_{punc}	[ROOT, like, .]	[]	$A_8 \cup \{punc(like, .)\} = A_9$

Shift-reduce dependency parsers can use information learned from a corpus to score the actions of a shift-reduce parser to resolve ambiguities, similar to the scoring method used to rank alternatives with a PCFG, by selecting actions that result in more commonly seen structures. The treebanks for training dependency parsers can either be ones that include dependency trees, or they can be adapted from phrase structures, as found in the Penn Treebank. There are also algorithms for translating dependency trees into phrase structures[27, 28]. In the more recent work of Lee and Wang[29] dependency structures are mapped to constituent trees in a two-phase process, as shown in Figure 4.25, where the first phase traverses the dependency structure to construct a partial set of constituent spans and the second phase applies a constraint-based maximum entropy parser[30], a type of statistical parser similar to a shift-reduce parser, to the original sentence to select the best phrase-level nodes.

Figure 4.25 Pseudocode for mapping dependencies to constituency trees, adapted from Lee and Wang (2016)

```
input: A dependency tree (DTree) with n input words
output: An unlabeled constituency tree (CTree) with POS tags and partial constituent brackets
Step 1: Identify the dependency span D_i of each word w_i
if w_i does not have any dependents
    then D_i contains only w_i
    else D_i subsumes all of its dependents recursively
Step 2: Convert each dependency span D_i to a constituent C_i
C_i is a node whose children are the head word and its immediate dependents
Step 3: Remove all constituent brackets containing only one word.
```

4.5 CLASSIFICATION-BASED PARSING

Most large-scale parsers developed since 2015 use sequence classification as the primary method rather than search. Most are also targeted to producing a dependency structure, because the structures are more language independent and sufficient for many downstream tasks. However, neural constituency parsers also exist. Versions exist that provide either a single best parse or a few best alternatives via a beam search. The training for a beam search is different than for a single-best parser. A single-best model only uses features or states that were associated with the correct parse found in the training set. A model that can return and rank multiple alternatives must also train negative features to prevent poorer quality alternatives from becoming part of the final set. Most approaches to supervised machine learning have been applied to model language at the sentence level, including linear models (such as Support Vector Machines), shallow neural networks (such as Perceptrons), and deep networks, which are fast emerging as the dominant approach [31].

4.5.1 Classification-Based Constituency Parsing

Modern classification-based constituency parsing uses deep neural networks. These networks do not require a grammar or lexicon, all knowledge is embedded in the language model that has been learned by processing a training dataset that includes parse trees. For a constituency parser, these parse trees must be constituency trees, such as found in the Penn Treebank. Current approaches often use an internal data representation similar to chart, consisting of labelled spans, e.g., (0, 2, NP). For an internal representation based on charts, there are three aspects: representations of tokenized input, representations of spans, and scoring mechanisms for labels. The input layer comprises representations for several types of information for each word: word meaning, word position in the sentence, and part of speech, usually as embeddings that are learned as part of the overall training with the treebank, but they can be learned separately and input pre-trained. The internal layers are often a bidirectional Long Short Term Memory (LSTM), which is one that operates on both a forward and a reversed version of the sentence[32], or a self-attentive encoder[33], to account for constraints from either side of the sentence surrounding the word. (In a self-attention model, nodes can focus on locations, and the weight of each is also a learned value, independent of the number of intervening words, to account for long-distance interactions, such as for questions where the wh-word seems to have been moved to the front.) These layers generate a score for each combination of a label and a span. The final stage of constituency parsing networks is typically a decoder to generate trees, by performing a CKY-style bottom up traversal that builds a tree comprising the highest-scoring labelled spans.

4.5.2 Classification-Based Dependency Parsing

Classification based approaches to dependency parsing also now use deep neural networks, trained using a dependency treebank. These networks are trained to jointly select: a) pairs of words that are optimally head and dependent and b) optimal dependency relations for candidate pairs (head and dependent words). In the final layer, the scores of all candidates are examined to select the best one. When training the network, the overall loss to be minimized is a combination of the loss (e.g., a sum) for the component subproblems. In intuitive terms, these networks are trained to provide a score that is akin to an estimated joint probability of the head, dependent, and relation, based on the *"context"* of the sentence. However, scores may not be limited to values between 0 and 1 and, for these networks, context is not a simple matter of nearby word or part of speech tag, but instead includes vector representations for a wide range of features such as part of speech tags, morphological features, character sequences, word types (as both a lemma and a semantic embedding), and sometimes scalar values to indicate the linear order and the distance between the head and the argument. These input vectors allow the networks to generalize over minor variations in spelling, meaning, or syntactic expression.

One of the most accurate (and most complex) exemplars of the neural classification approach has been developed by the Stanford NLP group. Their current implemented NLP pipeline is called Stanza and an illustration of the overall architecture is shown in Figure 4.26[34]. Designed to allow input as raw text, the pipeline of Stanza uses a complex neural architecture involving several layers to first create separate embeddings for each type of information (e.g., multiple layers of biLSTM, a final LSTM layer, several layers of Rectified Linear Units (ReLU), followed by additional layers to perform matrix operations that combine the separate vectors to select the optimal head, dependent, and relation combinations[35, 36]. Most of the processes listed on the left have been discussed previously, except "multi-word token expansion" which would handle things like mapping contractions onto separate tokens (e.g., "don't" onto "do and not") and named entity recognition, which is a type of shallow semantic processing that labels proper nouns and expressions with their general type, such as person, organization, location, etc. (We will discuss named entity recognition in a later chapter.)

Figure 4.26 The Stanza NLP processing pipeline (image from Qi et al (2020))

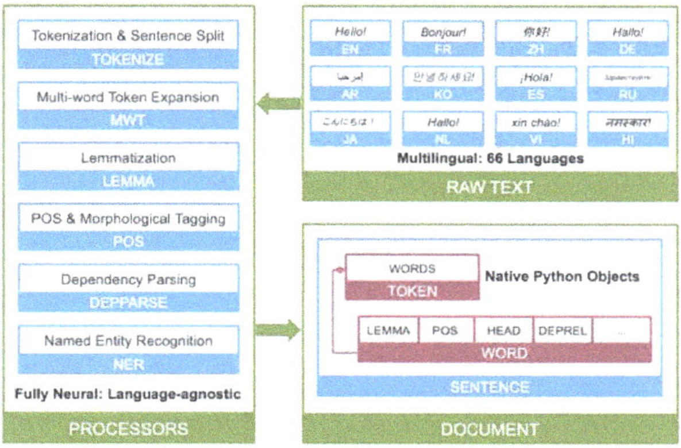

Stanza has has been implemented in Python, using the PyTorch software libraries for machine learning. It is open source, but may not be suitable for everyone, as it runs best on a GPU-enabled machine. Simpler architectures, using fewer layers, also do quite well, including UDPipe, which achieves 70 to 85% accuracy, runs on common laptops, and has libraries implemented for several programming languages[37, 38].

Classification-based parsers are available as parts of nearly all recent NLP software libraries. These libraries include one or more pretrained models for large widely used datasets, but also provide instructions and tools for updating or training models with new data. Data for training neural networks for dependency parsing must usually be provided in what is known as the CoNLL-U format, which is an ASCII format defined for a series of yearly task-based challenges (which are conferences with a common data set where participants submit results for prespecified tasks using the data)[39].

4.6 SHALLOW PARSING

Some applications do not require a full parse of the sentence, just a subdivision of the text into the top-level phrases. This process is called shallow parsing or **chunking**, Shallow parsing can involve either the creation of regular expressions to identify boundaries or the training of a classifier to find the end points of chunks.

4.6.1 Regular Expressions for Chunking

The grammars used for chunking are defined as complex regular expressions, which are similar to context free grammars, but typically do not involve recursion. For example to say that an NP chunk should be formed by a sequence of an optional determiner (DT) followed by any number of adjectives (JJ) and then a noun (NN) or as a sequence of proper nouns, one would use the regular expression "**NP: {<DT>?<JJ>*<NN>}{<NNP>+}**" in NLTK, where "?" indicates optional, "*" means occurs "zero or more" times, and "+" means "one or more" times.

When regular expression parser runs, it searches for sequences of tokens that match the pattern and produces a list, with each matched sequence labelled with the pattern type. To be able to define and use patterns recursively, one typically must iterate over the grammar multiple times, corresponding to the maximum depth of recursion that is allowed. Figure 4.27 shows an example, adapted from Figure 7.10 of Chapter 7 of the NLTK book[40], that illustrates the use of a recursive (cascaded) chunk grammar. NLTK does allow some recursion with regular expression-based chunking, but only if given a maximum depth, as done with the "loop=2" parameter in this example. By contrast, a CKY or Shift-Reduce parser will perform recursion to an arbitrary depth.

Figure 4.27 Example of a chunk grammar with recursion and its usage in NLTK

| RegEx grammar | ```
grammar = r"""
NP: {<DT|JJ|NN.*>+}
PP: {<IN><NP>}
VP: {<VB.*><RP|NP|PP|CLAUSE>+$}
CLAUSE: {<NP><VP>}"""
``` |
|---|---|
| Chunk grammar | ```
>>> sentence = [("John", "NNP"),
... ("thinks", "VBZ"), ("Mary", "NN"),
... ("saw", "VBD"), ("the", "DT"),
... ("cat", "NN"), ("sit", "VB") ("down", "RP")]
>>> cp = nltk.RegexpParser(grammar, loop=2)
>>> print(cp.parse(sentence)) (S
(NP John/NNP)
thinks/VBZ
(NP Mary/NN)
(VP saw/VBD (CLAUSE
(NP the/DT cat/NN)
(VP sit/VB down/RP))))
``` |

4.6.2 Classification-Based Chunking

To annotate chunks for training a classifier, some systems use an encoding that is called CoNLL 2000, because it is based on the encoding used from that conference. That encoding combines POS tags with labels that indicate the beginning (B) and inside (I) of the chunks, and use O tags to indicate "outside a chunk". An extended version of this encoding (CoNLL 2002) combines POS tags with semantic types for named entities, which are proper name expressions such as for people, organizations, or locations. Figure 4.28 shows examples of these two encodings with chunks on the left and named entities on the right. With training data labelled with CoNLL tags, a sequence classifier can be used to learn to tag unseen data, and expressions extracted by merging adjacent sequences of tokens that have related tags, e.g., [B-Loc, I-Loc, I-Loc], terminated by an "O" tag. Other similar encoding strategies are sometimes used.

Figure 4.28 Examples of CoNLL 2002 tags for named entities

Encoding of Chunks	Encoding of Named Entities
Michael NNP B-NP Lovell NNP I-NP accepted VBD B-VP the DT B-NP position NN I-NP of IN B-PP president NN I-NP of IN B-PP Marquette NNP B-NP University NNP I-NP	Michael NNP B-PER Lovell NNP I-PER accepted VBD O the DT O position NN O of IN O president NN O of IN O Marquette NNP B-ORG University NNP I-ORG

As a start, one might also try using a prettrained NER tagger, such as found in a software toolkit such as spaCy or CoreNLP. The taggers can be invoked by running the complete pipeline (the usual case), or one can call a tagger separately, after first splitting the text into separate words using "split()"[41].

4.7 SUMMARY

This chapter considered tasks associated with identifying the syntactic structure of natural language including tokenization, part-of-speech tagging, grammars, and parsing. We considered two types of analyses: parsing to identify syntactic constituents, such as phrases and clauses, and parsing to identify dependency structures, the sets of binary relations that connect the head words of constituents. Grammars describe what sequences comprise a language. Identifying how words or sequences match the grammar can be done by either a search process or classification. Creating datasets for classification is typically accomplished in a semi-automated manner: first, apply a search-based parser and then hand correct the analyses. Pretrained language models can sometimes be extended without adding new data, by enhancing the input representations to include semantic information (using word embeddings) or to include character-level embeddings where dense vectors are trained to map strings of characters (including those for non-standard spellings) onto known words. Although dependency structures provide information about syntactic function, it should be noted that this is not the same as a meaning representation or semantics. In the next chapter we will consider what sorts of semantic representations are possible and computational methods for creating them.

Notes

1. Universal Dependencies.org (2021) The English Web Treebank URL: https://universaldependencies.org/treebanks/en_ewt/index.html
2. Devlin, J., Chang, M., Lee, K., and Toutanova, K. (2019). BERT: Pre-training of Deep Bidirectional Transformers for Language Understanding. NAACL-HLT.
3. Google Research (2019) Github site for bert tokenizer URL: https://github.com/google-research/bert/blob/master/tokenization.py
4. A mapping from PTB tags to UD tags can be found online at: https://universaldependencies.org/tagset-conversion/en-penn-uposf.html
5. Marshall, I. (1983). Choice of Grammatical Word-Class without Global Syntactic Analysis: Tagging Words in the LOB Corpus. *Computers and the Humanities*, pp.139-150.
6. One can download the GENIA tree bank from https://nlp.stanford.edu/~mcclosky/biomedical.html CMU distributes POS taggers trained for either Twitter Data or data from the English Web Tree-

bank; you can find it at http://www.cs.cmu.edu/~ark/TweetNLP/#pos

7. Samuelsson, C. and Voutilainen, A. (1997). Comparing a Linguistic and a Stochastic Tagger. In *Proceedings of the 35th Annual Meeting of the Association for Computational Linguistics and Eighth Conference of the European Chapter of the Association for Computational Linguistics* Association for Computational Linguistics (pp. 246-253).

8. Young, S. and Bloothooft, G. eds. (2013). *Corpus-based methods in Language and Speech Processing (Vol. 2)*. Springer Science & Business Media.

9. Forney, G.D. (1973). The Viterbi Algorithm. In *Proceedings of the IEEE*, 61(3), doi: 10.1109/PROC.1973.9030, pp.268-278.

10. Zhai, C. and Lafferty, J. (2004). A Study of Smoothing Methods for Language Models Applied to Information Retrieval. *ACM Transactions on Information Systems* (TOIS), 22(2), pp.179-214.

11. Banga, R., and Mehndiratta, P. (2017). Tagging Efficiency Analysis on Part of Speech Taggers. (*2017). International Conference on Information Technology (ICIT)*, Bhubaneswar, doi: 10.1109/ICIT.2017.57. pp. 264-267.

12. Loria, S. (2020). Textblob: Simplified Text Processing, URL: https://textblob.readthedocs.io/en/dev/

13. Pytorch.org 2017. Sequence Models and Long-Short Term Memory Networks URL: https://pytorch.org/tutorials/beginner/nlp/sequence_models_tutorial.html

14. Meftah, S. and Semmar, N., (2018). A Neural Network Model for Part-of-Speech Tagging of Social Media Texts. In *Proceedings of the Eleventh International Conference on Language Resources and Evaluation* (LREC 2018).

15. Gui, T., Zhang, Q., Huang, H., Peng, M., and Huang, X.J. (2017). Part-of-Speech Tagging for Twitter with Adversarial Neural Networks. In *Proceedings of the 2017 Conference on Empirical Methods in Natural Language Processing* (pp. 2411-2420).

16. McCord, M.C. (1990). Slot Grammar. In *Natural Language and Logic* (pp. 118-145). Springer, Berlin, Heidelberg.

17. Alshawi, H. (1996). Head Automata and Bilingual Tiling: Translation with Minimal Representations. In *Proceedings of the 34th Annual Meeting on Association for Computational Linguistics* (pp. 167-176). Association for Computational Linguistics.

18. N. Chomsky, (1956) "Three Models for the Description of Language," in *IRE Transactions on Information Theory*, 2(3):113-124. doi: 10.1109/TIT.1956.1056813.

19. Collins, M. (1999). *Head-Driven Statistical Models for Natural Language Parsing*. Ph.D. thesis, University of Pennsylvania
20. Socher, R., Bauer, J., Manning, C.D. and Ng, A.Y. (2013). Parsing with Compositional Vector Grammars. In *Proceedings of the 51st Annual Meeting of the Association for Computational Linguistics (Volume 1: Long Papers)* (pp. 455-465).
21. Occurrences of some of some of these parts of speech are very rare and thus may not be familiar. For example, "horse" can be tagged as a noun (NN) as in "I saw a horse.", or an adjective (JJ) as in "I visited a horse farm." or a base form of verb (VB) as in "I wanted to horse around." or a present tense verb (VBP) as in "I horse around with my kids".
22. CKY assumes that all rules in the grammar (except lexical rules) have exactly two nonterminals on the right hand side - or has been binarized by adding extra nonterminal symbols.
23. McDonald, R., Pereira, F., Ribarov, K. and Hajič, J. (2005). Non-Projective Dependency Parsing using Spanning Tree Algorithms. In *Proceedings of the 2005 Conference on Human Language Technology and Empirical Methods in Natural Language Processing* (pp. 523-530). Association for Computational Linguistics.
24. Yamada, H. and Matsumoto, Y. (2003). Statistical Dependency Analysis with Support Vector Machines. In *Proceedings of the Eighth International Conference on Parsing Technologies* (pp. 195-206).
25. Nivre, J. (2008). Algorithms for Deterministic Incremental Dependency Parsing. *Computational Linguistics*,34(4), pp.513-553.
26. Note, this example traces a correct parse of "Happy children like to play with their friends." The Stanford CoreNLP.run online demo did not produce this parse when this example was written. It gave the following wrong one instead:
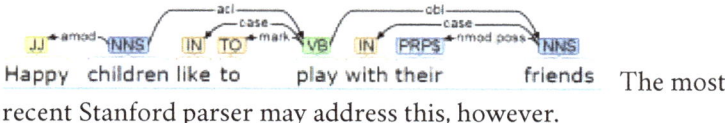
The most recent Stanford parser may address this, however.
27. Collins, M., Ramshaw, L., Hajič, J. and Tillmann, C., (1999). A Statistical Parser for Czech. In Proceedings of the 37th Annual Meeting of the Association for Computational Linguistics (pp. 505-512).
28. Xia, F. and Palmer, M. (2001). Converting Dependency Structures to Phrase Structures. In *Proceedings of the First International Conference on Human language Technology Research* (pp. 1-5). Association for Computational Linguistics.
29. Lee, Y. S., and Wang, Z. (2016). Language Independent Dependency to Constituent Tree conversion. In Proceedings of COLING 2016,

the 26th International Conference on Computational Linguistics: Technical Papers (pp. 421-428).

30. Adwait Ratnaparkhi. 1997. A Linear Observed Time Statistical Parser Based on Maximum Entropy Models. In *Proceedings of Empirical Methods in Natural Language Processing* (EMNLP). Also in ArXiv.org URL: https://arxiv.org/abs/cmp-lg/9706014

31. See Linzen, T. and Baroni, M. (2020). Syntactic Structure from Deep Learning. arXiv preprint arXiv:2004.10827. URL:https://arxiv.org/pdf/2004.10827

32. Gaddy, D., Stern, M. and Klein, D., 2018. What's Going on in Neural Constituency Parsers. An Analysis. In the *Proceedings of the 16th Annual Conference of the North American Chapter of the Association for Computational Linguistics: Human Language Technologies*. Also online as: https://arxiv.org/pdf/1804.07853.pdf

33. Kitaev, N. and Klein, D. (2018). Constituency Parsing with a Self-Attentive Encoder. arXiv preprint arXiv:1805.01052.

34. Qi, P., Zhang, Y., Zhang, Y., Bolton, J. and Manning, C. (2020). Stanza: A Python Natural Language Processing Toolkit for Many Human Languages. In the *Proceedings of the 58th Annual Meeting of the Association for Computational Linguistics (ACL) System Demonstrations*. Also see the STANZA Github website: https://stanfordnlp.github.io/stanza/

35. Dozat, T., Qi, P. and Manning, C.D. (2017). Stanford's Graph-Based Neural Dependency Parser at the CoNLL 2017 Shared Task. In *Proceedings of the CoNLL 2017 Shared Task: Multilingual Parsing from Raw Text to Universal Dependencies* (pp. 20-30).

36. Qi, P., Dozat, T., Zhang, Y. and Manning, C.D. (2019). Universal Dependency Parsing from Scratch. ArXiv preprint arXiv:1901.10457.

37. Straka, M. and Straková, J. (2017). Tokenizing, POS Tagging, Lemmatizing and Parsing UD 2.0 with UDpipe. In *Proceedings of the CoNLL 2017 Shared Task: Multilingual Parsing from Raw Text to Universal Dependencies* (pp. 88-99).

38. UDPipe is available from both a public Github and from CRAN. The CRAN site provides more extensive user-level documentation. Github URL: https://github.com/ufal/udpipe CRAN URL: https://cran.r-project.org/package=udpipe

39. Universaldepencies.org CONLL-U Format URL: https://universaldependencies.org/format.html

40. Bird, S., Klein, E., and Loper, E. (2009). Natural Language Processing with Python: Analyzing Text with the Natural Language Toolkit.

O'Reilly Media, Inc..

41. NLTK 3.5 Documentation URL http://www.nltk.org/api/nltk.tag.html#module-nltk.tag.stanford

CHAPTER 5.

SEMANTICS AND SEMANTIC INTERPRETATION

This chapter will consider how to capture the meanings that words and structures express, which is called semantics. The goal of a meaning representation is to provide a mapping between expressions of language to concepts in some computational model of a domain, which might be specified as a software application or as a set of well-formed formulas in a logic (or as some hybrid of the two, such as an AI frame system[1, 2, 3]). A reason to do semantic processing is that people can use a variety of expressions to describe the same situation. Having a semantic representation allows us to generalize away from the specific words and draw insights over the concepts to which they correspond. This makes it easier to store information in databases, which have a fixed structure. It also allows the reader or listener to connect what the language says with what they already know or believe.

As an example, consider what we might learn from the following sentence: "Malaysia's crude palm oil output is estimated to have risen by up to six percent."[4]. This sentence tells the reader (among other things) that countries have associated manufacturing and agricultural outputs, that one of Malaysia's outputs is "crude palm oil", and that some estimated measure of that output for some time period increased by "six percent or less". However, the reader might need to clarify what type of measure (e.g., volume or value) and what time period (e.g., month, year, or decade), or they might rely on background knowledge, such as knowing that this was an annual report of production volumes.

Semantic processing can be a precursor to later processes, such as question answering or knowledge acquisition (i.e., mapping unstructured content into structured content), which may involve additional processing to recover additional indirect (implied) aspects of meaning. The primary issues of concern for semantics are deciding a) what information needs to be represented b) what the target semantic representations are, including the valid mappings from input to output and c) what processing method can be used to map the input to the target representation.

Decisions about what needs to be represented will depend on the target task, but there are four main types of information that are typically included. These four things are:

- the entities that are being described,
- the types of events that are being mentioned and the roles that the entities fulfill with respect to the event,
- the type of propositional attitude that a sentence expresses, such as a statement, question, or request, and
- the intended word senses for each occurrence of a word in a sentence.

This information is determined by the noun phrases, the verb phrases, the overall sentence, and the general context. The background for mapping these linguistic structures to what needs to be represented comes from linguistics and the philosophy of language.

The target semantic representation will also depend on the target task. Shallow representations might identify the main verb and the spans of text that correspond to the entities that fulfill the functional parameters or semantic roles associated with the intended meaning of the verb. Deeper representations include the main verb, its semantic roles and the deeper semantics of the entities themselves, which might involve quantification, type restrictions, and various types of modifiers. The representation frameworks used for Natural Language semantics include formal logics, frame languages, and graph-based languages. Shallow representations might be sufficient for tasks related to mapping unstructured content into a structured representation (e.g. knowledge acquisition). Deep representations would be useful for tasks that require being able to go from a structured representation back into text via natural language generation, such as report generation or question answering from a knowledge base.

The processing methods for mapping raw text to a target representation will depend on the overall processing framework and the target representations. A basic approach is to write machine-readable rules that specify all the intended mappings explicitly and then create an algorithm for performing the mappings. An alternative is to express the rules as human-readable guidelines for annotation by people, have people create a corpus of annotated structures using an authoring tool, and then train classifiers to automatically select annotations for similar unlabeled data. The classifier approach can be used for either shallow representations or for subtasks of a deeper semantic analysis (such as identifying the type and boundaries of named entities or semantic roles) that can be combined to build up more complex semantic representations.

We will now consider each of these three aspects in greater detail. It should be noted that for some problems, a deep semantics such as described here is not necessary. In Chapter 8, we will discuss information extraction, which maps free text onto data structures without trying to provide any mapping between expressions in language and entities or events in an underlying model of a task domain or the "real world."

5.1 INFORMATION TO BE REPRESENTED

For sentences that are not specific to any domain, the most common approach to semantics is to focus on the verbs and how they are used to describe events, with some attention to the use of quantifiers (such as "a few", "many" or "all") to specify the entities that participate in those events. These models follow from work in linguistics (e.g. case grammars and theta roles) and philosophy (e.g., Montague Semantics[5] and Generalized Quantifiers[6]). Four types of information are identified to represent the meaning of individual sentences.

First, it is useful to know what entities are being described. These correspond to individuals or sets of individuals in the real world, that are specified using (possibly complex) quantifiers. Entities can be identified by their names (such as a sequence of proper nouns), by some complex description (such as a noun phrase that includes a head noun, a determiner, and various types of restrictive modifiers including possessive phrases, adjectives, nouns, prepositional phrases, and relative clauses), or by a pronoun.

Second, it is useful to know what types of events or states are being mentioned and their semantic roles, which is determined by our understanding of verbs and their senses, including their required arguments and typical modifiers. For example, the sentence "The duck ate a bug." describes an eating event that involved a duck as eater and a bug as the thing that was eaten. The most complete source of this information is the **Unified Verb Index**.

Third, semantic analysis might also consider what type of propositional attitude a sentence expresses, such as a statement, question, or request. The type of behavior can be determined by whether there are "wh" words in the sentence or some other special syntax (such as a sentence that begins with either an auxiliary or untensed main verb). These three types of information are represented together, as expressions in a logic or some variant.

Fourth, word sense discrimination determines what words senses are intended for tokens of a sentence. Discriminating among the possible senses of a word involves selecting a label from a given set (that is, a classification task). Alternatively, one can use a distributed representation of words, which are created using vectors of numerical values that are learned to accurately predict similarity and differences among words. One might also combine a symbolic label and a vector.

In some specialized domains, the primary focus is on the specification of ontologies of objects rather than events, where objects may have very complex requirements for their attributes. Ontologies specify definitions of concepts, place them into a hierarchy of subtypes, and define the various types of relations that they hold (e.g., "subclass-of", "instance-of", "part-of", etc.), and any restrictions on these relations. For example, in the domain of anatomy, there is a distinction between "shared" and "unshared" body parts. Below is an explanation from a paper describing one such ontology:

> "In modeling anatomy, we not only need to represent the part-of relations, but also we need to qualify relations between a part and a whole with additional attributes. For example, parts of an organ can be shared (that is, they belong to several anatomical entities) or unshared (they belong to one anatomical entity). Blood vessels and nerves that branch within a muscle must be considered a part of both that muscle and the vascular or neural trees to which they belong. In contrast, the fleshy part of the muscle (made of muscle tissue) and the tendon (made of connective tissue) are unshared". [7]

To represent this distinction properly, the researchers chose to "reify" the "has-parts" relation (which means defining it as a metaclass) and then create different instances of the "has-parts" relation for tendons (unshared) versus blood vessels (shared). Figure 5.1 shows a fragment of an ontology for defining a tendon, which is a type of tissue that connects a muscle to a bone. When the sentences describing a domain focus on the objects, the natural approach is to use a language that is specialized for this task, such as Description Logic[8] which is the formal basis for popular ontology tools, such as Protégé[9].

Figure 5.1 Fragment of the Foundational Model of Anatomy ontology for defining a tendon (example and image from Noy et al (2004))

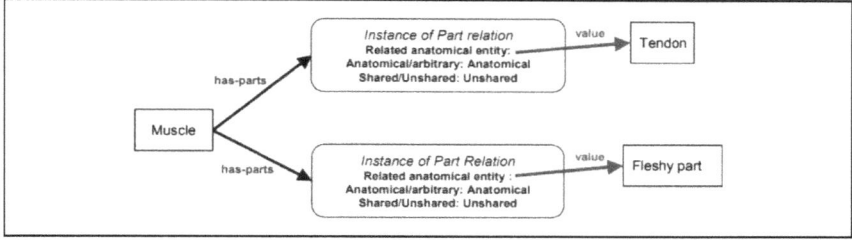

5.1.1 Case Grammar, Events, and Semantic Roles

Theories for what a semantics for natural language sentences should include have their basis in what linguists call a "case grammar". Case grammars describe the different roles that are associated with different verbs or types of verbs, for example action verbs have an agent and transitive verbs have a direct object, whose role might be described as either the theme or the patient depending on whether the verb affects the object in some way. Case grammars differ from typical representations given in a logic, where one might represent different types of events using different predicate symbols, where each predicate symbol is predefined to have a fixed number of arguments, each of which occurs in a fixed order. For example, the sentence "Rico visited Milwaukee." might be represented in a logic as "**visit(Rico, Milwaukee)**". The arguments of these predicates are *terms* in the logic, which can be either variables bound by quantifiers, or constants which name particular individuals in the domain. However, verbs can have both required arguments and optional modifiers. Case grammars involve naming the sets of required and modifying roles for each sense of a verb explicitly, for example "**[Agent Rico]**" or "**[Location Milwaukee]**". This is analogous to using keyword arguments in a programming language. Examples of semantic (thematic) roles include "Agent", which is a sentient being that performs an action and "Patient" which is an affected object of some action. Figures 5.2 to 5.5 include examples of roles, from VerbNet3.3, part of the **Unified Verb Index**.

Figure 5.2 Examples of semantic roles that commonly appear in the subject position

Subject relations	Example
Agent (+intentional, +sentient)	[The cat] chased a mouse.
Cause (-intentional, +nonsentient)	[The wind] rattled the windows.
Experiencer (+sentient) of perception	[The children] tasted the soup.
Pivot	[The bottle] contains seltzer water.
Theme (-affected)	[The ball] rolled down the hill.

Figure 5.3 Examples of semantic roles that commonly appear in the object position.

Object relations	Example
Attribute	Oil increased in [price].
Beneficiary	Claire sang a song for [her teacher].
Instrument	The chef baked a cake in [the oven].
Material	An oak tree will grow [from an acorn].
Patient (+affected)	The wind destroyed [the sand castles].
Product (+concrete)	Boeing builds [aircraft].
Recipient (+animate)	The teacher gave a book [to a student].
Result	The delay threw the project [into chaos].
Stimulus	The children saw [some clouds].
Theme (-affected)	The boy rolled [the ball] down the hill.
Topic	The teacher taught a class [about verbs.]

Figure 5.4 Examples of semantic roles that express a place (as a modifier).

Place relations	Example
Asset	Carmen purchased a dress [for $50].
Destination	I brought a book [to the meeting].
Extent (+measurable_change)	The top rotates [90 degrees].
Goal	I dedicated myself [to the cause].
Location (+concrete)	I searched [the cave] for treasure.
Source	The cleaner removes stains [from clothing].
Value (+scale)	He put the price [at 10 dollars].

Figure 5.5 Examples of semantic roles that express a time or span of time (as a modifier).

Temporal relations	Example
Time	He was happy [after receiving his marks].
Duration	The class continued [for two hours].

The set of roles associated with a verb by a case grammar are called "semantic frames". In linguistics, there have been several approaches to defining case grammars. The first case grammars were defined by Dr. Charles J. Fillmore in 1968, in his "The Case for Case". This work defined commonly occurring cases such as Agent, Object, Benefactor, Location, and Instrument, and provided examples for a small set of verbs for illustration. In 1997, Fillmore began the FrameNet project, a more comprehensive, data-driven effort to define a hierarchy of semantic frames and create a corpus of sentences annotated with semantic roles. FrameNet now includes over 1200 different frames. Software for labelling sentences with FrameNet roles is included in the Natural Language Toolkit. FrameNet is now also part of a larger resource called the Unified Verb Index (UVI). The UVI also includes verb types and annotated text from PropBank, OntoNotes, and VerbNet. The UVI is maintained by the creators of VerbNet at the University of Colorado.

There is an ISO standard for semantic roles which is part of ISO standard 24617, which is a standard for Language resource management — Semantic annotation framework (SemAF). When complete, ISO 24617 will consist of eight parts, of which the following six were the first to be completed:
— Part 1: Time and events (SemAF-Time, ISO-TimeML)
— Part 2: Dialogue acts
— Part 4: Semantic roles (SemAF-SR)
— Part 5: Discourse structure (SemAF-DS)
— Part 7: Spatial information (ISO-Space)

The last parts to be finalized are Part 8: Semantic relations in discourse (SemAF-DRel) and Part 6: Principles of semantic annotation (SemAF-Basics).

5.1.2 Quantification and Scoping

Quantifiers allow one to describe the properties of individuals and sets. In a first order logic of mathematics, there are just two quantifiers, the existential and the universal, and they bind only terms, which are expressions that denote individuals in the domain. Quantifiers introduce an additional type of ambiguity, related to the set of relations over which they bind variables, known as the "scope" of the quantifier. For example, the sentence "Every cat chased a mouse" might mean either that several cats all chased the same mouse, or each cat chased their own personal favorite mouse. Natural language systems can choose to leave quantifiers unscoped or to make a guess based on domain-specific knowledge. Other mechanisms are needed to address scoping across multiple sentences (e.g., some graphical representations use structure sharing, where each entity corresponds to a unique structure and all references to it point back to this same structure.)

The types of quantification that people express in natural language can be much more diverse than mere existence or universality, however. Natural language quantifiers can specify the size of a set at various levels of precision (e.g., "Exactly one", "At least two", or "Most") and they can specify a wide variety of type constraints, such as "most bears", "most hungry bears", "most bears that originated from Asia". To address this variety, the representation of semantics for natural language often involves a mechanism known as "Generalized Quantifiers"[10]. A generalized quantifier consists of the quantifier name, a set of quantified variables, and a constraint, which is a well-formed expression that uses the given variables. These quantifiers and property constraints will hold over any expressions within their scope. For example, "Most small dogs like toys" could be expressed in a logical framework as **[Most x, small(x) and dog(x) [All y toys(y): like(x,y)]]**. The interpretation of such quantifiers must be defined as some function, which might depend on the domain. For example, one might define "most" as either "more than 50%" or as "more than 60%". In some ontology tools, these are defined as "role-bounded" quantifiers (e.g., in Protege.)

5.2 COMPUTATIONAL FRAMEWORKS FOR SEMANTICS

There are two broad types of semantic frameworks: domain dependent and domain independent. Domain dependent semantics might be considered a mix of semantics and pragmatics – sentences are used to *do something* so the meaning is the procedure call or query that one would execute to do it. For this reason, these representations are sometimes also called Procedural Semantics[11,12]. Domain-independent semantics includes identifying the actions, participants, and objects described in language, and possibly other important information, such as when an event occurred and the manner or location in which it occurred. It may also include the interpretation of quantifiers to allow one to select the appropriate set of participants and objects. These representations might be used for a variety of applications, such as machine translation, knowledge acquisition (i.e., learning by reading), question answering, or the control of software. Domain independent semantics typically use some variant of mathematical logic or a graph-based equivalent.

5.2.1 Procedural Semantics

The notion of a procedural semantics was first conceived to describe the compilation and execution of computer programs when programming was still new. In the 1970's, psychologists, including George A. Miller[13] and Philip Johnson-Laird[14], described how this metaphor might better describe how language is used to communicate as it offered a uniform framework for describing how it is used "to make statements, to ask questions and to answer them, to make requests, and even to express invocations and imprecations" – unlike formal logics which ultimately reduce the meaning of all sentences to one of either "true" or "false". Of course, there is a total lack of uniformity across implementations, as it depends on how the software application has been defined. Figure 5.6 shows two possible procedural semantics for the query, "Find all customers with last name of Smith.", one as a database query in the Structured Query Language (SQL), and one implemented as a user-defined function in Python.

Figure 5.6 Examples of procedural semantics

Sentence: Find all customers with last name of Smith
SQL: SELECT * FROM Customers WHERE Last_Name='Smith'
Python: Customers.retrieveRows(last_name="Smith")

For SQL, we must assume that a database has been defined such that we can select columns from a table (called Customers) for rows where the Last_Name column (or relation) has 'Smith' for its value. For the Python expression we need to have an object with a defined member function that allows the keyword argument "last_name". Until recently, creating procedural semantics had only limited appeal to developers because the difficulty of using natural language to express commands did not justify the costs. However, the rise in chatbots and other applications that might be accessed by voice (such as smart speakers) creates new opportunities for considering procedural semantics, or procedural semantics intermediated by a domain independent semantics.

5.2.2 Methods for Creating Procedural Semantics

Procedural semantics can be created either using rule-based methods or by annotating a corpus with the target representation and then training a classifier. When the range of expressions is small, either approach is reasonable. For example, one can associate semantic annotations with particular parse trees by creating context free grammar rules with semantic features. Then, these annotations can be used either during a parse, as each structure is completed, or afterwards by traversing complete parse trees.

As an example, we will consider mapping queries to SQL where "city_table" is a table of cities, countries and populations (shown in Figure 5.7)

Figure 5.7 List of top four cities of Canada, Mexico, and the United States by population (according to Wikipedia)

City	Country	Population
Calgary	Canada	1238
Montreal	Canada	3519
Toronto	Canada	5429
Vancouver	Canada	2264
Mexico City	Mexico	8851
Ecatepec	Mexico	1655
Guadalajara	Mexico	1495
Puebla	Mexico	1434
New York	United_States	8623
Los Angeles	United_States	4000
Chicago	United_States	2716
Houston	United_States	2312

Figure 5.8 gives a set of CFG grammar rules with semantic features for creating SQL statements for queries like "What cities are located in Canada?" or "In what country is Houston?" where the target representations would be "**SELECT City FROM city_table WHERE Country = 'Canada'** " and "**SELECT Country FROM city_table WHERE City = 'Houston'** ", respectively.

Figure 5.8 Grammar for parsing a query into SQL

```
SBARQ[SEM=(?np WHERE ?sp)] -> WHNP[SEM=?np] SQ[SEM=?sp]
  SBARQ[SEM=(?wp WHERE ?sp)] -> WHPP[SEM=?wp] SQ[SEM=?sp]
  SQ[SEM=(?v ?np)] -> VBZ[SEM=?v] NP[SEM=?np]
  SQ[SEM=(?v ?pp)] -> VBP[SEM=?v] PP[SEM=?pp]
  SQ[SEM=(?v ?ap)] -> VBP[SEM=?v] JJP[SEM=?ap]
  WHNP[SEM=(?d ?n)] -> WDT[SEM=?d] NNS[SEM=?n] | WDT[SEM=?d]
NN[SEM=?n]
  WHPP[SEM=(?p ?wnp)] -> IN[SEM=?p] WHNP[SEM= ?wnp]
  PP[SEM=(?p ?np)] -> IN[SEM=?p] NP[SEM=?np]
  JJP[SEM=?pp] -> JJ[SEM=?a] P[SEM=?pp]
  NP[SEM="Country='Canada' "] -> NNP[SEM='Canada']
  NP[SEM="Country='Mexico' "] -> NNP[SEM='Mexico']
  NP[SEM="Country='United_States' "] -> DT NNP[SEM='United']
NNPS[SEM='States']
  NP[SEM="City='Calgary' "] -> NNP[SEM='Calgary']
  NP[SEM="City='Puebla' "] -> NNP[SEM='Puebla']
  NP[SEM="City='Houston' "] -> NNP[SEM='Houston']
  WDT[SEM='SELECT'] -> 'Which' | 'What'
  NNS[SEM="Country FROM city_table "] -> 'country'
  NNS[SEM="City FROM city_table "] -> 'cities'
  NNP[SEM=(?nnp)] -> 'Canada' | 'Calgary' | 'Houston' | 'Mexico' | 'Puebla' |
'United'
  NNPS[SEM=(?nnps)] -> 'States'
  VBP[SEM=" "] -> 'are'
  VBZ[SEM=" "] -> 'is'
  JJ[SEM=" "] -> 'located'
  IN[SEM=" "] -> 'in'
```

These rules are for a constituency–based grammar, however, a similar approach could be used for creating a semantic representation by traversing a dependency parse. Figure 5.9 shows dependency structures for two similar queries about the cities in Canada.

Figure 5.9 Dependency structures for "What cities are in Canada?" vs. "What cities are located in Canada?"

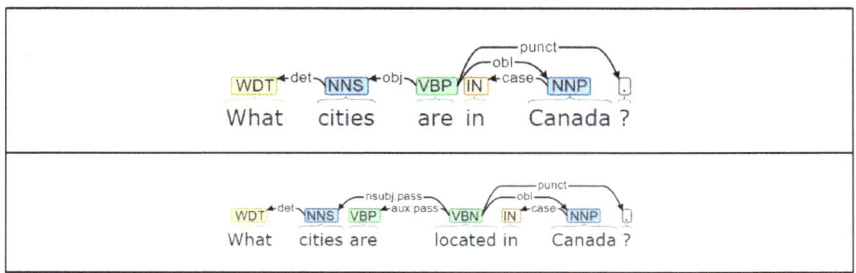

Notice that they both contain the dependencies "det" and "case". Thus, the result for "cities" and "in Canada" would be **SEM (det (WDT, cities))** = **"SELECT Cities from city_table WHERE"** and **SEM(case(IN, Canada))** = **"Country = Canada"**, respectively.

There are several existing corpora that include paired natural language sentences and SQL queries. One of the largest is the WikiSQL dataset which contains 80,654 pairs of the NL sentence-SQL query derived from 24,241 Wikipedia tables. There is also the Stack Exchange Natural Language Interface to Database (SENLIDB) corpus, which includes 24,890 NL sentence-SQL query pairs constructed using the Stack Exchange API. At the same time, new formats for databases are emerging, including "Graph Databases", which are optimized for retrieving relationship triples along with associated properties[15,16]. They also support a query language, Cypher, that is much closer to natural language than SQL, making it more straightforward to map NL sentences onto graph database languages[17]. Figure 5.10 shows an example of a query and an assertion in Cypher.

Figure 5.10 Examples of Cypher query language equivalents for natural language

MATCH (:Person {name: 'Jennifer'})-[:WORKS_FOR]->(company:Company) RETURN company.name *Cypher query for "What is the name of the company that Jennifer works for?"*
MATCH (jennifer:Person {name: 'Jennifer'}) MATCH (mark:Person {name: 'Mark'}) CREATE (jennifer)-[rel:IS_FRIENDS_WITH]->(mark) *Cypher assertion that "Jennifer is friends with Mark"*

Procedural semantics are possible for very restricted domains, but quickly become cumbersome and hard to maintain. People will naturally express the same idea in many different ways and so it is useful to consider approaches that generalize more easily, which is one of the goals of a domain independent representation.

5.3 DOMAIN INDEPENDENT FRAMEWORKS

Domain independent semantics tries to capture the type of state or event and its structure, which includes identifying the semantic roles associated with the event where the core roles would be action, subject, and object. It sometimes also tries to address the interpretation of quantifiers. Domain independent semantics are normally also compositional, which means they can be built up incrementally, with general mappings between corresponding syntactic and semantic constituent types. Composition can be defined formally, using the formalism of the lambda calculus[18], or procedurally, by providing explicit rules for composing objects of various types. The result can be either a well-formed expression in a logic, as an expression in an artificial intelligence frame language resembling a logic (sometimes also called a "quasi-logical form") or as a graph. Graph-based representations, also known as "semantic networks", offer many advantages, as they tend to be both more expressive than logic and more efficient, because their structure facilitates inference and supports sharing of structures across phrases and sentences.

5.3.1 Using First Order Predicate Logic for NL Semantics

Formal logics have a well-defined syntax, which includes the legal symbols for terms, relations, quantifiers, operators, conjunctions, and functions and how they can be combined. Well-formed expressions are defined recursively. Terms can be constants, variables, or the application of an n-ary function symbol to exactly n terms. Atomic formulas consist of an n-ary relation symbol with exactly n terms as arguments. (If a logic includes the equality symbol then $term_i = term_j$ is also a legal atomic formula.) Legal non-atomic formulas can be created by any of the following, where ¬ is the negation symbol (i.e., "not"), ∨ is the symbol for disjunction ("or"), ∧ is the symbol for conjunction ("and"), ∃ is the existential quantifier ("there exists"), and ∀ is the universal quantifier ("for all").

- If α is a formula then so is ¬α
- If α and β are formulas then so is α ∨ β and α ∧ β

- If x is a variable and α is a formula then so is ∃x.α and ∀x.α

Logic does not have a way of expressing the difference between statements and questions so logical frameworks for natural language sometimes add extra logical operators to describe the pragmatic force indicated by the syntax – such as ask, tell, or request. Logical notions of conjunction and quantification are also not always a good fit for natural language.

5.3.2 Compositionality in Logic-Based Representations

Domain independent semantics generally strive to be compositional, which in practice means that there is a consistent mapping between words and syntactic constituents and well-formed expressions in the semantic language. Most logical frameworks that support compositionality derive their mappings from Richard Montague[19] who first described the idea of using the lambda calculus as a mechanism for representing quantifiers and words that have complements. Subsequent work by others[20, 21] also clarified and promoted this approach among linguists.

Lambda expressions are function abstractions that can be applied to their arguments and then reduced, to perform substitutions for the lambda-bound variables. For example, **λx: (λy: loves (x,y) (Milwaukee)) = λx: loves (x, Milwaukee)**. Each lambda symbol can bind one or more variables, corresponding to a function that takes one of more arguments. With multiple lambda-bound variables, expressions may be nested, and then evaluated from the inside out, or a single lambda can bind multiple variables, in which case the order of values will determine to which variable they are bound, proceeding from left to right. Syntax for creating lambda expressions exists in Python, as "lambda", and in NLTK, using a slash operator, "\". Figure 5.11 shows what happens when lambdas with multiple variables versus multiple nested single variable lambdas are reduced using the NLTK lambda-reduction function, "simplify()": in each example, x1 is the unreduced lamda expression and x2 is the equivalent reduced, and we show their equality explicitly.

Figure 5.11 Examples of Lambda Expressions from NLTK HowTo nltk.logic

```
>>> x1 = read_expr(r'\a.sleep(a)(mia)').simplify()
>>> x2 = read_expr(r'sleep(mia)').simplify()
>>> x1 == x2
True
>>> x1 = read_expr(r'\a.\b.like(b,a)(mia)').simplify()
>>> x2 = read_expr(r'\b.like(b,mia)').simplify()
>>> x1 == x2
True
>>> x1 = read_expr(r'\a.(\b.like(b,a)(vincent))').simplify()
>>> x2 = read_expr(r'\a.like(vincent,a)').simplify()
>>> x1 == x2
True
>>> x1 = read_expr(r'\a.((\b.like(b,a)(vincent)) & sleep(a))').simplify()
>>> x2 = read_expr(r'\a.(like(vincent,a) & sleep(a))').simplify()
>>> x1 == x2
True
>>> x1 = read_expr(r'(\a.\b.like(b,a)(mia)(vincent))').simplify()
>>> x2 = read_expr(r'like(vincent,mia)').simplify()
>>> x1 == x2
True
```

There are two special cases. If the sentence within the scope of a lambda variable includes the same variable as one in its argument, then the variables in the argument should be renamed to eliminate the clash. The other special case is when the expression within the scope of a lambda involves what is known as "intensionality". Sentences that talk about things that might not be true in the world right now, such as statements about the past, statements that include a modal operator (e.g., "it is possible"), statements that include counterfactuals, and statements of "belief", such as "Rex believes that the cat is hungry." all require special care to separate what is true in the world versus some context of an alternate time, of the mental state of some agent, etc. Since the logics for these are quite complex and the circumstances for needing them rare, here we will consider only sentences that do not involve intensionality. In fact, the complexity of representing intensional contexts in logic is one of the reasons that researchers cite for using graph-based representations (which we consider later), as graphs can be partitioned to define different contexts explicitly. Figure 5.12 shows some example mappings used for compositional semantics and the lambda reductions used to reach the final form.

5.3.2.1 Linguistic and Logical Magic

Note that to combine multiple predicates at the same level via conjunction one must introduce a function to combine their semantics. Here we will call that function UNIFY_AND_CONJOIN. The intended result is to replace the variables in the predicates with the same (unique) lambda variable and to connect them using a conjunction symbol (*and*). The lambda variable will be used to substitute a variable from some other part of the sentence when combined with the conjunction.

Figure 5.12 Examples of lambda reduction using ad hoc functions to unify variables and raise conjunctions

Function with example parameters	Result
UNIFY_AND_CONJOIN((x, P1(x)), (y, P2(y)))	($\lambda x1$, [P1(x1) and P2(x1)])
RAISE_QUANT([s X NP Y])	[s NP [s X e_i Y]]
RAISE_INFL([s NP INFL X])	[s INFL [s NP X]]
ONLY_ONE(y,P(y))	$\exists y\ P(y)$ and $\forall z\ P(z)\ ?\ x = y$

Other necessary bits of magic include functions for raising quantifiers and negation (NEG) and tense (called "INFL") to the front of an expression. Raising INFL also assumes that either there were explicit words, such as "not" or "did", or that the parser creates "fake" words for ones given as a prefix (e.g., un-) or suffix (e.g., -ed) that it puts ahead of the verb. We can take the same approach when FOL is tricky, such as using equality to say that "there exists only one" of something. Figure 5.12 shows the arguments and results for several special functions that we might use to make a semantics for sentences based on logic more compositional.

In a logic, we must also assume that we represent verbs using a precise number of arguments in a precise order. As an alternative, one could represent the semantics of verbs by adding a term to represent the event and conjoining separate predicates for each of the semantic roles as in: **λx: λy: λz: ∃ ev1: [gives (ev1, x,y, z) and agent(ev1,x) and recipient(ev1,y) and theme(ev1,z)]**. Figure 5.13 shows the mapping between many common types of expressions in natural language, and a representation in a first order logic that includes lambda expressions.

Figure 5.13 Example mapping between natural language types and logical types

Natural language types	Logical type
Proper noun	A term expressed as either a constant, e.g., *Ashley* or a functional expression, e.g., *named_entity('Ashley')*
Adjectives and common nouns that occur with determiners	Lambda expressions with one variable: *λx: cat (x), λx: grey(x),*
Determiner	Lambda expressions with quantifiers, *e.g., "a" = λx: ∃y x(y)* where the later substitution with a noun provides the predicate symbol. See below.
Noun phrase of: DT JJ NN 　Where 　　if DT = a then Q y is ∃y 　　if DT = all then Qy is ∀y 　　if DT = the then Qy P(y) is ONLY_ONE(y, P(y)))	A quantified expression, e.g. for "a grey cat" which would be ∃ y [grey(y) and cat (y)] obtained as follows: *λx: Q y x(y) (UNIFY_AND_CONJOIN(SEM(JJ),SEM(NN)))* *λx: ∃y: x(y) (UNIFY_AND_CONJOIN((x, grey(x)), (y, cat (y))))* *λx: ∃y x(y) (λx1, [grey(x1) and cat (x1)])* ∃ y (λx1, [grey(x1) and cat (x1)]) (y) ∃ y [grey(y) and cat (y)]
Noun phrase with relative clause e.g. DT NN that S	A quantified expression, e.g., for "a cat that ate a big mouse" which would be *λx: Q y x(y) (UNIFY_AND_CONJOIN(SEM(NN),SEM(S))* obtained as follows: *λx: ∃y x(y) (UNIFY_AND_CONJOIN((x1, cat(x1)), (x2, ∃z [big(z) and mouse (z) and ate(x2,z)])))* *λx: ∃y x(y) (λu cat(u) and ∃z [big(z) and mouse (z) and ate(u,z)])* ∃y (λu cat(u) and ∃z [big(z) and mouse (z) and ate(u,z)) (y) ∃y (cat(y) and ∃z [big(z) and mouse (z) and ate(y,z)])
Verbs of N arguments (including the subject)	N nested Lambda expressions, expressed with N separate variables, e.g., for "sleep" or "eats" *λx: sleep(x); λy: λx: eats (x,y); λz: λy: λx: gives (x, y, z)*
Verb phrase (transitive) 　RAISE_QUANT(V NP) 　= NP [V e_i]	A lambda expression with a raised quantified expression, *λx NP [verb (x,y) (e_i)]* where e_i is the result of quantifier raising, *e.g. for "chases a mouse"* which would be *λx: (λw: ∃y mouse(y) andchases (x,w)) (y)* *λx: ∃y mouse(y) and chases (x,y)*

Verb phrase (ditransitive)
  RAISE_QUANT(V NP1) NP2
  = NP1, RAISE_QUANT(V NP2)
  = NP1 NP2 (V e1 e2)
	A lambda expression for a quantified expression, NP1 and [NP2 [λx verb (x, e_1, e_2)]] e.g., "gave a girl a book."
	λx ∃y [girl(y) and [∃z book (z) and gave(x, y, z)]]

Conjoined VP : VP CC VP	[[VP]] and [[VP]] where [[X]] gives the semantics of X
Sentence (NP VP)	λx: x (NP), e.g. "Ashley sleeps.", NP = Ashley and VP = λz sleep(z) λx: sleep(x) (Ashley) which reduces to sleeps(Ashley)

Sentence
  NP NP_{r1} VP where NP_{r1}
  is a previously raised NP
	λx Qy Ry and P(x, y)(NP), e.g. "Susan owns a grey cat."
	λx ∃y [grey(y) and cat (y) and owns(x, y)](Susan)
	∃y [grey(y) and cat (y) and owns(Susan, y)

Sentence
  NP NP_{r1} NP_{r2}VP where NP_{ri}
  are previously raised NP
	Q_1yRy and Q_2z Rz and λx P(x, y, z)(NP) e.g. "Sy gave a girl a book."
	λx ∃y[girl(y) and ∃z book (z) and gave(x, y, z)](Sy)
	∃y [girl(y) and ∃z book (z) and gave(Sy, y,z)]

Conjoined sentence: S CC S	[[S]] and [[S]] where [[X]] gives the semantics of X

5.3.2.2 Referring Expressions

Pure FOL, even with lambda expressions, does not fully capture the meaning of referring expressions such as pronouns, proper names, and definite descriptions (such as "the cat"), when we consider what would be needed by a database or a knowledge base (KB). A backend representation structure must be able to link referential expressions, such as "the cat" or "a cat", to some entity in the KB, either existing ("the") or newly asserted "a". Also, it is not always sufficient to use a constant for named entities, e.g., [[Susan]] = susan. Using a constant like this assumes uniqueness (e.g., that there is only one person named Susan), when in reality there are millions of people who share that name. At an abstract level, what we need is a representation of entities, distinct from the expressions (strings) used to name them and we need functions to map between the expressions at the logical level, with those in the underlying KB. We can express this at the logical level by defining function symbols that invoke these functions at the implementation level, such as Named_entity("Susan") or Pronoun("it"). Then to implement these at the backend we would need to define them with some new ad hoc function or database assertion or query. In Python we might build a dictionary with dynamically created identifiers as keys and asserted relations as values, e.g., relations[cat1] = [grey(cat1), cat(cat1), eat(cat1, mouse1)], when *"a grey cat ate a mouse"* is mentioned. Or we might use a database language, such as Cypher, with expressions like CREATE (susan:Person {name: 'Susan'}) or MATCH (:Person {name: 'Susan'}), respectively, when Susan is mentioned. Including KB entities within the semantics would also require making a change to representations involving an existential quantifier, where we remove the quantifier and substitute for the variable a new constant corresponding to the unnamed individual for which the predicate is true. In logic this notion is accomplished via a "skolem function"; for an NL semantics one might use an ad hoc function to create new symbols on the fly[22]. And, with possibly multiple symbols corresponding to the same real-world entity, a logic or KB would also need an equality operator, e.g., susan1 = susan2 or owl.sameAs(susan1,susan2). Similar issues (and solutions) would arise for references to entities that get their meaning from the context, such as indexicals ("I", "you", "here", or "there") or references that depend on time and location ("the president", "the teacher"). We will discuss these issues further in Chapter 7, when we consider how multiple sentences taken together form a coherent unit, known as a discourse.

5.3.3 Frame Languages and Logical Equivalents

Although first order logic offers many benefits (such as well-defined semantics and sound and complete inference strategies) they have critical deficiencies when it comes to representing objects, in addition to just referring to individuals as discussed in Section 5.3.2. It is also problematic that, in FOL, all categories and properties of objects are represented by atomic predicates. Description logic (DL)[23] provides a way of relating different predicates as part of their definition, independent of what facts one might assert with them. A DL knowledge base (KB) will include expressions that specify definitions by saying that some atomic concept is equivalent to a complex one. It will also include expressions that give names to partial definitions by saying that an atomic concept is subsumed by another one. Thirdly it will assert properties of individuals. The only types of inference are thus assertion and classification, but knowing whether one has defined a consistent ontology is important for many disciplines. DL systems have been used to create and manage very large ontologies (even millions of concepts). For example, they have been widely used in biology and medicine and many public ontologies exist (e.g., the US NCBO Bioportal lists over 900 public ontologies). DL systems can also provide an object-oriented frontend to a relational database.

The syntax of DL includes three main types: concepts, roles, and constants. In terms of the logic, concept names are unary predicates; however we can specify complex concepts as a conjunctions of simpler ones. Role names are binary predicates, e.g. hasMother(robert,susan). Constants are the names of individuals. One can also specify restrictions on the values of roles, and reify relations to define metaclasses and a metaclass hierarchy. In relation to natural language constituents, common (or category) nouns, such as "dog" are concepts; relational nouns, such as "age", "parent", or "area_of_study", are roles, and proper nouns are constants.

There are four types of logical symbols: punctuation (e.g.,

round and square brackets), positive integers, concept-forming operators (e.g., ALL, EXISTS, FILLS, AND), and three types of connectives (one concept is subsumed by another (d ⊆ e) ; one concept satisfies the description of another (d ? e); and one concept is equivalent to another (d ≡ e). Atomic concepts, roles, and constants are the only "nonlogical symbols" – that is, ones that the user defines. With these types and symbols, we can now define the well-formed formulas of DL, as shown in Figure 5.14. The rules define valid concepts and three types of sentences. One can say that two concepts are equivalent, using ≡, or that one concept is subsumed by another, using ⊆, or that a given constant (an instance) satisfies the description expressed by a concept, using ?.

Figure 5.14 Syntax of Description Logic

Syntax	Example
Every atomic concept is a concept.	cat
If r is a role and d is a concept, then [ALL r d] is a concept.	[ALL :weight cat]
If r is a role and n is an integer, then [EXISTS n r] is a concept.	[EXISTS 4 :legs]
If r is a role and c is a constant, then [FILLS r c] is a concept.	[FILLS :legs leg1]
If d1, ..., dk are concepts, then so is [AND d1, ..., dk].	[AND mammal predator [EXISTS 4 :legs] [EXISTS 1 :tail]]
If d and e are concepts, then (d ≡ e) is a sentence.	four_legged ≡ [EXISTS 4 :legs]
If d and e are concepts, then (d ⊆ e) is a sentence.	cat ⊆ four_legged
If c is a constant and d is a concept, then (c ? d) is a sentence.	TardarSauce ? cat

By default, every DL ontology contains the concept "Thing" as the globally superordinate concept, meaning that all concepts in the ontology are subclasses of "Thing". The quantifiers each specify particular subsets of the domain. [ALL x y] where x is a role and y is a concept, refers to the subset of all individuals x such that if the pair <x, y> is in the role relation, then y is in the subset corresponding to the description. [EXISTS n x] where n is an integer is a role refers to the subset of individuals x where at least n pairs <x,y> are in the role relation. [FILLS x y] where x is a role and y is a constant, refers to the subset of individuals x, where the pair x and the interpretation of the concept is in the role relation. [AND x_1 x_2 ..x_n] where x_1 to x_n are concepts, refers to the conjunction of subsets corresponding to each of the component concepts. Figure 5.15 includes examples of DL expressions for some complex concept definitions.

Figure 5.15 Examples of a complex concept in description logic and some example sentences

"a company with at least 7 directors, whose managers are all women with PhDs, and whose minimum salary is $100/hr" 　[AND Company 　[EXISTS 7 :Director] 　[ALL :Manager [AND Woman [FILLS :Degree PhD] [FILLS :MinSalary '$100/hour']]]
"A dog is among other things a mammal that is a pet and a carnivorous animal whose voice call includes barking" 　(Dog [AND Mammal Pet CarnivorousAnimal [FILLS :VoiceCall barking]])
"A FatherOfDaughters is a male with at least one child and all of whose children are female" 　(FatherOfDaughters ≡ [AND Male [EXISTS 1 :Child] [ALL :Child Female]])
"Joe is a FatherOfDaughters and a Surgeon" 　(joe → [AND FatherOfDaughters Surgeon]])

Description logics separate the knowledge one wants to represent from the implementation of underlying inference. Inference services include asserting or classifying objects and performing queries. There is no notion of implication and there are no explicit variables, allowing inference to be highly optimized and efficient. Instead, inferences are implemented using structure matching and subsumption among complex concepts. One concept will subsume all other concepts that include the same, or more specific versions of, its constraints. These processes are made more efficient by first normalizing all the concept definitions so that constraints appear in a canonical order and any information about a particular role is merged together. These aspects are handled by the ontology software systems themselves, rather than coded by the user.

Ontology editing tools are freely available; the most widely used is Protégé, which claims to have over 300,000 registered users. Protégé also allows one to export ontologies into a variety of formats including RDF (Resource Description Framework)[24,25] and its textual format Turtle, OWL (Web Ontology Language)[26, 27], and XML Schema[28], so that the knowledge can be integrated with rule systems or other problem solvers.

Another logical language that captures many aspects of frames is CycL, the language used in the Cyc ontology and knowledge base. The Cyc KB is a resource of real world knowledge in machine-readable format. While early versions of CycL were described as being a frame language, more recent versions are described as a logic that supports frame-like structures and inferences. Cycorp, started by Douglas Lenat in 1984, has been an ongoing project for more than 35 years and they claim that it is now the longest-lived artificial intelligence project[29].

5.3.4 Compositionality using Frame Languages

Compositionality in a frame language can be achieved by mapping the constituent types of syntax to the concepts, roles, and instances of a frame language. For the purposes of illustration, we will consider the mappings from phrase types to frame expressions provided by Graeme Hirst[30] who was the first to specify a correspondence between natural language constituents and the syntax of a frame language, FRAIL[31]. Figure 5.16 shows the mappings for the most common types of phrases. These mappings, like the ones described for mapping phrase constituents to a logic using lambda expressions, were inspired by Montague Semantics. The frame language syntax used here includes symbols for variables and constants, which might name entities, the values of attributes, or instances (e.g., "Newton", "black", or cat01); symbols for frame types, which include both entities and actions (e.g., "cat" or "eat"); symbols for slots, which might be properties or semantic roles (e.g., "color" or "agent"); and symbols for frame determiners, which are functions for either storing or querying the frame system. Well-formed frame expressions include frame instances and frame statements (FS), where a FS consists of a frame determiner, a variable, and a frame descriptor that uses that variable. A frame descriptor is a frame symbol and variable along with zero or more slot-filler pairs. A slot-filler pair includes a slot symbol (like a role in Description Logic) and a slot filler which can either be the name of an attribute or a frame statement. The language supported only the storing and retrieving of simple frame descriptions without either a universal quantifier or generalized quantifiers. More complex mappings between natural language expressions and frame constructs have been provided using more expressive graph-based approaches to frames, where the actually mapping is produced by annotating grammar rules with frame assertion and inference operations.

Figure 5.16 Example mappings between syntactic types and frame expression types

Syntactic type and examples	Frame expression	Examples
Determiner, "the", "a"	Frame determiner	(the ?x), (a ?x)
Common noun, "cat", "mat"	Frame	(cat ?x), (mat ?x)
Pronoun, "he"	Frame statement, Instance	(the ?x (being ?x (gender = male)), man87
WH Pronoun, "what", "which"	Variable	?wh
Noun phrase, "the cat"	Frame statement, Instance	(the ?x (cat ?x)), cat01
Proper noun phrase, "Newton"	Frame statement, Instance	(the ?x (thing ?x (name = Newton)), thing01
Main verb, "chase", "sleep"	Frame	(chase ?x) , (sleep ?x)
Adjective, "black"	Slot-filler pair	(color = black)
Preposition, "on"	Slot name	location
Prepositional phrase, "on the mat"	Slot-filler pair	(location = mat93)
Auxiliary verb, "was"	Slot-filler pair	(tense = past)
Adverb, "quietly"	Slot-filler pair	(manner = quietly)
Verb phrase, "chase a mouse"	Frame descriptor	(chase ?x (patient = (a ?y (mouse ?y))))
Clause-end punctuation, ".", "?"	Frame determiner	(a ?x), (question ?x)
Sentence "The cat ate the mouse", "What did he eat?"	Frame statement, Instance	(a ?x (eat ?x (agent = cat01) (patient = mouse19))), (question ?x (eat ?x (agent = cat01) (patient = ?wh)))

5.3.5 Graph-Based Representation Frameworks

Graph-based representation frameworks for semantics have drawn wider attention with the commercial success of Amazon

Alexa[32]. Although application developers define intents in terms of natural language sentences, it was reported in June 2018 that Alexa's internal representation – before accessing the applications – would use a new graph-based framework called the "Alexa Meaning Representation Language"[33, 34]. Figure 5.17 shows the graph for a request to find a restaurant that includes a complex spatial relation "near the Sharks game". Graph-based representations of knowledge have had a longstanding following, including *The International Conference on Conceptual Structures*, which has origins going back to 1986. The focus of the meeting is a semantic framework called Conceptual Graphs. Figure 5.18 shows an example by John Sowa, illustrating one of the three possible interpretations of "Tom believes Mary wants to marry a sailor." along with its text-based representation in the Conceptual Graph Interchange Format, part of the ISO standard for Common Logic. Other currently active graph-based projects for NL include the FRED machine reading project which generates representations as RDF/OWL ontologies and linked data, and the Cogitant project which distributed libraries for editing Conceptual Graphs. There are also freely available datasets of text annotated with CG that have been used for supervised (reinforcement) learning[35, 36].

Figure 5.17 AMRL Graph for "Find restaurants near the Sharks game" (Image from Perera et al 2018)

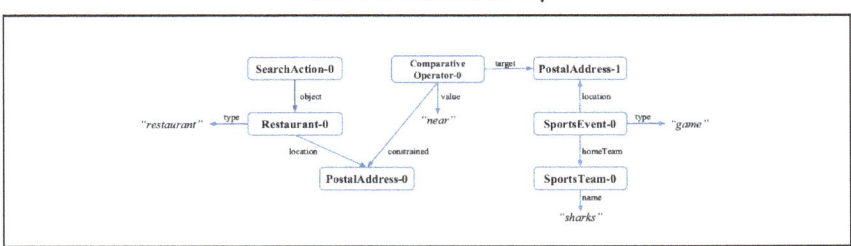

The Conceptual Graph shown in Figure 5.18 shows how to capture a resolved ambiguity about the existence of "a sailor", which might be in the real world, or possibly just one agent's belief context. The graph and its CGIF equivalent express that it is in both Tom and Mary's belief context, but not necessarily the real world. Conceptual graphs have also been used to represent sentences in legal statutes, which can have complex quantification in the form of exceptions or exclusions, e.g., "The Plaintiff by a warranty deed conveyed the land to the Defendant, save and except for all oil, gas and other minerals.", which might be handled by creating a negated type restriction or a negated context.

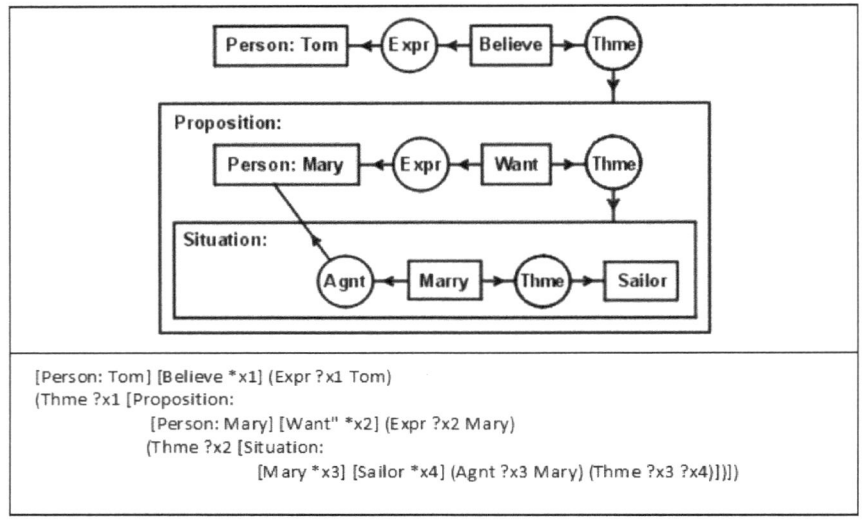

Figure 5.18 Conceptual Graph illustration and CGIF notation for one scoping of "Tom believes Mary wants to marry a sailor."

[Person: Tom] [Believe *x1] (Expr ?x1 Tom)
(Thme ?x1 [Proposition:
          [Person: Mary] [Want" *x2] (Expr ?x2 Mary)
          (Thme ?x2 [Situation:
                    [Mary *x3] [Sailor *x4] (Agnt ?x3 Mary) (Thme ?x3 ?x4)])])

Graph-based semantic representation for Natural Language have a long history, including work by many pioneers of Computer Science and Artificial Intelligence including John Sowa[37], Roger Schank, Ronald Brachman, and Stuart Shapiro[38], who themselves drew inspiration from the work of Charles S. Pierce in the 1880's on "Existential Graphs" and graph-based inference. The advantages that graphs offer over logics are that the mapping of natural language sentences to graphs can be more direct and structure sharing can be used to make it clear when the interpretation of two expressions correspond to the same entity, which allows quantifiers to span multiple clauses. Graphs can also be more expressive, while preserving the sound inference of logic. One can distinguish the name of a concept or instance from the words that were used in an utterance. Also, many known restrictions of first order logic, such as its limited set of quantifiers and connectives, the reliance on implication and inference to express class membership, the limited scope of quantifiers, and difficulties in representing questions and requests can all be addressed in a graphical representation. Other scope issues, such as subjective context can also be disambiguated.

The SNePS framework has been used to address representations of a variety of complex quantifiers, connectives, and actions, which are described in *The SNePS Case Frame Dictionary* and related papers. For example, Figure 5.19 shows how a graph might represent the sentence "All men are mortal" without implication (or its equivalent as disjunction), how a graph might represent the correct quantifier scope in the expression "Every farmer that owns a donkey beats it.", and a graph for expressing a quantifier that means that "at least I and at most j of a given set of statements are true". SNePS also included a mechanism for embedding procedural semantics, such as using an iteration mechanism to express a concept like, "While the knob is turned, open the door".

Figure 5.19 Example of Analog graphs for representing "All men are mortal" (top); "Every farmer that owns a donkey beats it" (middle); the complex quantifier "AndOr" where at least l and at most j are true (bottom)

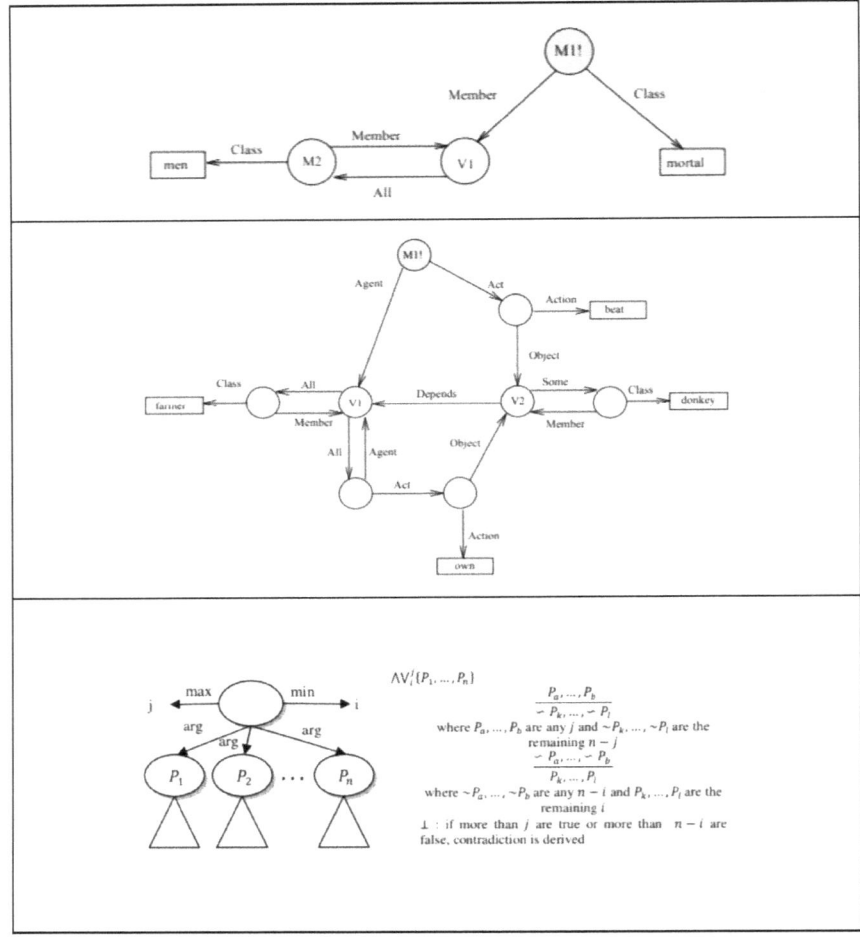

The most recent projects based on SNePS include an implementation using the Lisp-like programming language, Clojure, known as CSNePS or Inference Graphs[39, 40]. It is being used to represent clinical practice guidelines[41]. Clinical guidelines are statements like "Fluoxetine (20–80 mg/day) should be considered for the treatment of patients with fibromyalgia."[42], which are disseminated in medical journals and the websites of professional organizations and national health agencies, such as the U.S. Preventive Services Task Force and the U.S. Agency for

Health Research Quality (AHRQ), respectively as sentences, but must be mapped onto some actionable format if they are to be used to generate notifications within a clinical decision support system or to automatically embed so-called "infobuttons" within electronic medical records[43, 44].

5.4 SUMMARY

This chapter discussed the kinds of information one would want a semantics for natural language to include, several computational approaches to representing this information, and methods for mapping between sequences of words and representations. From a conceptual perspective, the four main types of information that one would want to capture are: 1) the entities that are being described, 2) the types of events that are being mentioned and the roles that the entities fulfill with respect to the event, 3) the propositional attitude that a sentence expresses, such as a statement, question, or request, and 4) the intended word senses for each occurrence of a word in a sentence. To capture all of these elements in a domain-independent way is to create what is known as a "deep semantics", which is usually expressed in a logic (or comparable framework such as a graph or ontology language). Such a semantics would allow one to distinguish between differences among what is asserted as true in the real world, what agents are asserting about their own beliefs, and what beliefs they are ascribing to others. These differences would be essential to understanding complex texts such as personal histories or legal briefs.

For some applications, such as supporting NL queries to a database, deep meaning is not required and interpretation can comprise finding the command that best represents the content of a natural language expression. In these cases, it is sufficient to create a "procedural semantics" that maps natural language expressions directly onto a database query language or the API of some backend software system. Mapping to procedure calls and queries shifts the burden of resolving ambiguous expressions onto the natural language processing components, whereas with a domain independent semantics one can leave the representation ambiguous and allow the backend application to make decisions based on its understanding of the user's tasks and goals. Another form of shallow understanding is to consider different ways we might label texts, such as "grammatical" versus "ungrammatical" or "positive" versus "negative", etc. While there are an innumerable number of ways we might label text, a few such classification problems have been used as benchmark tasks for comparing the generality of language models, espcially ones that use deep learning to implement an entire NLP pipeline. Before we continue our discussion of classical levels of language processing, such as discouse and dialog (which might be considered subareas of pragmatics), we will first discuss the classification tasks that are now considered benchmarks for NLP systems.

Notes

1. Minsky, M. (1975). A Framework for Representing Knowledge. In P. Winston, Ed., *The Psychology of Computer Vision*. New York: McGraw-Hill, pp. 211-277. A copy of the original paper, published as an MIT Memo, can be found online as https://courses.media.mit.edu/2004spring/mas966/Minsky%201974%20Framework%20for%20knowledge.pdf
2. Brewka, G. (1987). The Logic of Inheritance in Frame Systems. In *Proceedings of the International Joint Conference on Artificial Intelligence*.
3. AI frame systems are similar to object oriented programs (OOP), as AI frames provided much of the basis for early OOP.
4. Bar-Haim, R., Dagan, I., Greental, I., & Shnarch, E. (2007). Semantic Inference at the Lexical-Syntactic Level. In *Proceedings of the National Conference on Artificial Intelligence* (Vol. 22, No. 1, p. 871). Menlo Park, CA; Cambridge, MA; London; AAAI Press; MIT Press.
5. Dowty, D. R., Wall, R., & Peters, S. (2012). Introduction to Montague semantics (Vol. 11). Springer Science & Business Media.
6. Barwise, J., & Cooper, R. (1981). Generalized Quantifiers and Nat-

ural Language. In Philosophy, language, and artificial intelligence (pp. 241-301). Springer, Dordrecht.

7. Noy, N. F., Musen, M. A., Mejino Jr., J.L.V, and Rosse, C. (2004). Pushing the Envelope: Challenges in a Frame-Based Representation of Human Anatomy. *Data & Knowledge Engineering* Volume 48, Issue 3, March 2004, Pages 335-359

8. Baader, F., Calvanese, D., McGuinness, D., Patel-Schneider, P., and Nardi, D. (Eds.). (2003). *The Description Logic Handbook: Theory, Implementation and Applications*. Cambridge University Press.

9. Musen, M. A., and the Protégé Team (2015). The Protégé Project: A Look Back and a Look Forward. AI Matters, 1(4), 4–12. https://doi.org/10.1145/2757001.2757003. PMID: 27239556

10. Barwise, J. and Cooper, R. (1981). Generalized Quantifiers and Natural Language. *Linguistics and Philosophy* Vol. 4

11. Johnson-Laird, P. N. (1977). Procedural Semantics. Cognition, 5(3), 189-214.

12. Woods, W. A. (1981). Procedural Semantics as a Theory of Meaning. Bolt, Beranek and Newman, Inc. Cambridge, MA.

13. Miller, G. A. (1974). Toward a Third Metaphor for Psycholinguistics. In W. B. Weimer & D. S. Palermo (Eds.), *Cognition and the Symbolic Processes*. Lawrence Erlbaum.

14. Johnson-Laird, P. N. (1977). Procedural Semantics. *Cognition*, 5(3), 189-214.

15. Besta, M., Peter, E., Gerstenberger, R., Fischer, M., Podstawski, M., Barthels, C., ... & Hoefler, T. (2020). Demystifying Graph Databases: Analysis and Taxonomy of Data Organization, System Designs, and Graph Queries. arXiv preprint arXiv:1910.09017v4 URL https://arxiv.org/abs/1910.09017v4 (Accessed March 2021).

16. Hogan, A., Blomqvist, E., Cochez, M., d'Amato, C., de Melo, G., Gutierrez, C., ... & Zimmermann, A. (2020). Knowledge Graphs. arXiv preprint arXiv:2003.02320.

17. Sun, C. (2018) *A Natural Language Interface for Querying Graph Databases* Masters Thesis, Computer Science and Engineering, Massachusetts Institute of Technology.

18. Church, A. (1941). *The Calculi of Lambda-Conversion*. Princeton University Press.

19. Montague, R. (1974). Formal Philosophy: Selected Papers of Richard Montague. Yale University Press

20. Dowty, D., Wall, R. and Peters, S. (1981) *Introduction to Montague Semantics*. Dordrecht: D. Reidel.

21. Chierchia G. and McConnell-Ginet, S. (1990). *Meaning and Grammar - 2nd Edition: An Introduction to Semantics*. The MIT Press.
22. . By new symbols, I mean things like cat1, cat2, etc. which are returned by the Common Lisp function gensym().
23. Baader, F., Calvanese, D., McGuinness, D., Patel-Schneider, P., Nardi, D. (eds.) (2003) *The Description Logic Handbook: Theory, Implementation and Applications*. Cambridge University Press.
24. Lassila, O. and Swick, R.R. (1998). Resource description framework (RDF) model and syntax specification.
25. McBride, B. (2004). The Resource Description Framework (RDF) and Its Vocabulary Description Language RDFS. In *Handbook on Ontologies* (pp. 51-65). Springer, Berlin, Heidelberg.
26. Bechhofer, S., Van Harmelen, F., Hendler, J., Horrocks, I., McGuinness, D.L., Patel-Schneider, P.F. and Stein, L.A. (2004). OWL Web Ontology Language Reference. W3C recommendation, 10(02).
27. Antoniou, G. and Van Harmelen, F. (2004). Web Ontology Language: OWL. In *Handbook on Ontologies* (pp. 67-92). Springer, Berlin, Heidelberg.
28. Roy, J. and Ramanujan, A. (2001). XML Schema Language: Taking XML to the Next Level. *IT Professional*, 3(2), pp.37-40.
29. Cycorp is the company that maintains and distributes Cyc. See https://www.cyc.com/. For a technical overview, see https://www.cyc.com/cyc-technology-overview/
30. Hirst, G. (1992). *Semantic Interpretation and the Resolution of Ambiguity*. Cambridge University Press.
31. Charniak, E. (1981). A common representation for problem-solving and language-comprehension information. Artificial Intelligence, 16(3), 225-255.
32. Lopatovska, I., Rink, K., Knight, I., Raines, K., Cosenza, K., Williams, H., Sorsche, P., Hirsch, D., Li, Q., and Martinez, A. (2019). Talk to Me: Exploring User Interactions with the Amazon Alexa. *Journal of Librarianship and Information Science*, 51(4), 984-997.
33. Kollar, T., Berry, D., Stuart, L., Owczarzak, K., Chung, T., Kayser, M., Snow, B., and Matsoukas, S. (2018). The Alexa Meaning Representation Language. In *Proceedings of the 16th Annual Conference of the North American Chapter of the Association for Computational Linguistics: Human Language Technologies (NAACL-HLT 2018)*, pages 177–184
34. Perera, V., Chung, T., Kollar, T., & Strubell, E. (2018). Multi-Task Learning For Parsing The Alexa Meaning Representation Language. Proceedings of the AAAI Conference on Artificial Intelligence, 32(1).
35. Gkiokas, A., & Cristea, A. I. (2014). Training a Cognitive Agent to

Acquire and Represent Knowledge from RSS Feeds onto Conceptual Graphs. IARIA COGNITIVE, pp. 184-194.

36. From their 2014 work, Gkiokas and Cristea provide 7MB of manually transcribed CG structures for data obtained from RSS feeds from BBC, SkyNews, KnoxNews, USA Today and Science Daily that they make available online at: https://github.com/alexge233/conceptual_graph_set

37. John Sowa is most associated with Conceptual Graphs, which he summarizes on his webpage: http://www.jfsowa.com/cg/cgif.htm

38. Stuart Shapiro is most associated with SNePs. An excellent summary of Semantic Networks, including SNePS was written by J. Martins. It is available online at: https://web.archive.org/web/20190413011355/https://fenix.tecnico.ulisboa.pt/downloadFile/3779571243569/Cap6.pdf

39. Schlegel, D. R., and Shapiro, S. C. (2013). Inference Graphs: A Roadmap. In Poster collection of the Second Annual Conference on Advances in Cognitive Systems (pp. 217-234).

40. Schlegel, D., and Shapiro, S. (2015). Inference Graphs: Combining Natural Deduction and Subsumption Inference in a Concurrent Reasoner. In *Proceedings of the AAAI Conference on Artificial Intelligence* (Vol. 29, No. 1).

41. Schlegel, D. R., Gordon, K., Gaudioso, C., and Peleg, M. (2019). Clinical Tractor: A Framework for Automatic Natural Language Understanding of Clinical Practice Guidelines. In *AMIA Annual Symposium Proceedings* (Vol. 2019, p. 784). American Medical Informatics Association.

42. Gad El-Rab, W., Zaïane, O. R., & El-Hajj, M. (2017). Formalizing Clinical Practice Guideline for Clinical Decision Support Systems. *Health Informatics Journal*, 23(2), 146-156.

43. Cook, D. A., Teixeira, M. T., Heale, B. S., Cimino, J. J., & Del Fiol, G. (2017). Context-Sensitive Decision Support (Infobuttons) in Electronic Health Records: A Systematic Review. *Journal of the American Medical Informatics Association : JAMIA*, 24(2), 460–468. https://doi.org/10.1093/jamia/ocw104

44. Hematialam, H., & Zadrozny, W. (2017). Identifying Condition-Action Statements in Medical Guidelines Using Domain-Independent Features. ArXiv, abs/1706.04206.

CHAPTER 6.

BENCHMARK TASKS FOR LANGUAGE MODELLING

This chapter assesses the progress of Natural Language Processing as a scientific discipline. We do so by considering applications of NLP that test the generality of a system or language model. The field of NLP comprises both practical applications and basic science.

Basic science refers to investigations where the primary goal is to predict phenomena or to understand nature. Basic science outcomes help us to develop technologies that alter events or outcomes. Early qualitative science NLP involved researchers looking at small examples of language phenomena and using them to better understand how human language processing works. This research has looked at what people do well and also when they make mistakes and seeing under what conditions computation models exhibit similar behavior. Inspiration for computational approaches comes from research in other disciplines, primarily psycholinguistics. Early work involved asking people to make judgements about whether they think a sentence is grammatical. More modern approaches use biosensors to track movements of the eyes or event-related potentials of the brain, as they process ambiguous sentences or resolve long distance dependencies, such as referring expressions[1].

Basic science for NLP also includes developing models of human language. Language modeling involves learning parameters for complex mathematical expressions that measure or predict the likelihood of occurrences of a word or sentence for a given context. These models are used to implement methods for solving low-level NLP tasks that form the basis of more complex software applications. Four important examples of low-level NLP tasks include:

1. Labelling language units or pairs of units according to their grammaticality,

2. Labelling units with the type of sentiment or emotion they express

3. Labelling pairs of units as two whether they are semantically similar and

4. Labelling pairs of units as to their logical relationship.

They are sometimes called "benchmark" tasks for language processing because they are tasks that can be defined independent of a specific computational approach and thus offer a way to make them comparable.[2] For example, having a method of correctly classifying sentences as ungrammatical might be useful for helping writers, teaching second language learners, or providing input to a classification-based parser. To date, there is no one modelling approach that can handle all these benchmark tasks well, which is a sign that the field of NLP has not yet solved the problem of creating general-purpose models of human language. In this chapter, we will consider each of the four tasks.

6.1 GRAMMATICALITY ANALYSIS

Grammaticality refers to whether an expression obeys the accepted syntactic conventions of a language, independent of whether those sentences make "sense". A sentence can be both grammatical and meaningless; a classic example is "Colorless green ideas sleep furiously."[3, 4]. Grammaticality judgements are binary (yes or no). Since grammars are descriptions developed by observing the language of native speakers, decisions about what counts as grammatical must also come from native speakers of a language or expert observations. Grammaticality analysis can be used directly, such as for tools to support writing or to grade the writing of language learners, or it can be used to generate features for other tasks, such as assessing some cognitive disorders (e.g., the frequency of ungrammaticality has been associated with particular subtypes of autism spectrum disorder[5]).

Approaches to grammaticality involve either comparing a given sentence against some model of perfect grammar or comparing a given sentence against some model of common errors, or a combination[6]. Models of perfect grammar can consist of rules that enforce syntactic constraints at the sentence level. These constraints include that the subject and verb must agree (e.g., both be plural or singular); the pronoun must be correct form (case) for its role in the sentence (e.g., a subject "I" versus the object "me"); the noun must agree with its determiner (e.g., "This book" but not "These book"); the verb must in in the correct tense given its role (e.g. the present form of "be" expects the present participle, as in "am/is/are walking"); conjoined phrases should all have the same (parallel) structure; and words that take arguments, that is create requirements for the co-occurrence of other constructs, must occur with the correct pattern of arguments. There are also rules about the location of apostrophe when forming the possessive. Models of common errors can be rules that describe examples of violations of syntactic constraints and also rules for detecting problems that are primarily semantic, such as dangling modifiers, which are constructions where the entity being modified is either missing or ambiguous.

There are also specialized models of common errors, for different types of learners, such as children or people who are learning a second language. Children often have difficulty with homophones (such as "there", "their" and "they're") or near-homophones (such as "then" and "than") which sound similar, but are spelled differently. Second language learners have errors that occur when they mistakenly apply grammatical constraints from their first language that do not hold in the second language. For example, native speakers of Arabic sometimes omit the present form of "be" before an adjective or an indefinite article before a noun, because they are not used in these constructions in Arabic.

One of the first automated grammar checkers was EPISTLE[7]. It takes what we would now consider to be a standard relaxation approach. The algorithm first attempts to parse a sentence while enforcing grammaticality constraints expressed as rules written by experts and then selectively relaxing some of the constraints, while noting the type and location of a violated condition. (The reason to look for known types of errors is to be able to decide whether a parser failed to derive a sentence because it lacks coverage or failed because the sentence being parsed has an error.) An alternative rule-based approach is based on extending a rule-based grammar to include explicit "malrules" that cover known types of errors and are marked with extra features that flag them as errors[8, 9]. For example, a malrule might say that an erroneous noun phrase is one with a plural determiner and a singular head noun.

Both relaxation and malrules rely on search to find a rule that matches the suspect sentences. More recent approaches to grammaticality analysis use classification rather than search to determine the existence and type of the error. One approach is to train models using a large corpus of grammatical text, then score unseen examples with a measure of their likelihood of being one of the training sentences and applying thresholds of similarity to determine if a writer's usage is correct "enough" (that is close enough to a predicted example) given the context. More recent approaches use a corpus of erroneous examples to train models and then classify unseen sentences as one of the erroneous ones. Figure 6.1 shows some examples of errors found in writing assignments submitted by learners of English.

Figure 6.1 Grammatical errors annotated in NUCLE with ERRANT from Ng et al (2014)

Type	Description	Example
Vt	Verb tense	Medical technology during that time [is→was] not advanced enough to cure him.
Vm	Verb modal	Although the problem [would→may] not be serious, people [would→might] still be afraid.
V0	Missing verb	However, there are also a great number of people [who → who are] against this technology.
Vform	Verb form	A study in 2010 [shown → showed] that patients recover faster when surrounded by family members.
SVA	Subject-verb agreement	The benefits of disclosing genetic risk information [outweighs → outweigh] the costs.
ArtOrDet	Article or determiner	It is obvious to see that [internet → the internet] saves people time and also connects people globally.
Nn	Noun number	A carrier may consider not having any [child → children] after getting married.
Npos	Noun possessive	Someone should tell the [carriers → carrier's] relatives about the genetic problem.
Pform	Pronoun form	A couple should run a few tests to see if [their → they] have any genetic diseases beforehand.
Pref	Pronoun reference	It is everyone's duty to ensure that [he or she → they] undergo regular health checks.
Prep	Preposition	This essay will [discuss about → discuss] whether a carrier should tell his relatives or not.
Wci	Wrong collocation/idiom	Early examination is [healthy → advisable] and will cast away unwanted doubts.
Wa	Acronyms	After [WOWII → World War II], the population of China decreased rapidly.
Wform	Word form	The sense of [guilty → guilt] can be more than expected.
Wtone	Tone (formal/informal)	[It's → It is] our family and relatives that bring us up.
Srun	Run-on sentences, comma splices	The issue is highly [debatable, a → debatable. A] genetic risk could come from either side of the family.
Smod	Dangling modifiers	[Undeniable, → It is undeniable that] it becomes addictive when we spend more time socializing virtually.
Spar	Parallelism	We must pay attention to this information and [assisting → assist] those who are at risk.

Sfrag	Sentence fragment	However, from the ethical point of view.
Ssub	Subordinate clause	This is an issue [needs → that needs] to be addressed.
WOinc	Incorrect word order	Someone having what kind of disease → What kind of disease someone [has] is a matter of their own privacy.
WOadv	Incorrect adjective/adverb order	In conclusion, [personally I → I personally] feel that it is important to tell one's family members.
Trans	Linking words/phrases	It is sometimes hard to find [out → out if] one has this disease.
Mec	Spelling, punctuation, capitalization, etc.	This knowledge [maybe relevant → may be relevant] to them.
Rloc–	Redundancy	It is up to the [patient's own choice → patient] to disclose information.
Cit	Citation	Poor citation practice.
Others	Other errors	An error that does not fit into any other category but can still be corrected.
Um	Unclear meaning	Genetic disease has a close relationship with the born gene. (i.e., no correction possible without further clarification.)

Resources for building models of correct grammar from data include syntactic tree banks (which are collections of sentences annotated with parse trees that have been vetted by experts)[10]. Resources for building models of errors include sentences collected from published articles by trained scholars of linguistics that include examples of grammatical or ungrammatical sentences. One such collection is the Corpus of Linguistic Acceptability[11]. Other collections of erroneous sentences include the NUS Corpus of Learner English (NUCLE)[12], the Cambridge English Write & Improve (W&I) corpus, and the LOCNESS corpus, which are collections of essays written by second language learners that have been annotated. Another resource is ERRANT, a grammatical ERRor ANnotation Toolkit designed to automatically extract edits from parallel original and corrected sentences and classify them according to the type of error. Figure 6.1 shows 28 error types along with examples for each from the NUCLE corpus that have been annotated using ERRANT[13].

6.2 SENTIMENT ANALYSIS AND EMOTION

RECOGNITION

Sentiment Analysis attempts to capture the emotional aspects of language including opinions and evaluation. It originated from work that classified sentences as subjective or objective based on the particular words that they contain[14,15,16,17]. Particular words express the polarity of opinions expressed by a language unit, which might be positive (e.g., "liking"), negative (e.g., "not liking"), or neutral, which is often expressed using adjectives, such as "beautiful" vs "ugly". Sentences are considered "objective" if they do not include any expressed opinions. Figure 6.2 shows examples of subjective and objective sentences. The sentence on the left is considered subjective because the word "fascinating" is considered positive (in contrast to saying "boring" or "trite"); the sentence on the right is objective because "increase" is considered factual (without implying the increase was too much or too little).

Figure 6.2 Examples of subjective versus objective sentences

Subjective sentence	Objective sentence
At several different layers, it's a fascinating tale.	Bell Industries Inc. increased its quarterly to 10 cents from 7 cents a share.

Sentiment often involves just labelling the general polarity, which might be positive, negative, or neutral. More fine-grained approaches classify particular levels of sentiment. For example, the Stanford Sentiment Treebank uses continuous values ranging from 1 to 25, where 1 is the most negative and 25 is the most positive. Figure 3 below shows some examples (taken from movie reviews) and the scores that the sentences received using their algorithm.

Figure 6.3 Stanford Sentiment Treebank example score values

Example	Score (rounded)
The performances are an absolute joy.	21
Yet the act is still charming here	18
A big fat pain	5
Something must have been lost in the translation	7

Beyond sentiment, there are also approaches that try to capture various types of emotion, such as anger, excitement, fear, joy, sadness, etc. These tasks are not included in the benchmarks, but might be in the future. Training data would be more difficult to create as labelling examples with such categories requires specialized expertise. However, associating words with emotions has long been part of the qualitative analysis of human language performed by some psychologists[18,19] and incorporated into some tools, such as Linguistic Inquiry and Word Count (LIWC)[20].

Freely available tools for sentiment analysis include VADER, TextBlob, and Sentistrength. Some of the most recent open source tools use Deep Learning (e.g., from the Open Data Hub). Resources for building sentiment analysis include movie and product reviews in the public domain, which typically include an explicit rating that can be mapped to a sentiment polarity value. Examples of public standardized corpora includes the Stanford Sentiment Treebank[21] which was derived from a sentence-level corpus of movie reviews[22]. The LIWC tools mentioned above are available for a licensing fee.

6.3 SEMANTIC SIMILARITY

Semantic similarity, also called semantic textual similarity, is the notion that two expressions mean approximately the same thing (e.g., they are paraphrases of each other). Similarity is thus a symmetric relationship – when comparing two units neither would be more general or specific than the other. Similarity can arise at the word level, through the synonyms, or at the sentence level, where one might reorder the parts of a conjunction or substitute an active construction for a passive one. Being able to detect when two expressions mean "nearly" the same thing is useful for assessing whether a student has answered a test question correctly, or when trying to determine the intent of a question or command without requiring the designer to list every possible expression explicitly. Systems that require one to say things in exactly one way make it difficult for users to learn or remember the required phrasing.

Systems that map expressions onto sentences in a formal logic to test subsumption (which they refer to as classification inference) are performing a type of semantic similarity analysis. A rule-based approach would create a deep-semantics (such as an expression in first order logic or description logic) and then test whether a pair of concepts (A, B) are equivalent, that is, both A $\subseteq$ B and B $\subseteq$ A hold. Today, semantic similarity is a task that can be learned from data that includes pairs of expressions that have been previously deemed to be similar. Figure 6.4 includes some examples of similarity judgements given by staff at Microsoft.

Figure 6.4 Examples of similarity judgements from the Microsoft Research Paraphrase Corpus (2005)

Sentence 1	Sentence 2	Similarity class
Amrozi accused his brother, whom he called "the witness", of deliberately distorting his evidence.	Referring to him as only "the witness", Amrozi accused his brother of deliberately distorting his evidence.	Yes
Yucaipa owned Dominick's before selling the chain to Safeway in 1998 for $2.5 billion.	Yucaipa bought Dominick's in 1995 for $693 million and sold it to Safeway for $1.8 billion in 1998.	No

Three resources for semantic similarity that have been proposed as a standard for evaluating work on similarity are: The Microsoft Research Paraphrase Corpus[23], the Quora Question Pairs dataset[24, 25], and the Semantic Similarity Benchmark corpus from SemEval 2017[26]. The first two of these corpora include text collected from online news and questions posted to a community question answering website where equivalence judgements were provided by staff at the respective organizations (e.g., Microsoft and Quora). The SemEval data includes video and image captions created via crowdsourcing and judged by organizers and participants of the conference. One newer dataset that may prove useful is the multi-domain question rewriting dataset, which was created from Stack Exchange question edit histories by researchers at Google, University of Chicago, and Toyota Technological Institute[27].

6.4 TEXTUAL ENTAILMENT

Textual entailment, also known as natural language inference, is an approximation of real inference that has been formalized to allow for using classification as a solution. There are three categories: a given text either entails another text, contradicts another text, or neither, which is classified as "neutral". (There are examples in Figure 6.5.) By convention, the entailing text is known as "the text" or "the premise" and the other text is known as "the hypothesis". A search-based system might create a semantics using first order logic and apply a theorem prover. A more efficient approach would use a graph-based representation, such as a subsumption hierarchy. Recent work by Young et al. (2014) explores combining a statistical measure (conditional probability or mutual information) and a graph structure, to form a hybrid structure that they call a Denotation Graph[28].

Classification-based approaches for Textual Entailment have also been devised, using a training set where items have both generated and then labelled by hand for different entailment relations, typically by crowdsourcing, using the Amazon Mechanical Turk platform. The conventionally used entailment categories for this approach are defined as follows:

Entailment: the hypothesis states something that is definitely correct about the situation or event in the premise.

Neutral: the hypothesis states something that might be correct about the situation or event in the premise.

Contradiction: the hypothesis states something that is definitely incorrect about the situation or event in the premise.

The collections of sentence pairs that have been created are designed to exemplify several known sources of entailment, from low-level word meanings and sentence structure to high-level reasoning and application of world knowledge. They capture four broad categories of phenomena: lexical semantics, predicate-argument structure, logic, and world and common sense knowledge, where each category may have several subtypes. We will now consider the general idea for each.

Lexical semantics or word meaning includes entailments based on concept abstraction or exclusivity, such as that a cat is a type of mammal and a cat is not a dog. It also includes morphological negation (e.g. agree vs. disagree, happy vs. unhappy, etc). It also includes entailments based on verbs, that in normal usage warrant certain inferences, such as saying "I stopped doing X" entails one was doing X previously and saying "I recognize that X" entails X. Also, saying "The cat is fat." entails that the cat exists. (Linguists sometimes refer to these various types of expressions as presuppositions or factives.)

Predicate-argument structure includes a verb and its subject and object, which may tell you who did something and what was acted upon (their semantic role). The order of the roles depends on the syntax. For example both "The cat broke the vase." and "The vase was broken by the cat." entail that the vase broke.

Logic includes entailments that may arise because of connectives (conjunction, disjunction), negation, double negation, conditionals, and quantifiers. Logic also includes entailments based on specific types of entities, such as numbers and intervals of time, which have an associated magnitude and sequential order, and operators defined on them, such as less than or greater than, and before or after. Logic-based entailments (mostly) follow the semantics of mathematical logic. For example, "the cat sat on the mat and slept" entails "the cat slept" and "the cat slept" entails "the cat slept or the cat ate", but "the cat slept or ate" is neutral about "the cat slept". Conditionals include sentences like "if it is raining, the grass will be wet", which would not entail that "the grass is wet" or "it is raining" or even "it is raining and the grass is wet"; however, a complex conditional such as "It is raining and if it is raining, then the grass will be wet" would entail that "the grass is wet." Quantifiers of logic include the universal (all) and the existential (some) which create entailments based on their semantics, e.g., "All cats have fur." entails "my cat has fur" and "my cat likes fish" entails that "some cats like fish". Natural language includes additional quantifiers such as "most" or "most X in the Y". Determining the entailments of these quantifiers requires judgements that combine an understanding of their general meaning and world or common sense knowledge.

World and common sense knowledge includes entailment relations based on knowledge of history, geography, law, politics, science, technology, culture, other aspects of human experience. An example might be that "Milwaukee has some beautiful parks." entails that "Wisconsin has some beautiful parks." Common sense includes entailment relations that are not exactly factual, but do not depend on either cultural or educational background. For example, "A girl was making snow angels" entails "a girl is playing in the snow" and "the grass is wet" entails "it might have rained". Some examples from the Stanford Natural Language Inference dataset, showing the Text-Hypothesis pairs and the crowdsourced inference type, are shown in Figure 6.5

Figure 6.5 Examples of textual entailment types

Text	Hypothesis	Class label
A man inspects the uniform of a figure in some East Asian country.	The man is sleeping	contradiction
An older and younger man smiling.	Two men are smiling and laughing at the cats playing on the floor.	neutral
A black race car starts up in front of a crowd of people.	A man is driving down a lonely road.	contradiction
A soccer game with multiple males playing.	Some men are playing a sport.	entailment
A smiling costumed woman is holding an umbrella.	A happy woman in a fairy costume holds an umbrella.	neutral

Textual entailment recognition is a classification task that can support several different software applications including text summarization, question answering, information retrieval, and machine translation. For example, summaries can be shortened by removing any sentences that are already entailed by other sentences in the summary. In question answering, any acceptable candidate answer found in a source document must entail the ideal answer, which we are presumed to already know. In information retrieval, search criteria might be given in terms of sentences that the desired documents must entail. Textual entailment being independent of any application has also been used as a benchmark task for natural language, one that could be used to evaluate and compare the effectiveness of natural language models across a variety of applications. Currently there are a number of software tools and datasets available for creating and evaluating systems for textual entailments. Functions for performing textual entailment are included in (or available for) AllenNLP and spaCy.

Some resources that have been proposed as a standard for evaluation include: the Multi-Genre Natural Language Inference Corpus, which includes examples drawn from transcribed speech, popular fiction, and government reports which were labelled via crowdsourcing[29]; the Stanford Natural Language Inference corpus[30]; the Stanford Question Answering Dataset[31]; the Recognizing Textual Entailment datasets, which come from a series of annual challenges, first held in 2004[32]; and the data from the Winograd Schema Challenge[33].

6.5 SUMMARY

Four tasks have emerged as benchmarks tasks for language modelling. These tasks are grammaticality analysis, sentiment analysis, semantic textual similarity, and recognizing textual entailment. Language models can address these tasks by training on data that represents the set of class types for that task. Much of this data was created "naturally", for example extracted from collections of student writing graded by instructors, from online reviews of products, or from captions posted to online image databases (e.g., Flickr). When examples of entailments did not otherwise exist, the data has been crowdsourced. These benchmark tasks, while not always useful on their own, are useful for many downstream applications. For example, a training system might evaluate the similarity or entailment relation of the response to an expected answer. A question-answering system might use textual similarity to group together related questions. A combination of grammaticality and textual similarity would be helpful for assessing or improving writing, for example to identify grammatical mistakes, excessive repetition, or potential plagiarism. Single or cross-language similarity classification might be used as an objective function for training systems that summarize texts or that translate from one language to another.
In addition to supporting better applications, benchmark tasks serve as a guiding force for advancing the basic science of NLP. Language models and the architectures for constructing them are becoming more powerful and more complex every day. To compare alternatives or to measure progress over time, common datasets and tasks like the ones discussed in this chapter are often used. Because these tasks do not depend on a particu-

lar domain, such as medicine or manufacturing, they are also used to test generality. Already, some have become concerned that these tasks are not sufficiently general or appropriate, however[34]. To increase generality, additional benchmarks have been proposed, e.g., SuperGLUE[35]. Concerns about how to address the ethics of creating language models have yet to be resolved and so each NLP projectmust be careful to avoid or reduce potentially harmful consequences.

Notes

1. Barkley, C., Kluender, R. and Kutas, M. (2015). Referential Processing in the Human Bain: An Event-Related Potential (ERP) Study. *Brain Research*, 1629, pp.143-159. (Online at: http://kutaslab.ucsd.edu/people/kutas/pdfs/2015.BR.143.pdf)
2. Wang, A., Singh, A., Michael, J., Hill, F., Levy, O. and Bowman, S.R. (2018). Glue: A Multi-Task Benchmark and Analysis Platform for Natural Language Understanding. *ArXiv preprint* arXiv:1804.07461.
3. Chomsky, N. (1957). Syntactic Structures (The Hague: Mouton, 1957). Review of Verbal Behavior by BF Skinner, Language, 35, 26-58.
4. Erard, M. (2010). The Life and Times of "Colorless Green Ideas Sleep Furiously". Southwest Review, 95(3), 418-425. Accessed July2021, from http://www.jstor.org/stable/43473072
5. Wittke K, Mastergeorge AM, Ozonoff S, Rogers SJ, Naigles LR. (2017). Grammatical Language Impairment in Autism Spectrum Disorder: Exploring Language Phenotypes Beyond Standardized Testing. *Frontiers in Psychology*. 8:532. DOI: 10.3389/fpsyg.2017.00532.
6. Dale, R. (2011). Automated Writing Assistance: Grammar Checking and Beyond. (manuscript) Online at: http://web.science.mq.edu.au/~rdale/teaching/icon2011/iconbib.pdf)
7. Heidorn, G.E., Jensen, K., Miller, L.A., Byrd, R.J., and Chodorow, M. (1982). The EPISTLE Text-Critiquing System. *IBM Systems Journal*, 21, pp. 305-326.
8. Sleeman. D. (1982). Inferring (mal) Rules from Pupil's Protocols. In *Proceedings of the 1982 European Conference on Artificial Intelligence (ECAI-82)*, Orsay, France, pp. 160–164.
9. Schneider, D., & McCoy, K. F. (1998). Recognizing Syntactic Errors

in the Writing of Second Language Learners. In *COLING 1998 Volume 2: The 17th International Conference on Computational Linguistics*. Also online at: arXiv.org/abs/cmp-lg/9805012.

10. Taylor, A., Marcus, M., and Santorini, B. (2003). The Penn Treebank: An Overview. *Treebanks: Building and Using Parsed Corpora,* Abeillé, A. *(Ed.),* pp. 5-22.

11. Warstadt, A., Singh, A. and Bowman, S.R. (2019). Neural Network Acceptability Judgments. *Transactions of the Association for Computational Linguistics,* 7, pp. 625-641.

12. Dahlmeier, D., Ng, H.T. and Wu, S.M. (2013). Building a Large Annotated Corpus of Learner English: The NUS Corpus of Learner English. In *Proceedings of the Eighth Workshop on Innovative Use of NLP for Building Educational Applications,* pp. 22-31.

13. Ng, H.T., Wu, S.M., Briscoe, T., Hadiwinoto, C., Susanto, R.H. and Bryant, C. (2014). The CoNLL-2014 Shared Task on Grammatical Error Correction. In *Proceedings of the Eighteenth Conference on Computational Natural Language Learning: Shared Task,* pp. 1-14.

14. Hatzivassiloglou, V., and McKeown, K. (1997). Predicting the Semantic Orientation of Adjectives. In *Proceedings of the 35th Annual Meeting of the Association for Computational Linguistics and 8th Conference of the European Chapter of the Association for Computational Linguistics* (ACL-EACL 1997), pp. 174–181.

15. Wiebe, J., Bruce, R., and O'Hara, T. (1999). Development and Use of a Gold Standard Data Set for Subjectivity Classifications. In *Proceedings of the 37th Annual Meeting of the Association for Computational Linguistics* (ACL-99), 246–253. University of Maryland: ACL.

16. Wiebe, J. (2000). Learning Subjective Adjectives from Corpora. In *Proceedings of the Seventeenth National Conference on Artificial Intelligence and Twelfth Conference on Innovative Applications of Artificial Intelligence.* AAAI Press, 735–740.

17. Wiebe, J., Wilson, T., Bruce, R., Bell, M. and Martin, M. (2004). Learning Subjective Language. *Computational linguistics,* 30(3), pp.277-308.

18. Gottschalk, L. A., and Gleser, G. C. (1969). *The Measurement of Psychological States through the Content Analysis of Verbal Behavior.* CA: University of California Press.

19. Weintraub, W. (1989). *Verbal Behavior in Everyday Life.* NY: Springer.

20. Pennebaker, J.W., Boyd, R.L., Jordan, K., and Blackburn, K. (2015). *The Development and Psychometric Properties of LIWC2015.* Austin, TX: University of Texas at Austin.

21. Socher, R., Perelygin, A., Wu, J., Chuang, J., Manning, C.D., Ng, A.Y.

and Potts, C. (2013). Recursive Deep Models for Semantic Compositionality over a Sentiment Treebank. In *Proceedings of the 2013 Conference on Empirical Methods in Natural Language Processing* pp. 1631-1642.

22. Pang, B., Lee, L. and Vaithyanathan, S. (2002). Thumbs Up?: Sentiment Classification using Machine Learning Techniques. In *Proceedings of the 2002 Conference on Empirical Methods in Natural Language Processing*. Volume 10 (pp. 79-86). Association for Computational Linguistics.

23. Dolan, W.B. and Brockett, C. (2005). Automatically Constructing a Corpus of Sentential Paraphrases. In *Proceedings of the Third International Workshop on Paraphrasing* (IWP2005).

24. Csernai, K. (2017). Data @ Quora: First Quora Dataset Release: Question Pairs. URL: https://www.quora.com/q/quoradata/First-Quora-Dataset-Release-Question-Pairs (Accessed March 2021).

25. An archived copy of the Quora Question Pairs dataset, as a 55.5MB tsv file, can be found here: http://web.archive.org/web/20181122142727/http://qim.fs.quoracdn.net/quora_duplicate_questions.tsv

26. Cer, D., Diab, M., Agirre, E., Lopez-Gazpio, I. and Specia, L. (2017). Semeval-2017 Task 1: Semantic Textual Similarity Multilingual and Cross-Lingual Focused Evaluation. *arXiv preprint* arXiv:1708.00055.

27. Chu, Z., Chen, M., Chen, J., Wang, M., Gimpel, K., Faruqui, M., & Si, X. (2020). How to Ask Better Questions? A Large-Scale Multi-Domain Dataset for Rewriting Ill-Formed Questions. Proceedings of the AAAI Conference on Artificial Intelligence, 34(05), 7586-7593. https://doi.org/10.1609/aaai.v34i05.6258

28. Young, P., Lai, A., Hodosh, M. and Hockenmaier, J. (2014). From Image Descriptions to Visual Denotations: New Similarity Metrics for Semantic Inference over Event Descriptions. *Transactions of the Association for Computational Linguistics*, 2, pp.67-78.

29. Williams, A., Nangia, N. and Bowman, S.R. (2017). A Broad-Coverage Challenge Corpus for Sentence Understanding through Inference. *ArXiv preprint* arXiv:1704.05426.

30. Bowman, S., Angeli, G., Potts, C., ,and Manning, C. (2015). A Large Annotated Corpus for Learning Natural Language Inference. In *Proceedings of the 2015 Conference on Empirical Methods in Natural Language Processing*, pp. 632–642. Association for Computational Linguistics.

31. Rajpurkar, P., Zhang, J., Lopyrev, K., and Liang, P. (2016). SQuAD: 100,000+ Questions for Machine Comprehension of Text. In *Proceedings of the 2016 Conference on Empirical Methods in Natural Lan-*

guage Processing, pp. 2383–2392. Association for Computational Linguistics.

32. Dagan, I., Glickman, O., and Magnini, B. (2006). The PASCAL Recognising Textual Entailment Challenge. In *Machine Learning Challenges: Evaluating Predictive Uncertainty, Visual Object Classification, and Recognising Textual Entailment*, pp. 177–190. Springer.

33. Davis, E., Morgenstern, L., and Ortiz Jr., C. (2017). The First Winograd Schema Challenge at IJCAI-16. *AI Magazine*, *38*(3), 97-98. (Link to data: https://cs.nyu.edu/faculty/davise/papers/Winograd-Schemas/WSCollection.html)

34. Floridi, L., Chiriatti, M. GPT-3: Its Nature, Scope, Limits, and Consequences.(2020) Minds & Machines 30, 681–694. https://doi.org/10.1007/s11023-020-09548-1

35. Wang, A., Pruksachatkun, Y., Nangia, N., Singh, A., Michael, J., Hill, F., Levy, O. and Bowman, S.R., (2019). SuperGLUE A stickier benchmark for general-purpose language understanding systems. In *Proceedings of the 33rd International Conference on Neural Information Processing Systems* (pp. 3266-3280) Also available as: arXiv preprint arXiv:1905.00537.

CHAPTER 7.

DISCOURSE AND DIALOG

In this chapter, we will consider language above the level of a single clause. In conversation, people communicate over several exchanges, depending on what they are trying to do or whether they think they have been understood. In writing, people construct paragraphs, sections, chapters, books, etc., organizing the content into aggregated units of varying sizes to help present their thoughts in a way that will be understandable and convincing to their intended audience.

Within NLP, the term used to describe aggregated forms of language is discourse. The term encompasses both written text, such as stories, and spoken communication among multiple people or artificial agents. When the communication involves multiple parties engaging in interactive communication, we refer to these extended exchanges as dialog.

NLP pipelines are applied to discourse for the following representative tasks (among others):

- To extract information,
- To find documents or information within larger collections,
- To convey distributed, structured information, such as found in a database, in a more understandable form, and
- To translate from one form or language into another.

Computational models of dialog are also used to manage complex devices or to elicit social behaviors from people (e.g., as a diagnostic, monitoring, or treatment tool for depression[1]). The participants in a dialog can all be people, in which case the role of NLP might be to extract knowledge from their interaction, or to provide mediating services. Or, the parties might be a heterogeneous group of people and an automated system, such as a chatbot. Because dialog involves multiple parties, it brings additional complexity to manage the flow of control among participants and also to assure that participants' understandings of the dialog are similar. Applications of dialog include interactive voice response systems (IVR), question answering systems, chatbots, and information retrieval systems. Applications of discourse that do not require interaction include text summarization systems and machine translation systems.

When we think of the meaning of discourse, we might think about the "story" that the discourse is trying to convey. Understanding a story requires a deeper level of understanding than found in the benchmark tasks we discussed in an earlier chapter. Story understanding was among the tasks that concerned many AI and NLP researchers in the 1970's, before access to large electronic corpora became widely available[2]. Some of the key ideas of understanding a story are similar to what might be captured in a deep, logic-based semantics, as we discussed in Chapter 5, including wanting to know what people or things are involved in the story. (In a logic, these would be referents associated with logical terms.) One might also want to know the various sorts of properties and relations that hold among characters, objects, and events, for example, where things are located, when events happened, what caused the events to happen, and why the characters did what they did. In a 2020 article in the MIT Technology Review, these elements of story understanding were noted as being totally missed by current research in natural language processing[3]. One reason that story understanding remains unsolved is that these tasks were found to be much more difficult than anticipated, were hard to evaluate, and did not generalize from one application to another. Thus, with rare exception, the consensus view became that it was better to leave these problems to future work[4]. One notable exception has been the work of Doug Lenat, and others at Cyc.com (originally Cycorp), who have been building deep representations of human knowledge since 1984. There is an opportunity to move forward again, by considering approaches that combine the evidence provided by data with the data abstractions provided by knowledge-based methods, such as ontologies and inference.

All types of multi-sentence discourse share certain properties. In a non-interactive discourse, there is a singular narrative voice, or perspective, that represents the author(s) of the document (or one of the characters in the story). The sequences of clauses and aggregated structures form coherent units so that the structure is identifiable. There are also identifiable meaning relationships that hold between units of discourse, such as between a cause and effect. Evidence that these structures exist includes the author's use of explicit words like "because" or "and", but sometimes the relations are just left to be inferred based on their close proximity and the expectations shared by writers and readers that they exist. Within a discourse unit, authors or speakers can make references to entities and expressions, even ones that span beyond a single clause. Understanding a discourse requires being able to recover these relationships and references; generating coherent discourse requires selecting appropriate referring expressions to use.

This chapter considers the meaning, structure, and coherence of discourse and dialog. It includes tasks of interpretation and generation and some applications. We will start by considering some general challenges for systems that process discourse and dialog.We will consider additional applications in Chapter 8 (on Question Answering) and Chapter 9 (on Natural Language Generation).

7.1 COMPUTATIONAL CHALLENGES FOR DISCOURSE PROCESSING

The reason to consider discourse and dialog rather than just the sentences that comprise them is that sometimes information is presented or requested over multiple sentences, and we want to recognize various phrases or relations among them that identify the who, what, when, where and why of the event. For discourse, we might extract information found in articles in newspapers or magazines or the chapters of books and store it in tables that are more easily searchable. For dialog, we might want to extract information from interactions to achieve tasks, such as booking travel or making a restaurant reservation, or tutoring a student[5]. Or, we might want to be able to identify direct or implied requests within purely social conversations that unfold without specified goals or roles among the participants. Many of these tasks have been the focus of recent dialog state tracking and dialog system technology challenges[6, 7]

Figure 7.1 Fragment of text from MUC-3 challenge dataset

A MEDIUM-SIZED BOMB EXPLODED SHORTLY BEFORE 1700 AT THE PRESTO INSTALLATIONS LOCATED ON [WORDS INDISTINCT] AND PLAYA AVENUE. APPROXIMATELY 35 PEOPLE WER~! INSIDE THE RESTAURANT AT THE TIME. A WORKER NOTICED A SUSPICIOUS PACKAGE UNDER A TABLE WHERE MINUTES BEFORE TWO MEN HAD BEEN SEATED. AFTER AN INITIAL MINOR EXPLOSION, THE PACKAGE EXPLODED. THE 35 PEOPLE HAD ALREADY BEEN EVACUATED FROM THE BUILDING, AND ONLY 1 POLICEMAN WAS SLIGHTLY INJURED; HE WAS THROWN TO THE GROUND BY THE SHOCK WAVE. THE AREA WAS IMMEDIATELY CORDONED OFF BY THE AUTHORITIES WHILE THE OTHER BUSINESSES CLOSED THEIR DOORS. IT IS NOT KNOWN HOW MUCH DAMAGE WAS CAUSED; HOWEVER, MOST OF THE DAMAGE WAS OCCURRED INSIDE THE RESTAURANT. THE MEN WHO LEFT THE BOMB FLED AND THERE ARE NO CLUES AS TO THEIR WHEREABOUTS.

One example of complex event extraction from discourse would be to identify the various parts of a terrorist incident, which was one of the early challenges posed for the Message Understanding Conference (MUC) series, held from 1987 to 1997[8]. Figure 7.1 shows a sample of text from the MUC-3 dataset (this is verbatim from the source data, including the capitalization and any errors). A structure for storing events of terrorism might have associated roles for the type of incident, the perpetrators, the targets, including physical, human or national, the location and the effects on the targets. Figure 7.2 shows the main parts of the target template, and the values that would be assigned to the roles based on the fragment of text where a "-" value means that no filler for the role was found in the text.

Figure 7.2 Some filled roles for the terrorism template from MUC-3

Selected Roles	Fillers based on text of Figure 1
DATE OF INCIDENT	2 07 SEP 89
TYPE OF INCIDENT	BOMBING
CATEGORY OF INCIDENT	TERRORIST ACT
PERPETRATOR: ID OF INDIV(S)	"TWO MEN" / "MEN"
PERPETRATOR: ID OF ORG(S)	-
PERPETRATOR: CONFIDENCE	-
PHYSICAL TARGET: ID(S)	"FAST-FOOD RESTAURANT" / "PRESTO INSTALLATIONS" / "RESTAURANT"
PHYSICAL TARGET: TOTAL NUM	1
PHYSICAL TARGET: TYPE(S)	COMMERCIAL: "FAST-FOOD RESTAURANT" / "PRESTO INSTALLATIONS" / "RESTAURANT"
HUMAN TARGET: ID(S)	"PEOPLE" "POLICEMAN"
HUMAN TARGET: TOTAL NUM	36
HUMAN TARGET: TYPE(S)	CIVILIAN: "PEOPLE" LAW ENFORCEMENT: "POLICEMAN"
TARGET: FOREIGN NATION(S)	-
INSTRUMENT: TYPES(S)	-
LOCATION OF INCIDENT	COLOMBIA: MEDELLIN (CITY)
EFFECT ON PHYSICAL TARGET(S)	SOME DAMAGE: "FAST-FOOD RESTAURANT" / "PRESTO INSTALLATIONS" / "RESTAURANT"
EFFECT ON HUMAN TARGET(S)	INJURY: "POLICEMAN" NO INJURY: "PEOPLE"

A more recent example of a complex task-oriented dialog would be to create a chatbot that acts as a health coach that encourages its clients to adopt SMART (specific, measurable, attainable, realistic, time-bound) goals and to address barriers to achieving those goals[9]. One subtask of this is to find expressions that correspond to Measurability (M), Specificity (S), Attainability (A) and Realism (R), such as times, activities, and scores and the utterances that express an intent to elicit a SMART attribute, as shown in Figure 7.3 from the Gupta dataset of human-human coaching dialogs[10].

Figure 7.3 Examples of tagged goal attributes in Gupta et al (2020) dataset

Coach: What goal could you make that would allow you to do more walking?
Patient: Maybe walk (S activity) more in the evening after work (S time).
Coach: Ok sounds good. [How many days after work (S time) would you like to walk (S activity)?] (M days number intent)
Coach: [And which days would be best?] (M days name intent)
Patient: 2 days (M days number). Thursday (M days name), maybe Tuesday (M days name update)
Coach: [Think about how much walking (S activity) you like to do for example 2 block (M quantity distance other)]
(M quantity intent)
Patient: At least around the block (M quantity distance) to start.
Coach: [On a scale of 1 – 10 with 10 being very sure. How sure are you that you will accomplish your goal?](A intent)
Patient: 5 (A score)

In this section, we have presented two examples (one older, one recent) of applications of dialog modelling. In the next section, we will consider more theoretical approaches to models of discourse.

7.2 MODELS OF DISCOURSE

Discourse has both a surface structure and an intended meaning. Discourse structure, like sentence structure, has both a linear and hierarchical structure of constituents that in computer science we generally describe as a tree. Discourse has identifiable segments, associated either with content (topics and subtopics) or dialog management (begin, end). As a computational abstraction, processing this structure can be performed using a stack, where topics are pushed when they are introduced and popped when they are completed. (Sequences of pushes and pops reflect parent-child relationships in a tree.)

Evidence for the existence of boundaries between segments and between higher-level discourse units include both cues in the surface forms and in the explicit and implicit semantics. Evidence for the *lack* of a boundary is known as coherence. Discourse coherence is maintained by language users through their choices of words or references to concepts and entities that give the reader or listener the sense that the topic, and the reason that they are talking about the topic, has not changed from when it was introduced. Coherence is related to structure, because segments will correspond to coherent groups and boundaries are indicated by expressions that disrupt the coherence. One way to create coherence is by using referring expressions, such as expressions that begin with the definite determiner "the". Another way to create coherence that is through repetition of words and phrases that refer to the same or to a related concept. We call these devices and the resulting phenomena cohesion[11]. Words can be related by being synonyms, paraphrases, or hypernyms (which are subtypes of something), by being in part-whole relations with each other in some model of a domain, or by being associated with some well-known scenario, such as eating in a restaurant. These word groupings can be obtained from hand-built resources such WordNet, or by counting examples in a corpus.

Another way to create coherence is by organizing adjacent expressions into binary relations that hold between two events or states of affairs that are being described. There are several approaches to specifying these relations. One popular approach uses the terminology of discourse relations, where the words that signal the relation are known as discourse connectives. Another approach is to focus on the writer's own purpose for including a clause or larger unit; the relations based on the writer's purpose are called rhetorical relations. A third approach for analyzing discourse (or annotating discourse data) is to focus on representing the meaning as a variant of a logic that extends beyond a single sentence. Two examples of a logic-based approach are Discourse Representation Theory (discussed later in this section) and SNePS[12, 13, 14].

The remainder of Section 7.2 discusses discourse relations, rhetorical relations, Discourse Representation Theory, referring expressions, and entailments of discourse. While not exhaustive, this group of approaches to discourse covers the most challenging tasks and well-developed computational models for addressing them.

7.2.1 Discourse Relations

Discourse relations are binary relations that hold between adjacent clauses or between a clause and a larger coherent unit based on the semantics of the expressions themselves (rather than the author's intentions in making them). The elements of the binary relation are joined by an implicit or explicit discourse connective that indicates the type of semantic relation that holds between the two parts. Discourse connectives include words like "so" and "because" whose lexical meaning specifies the type of discourse relation (such as "explanation" or "justification"). The two related expressions are typically complete clauses, but one of them might be a complex noun phrase derived from a clause, such as "the occurrence of a pandemic" which is derived from "a pandemic occurred". We call such derived noun phrases "nominalizations". Figure 7.4 includes some examples of discourse relations that occur within a single sentence. In the figure, the discourse connective has been underlined, Argument 1 (like the subject) of the binary relation is in italics, and Argument 2 (the object of the connective) is in bold font, following the conventions of the Penn Discourse Treebank (PDTB)[15]. The semantics of the connective is shown in the second column with its top-level category and the subcategory to which it belongs. So in the second example, Argument 2 is the Reason for the state of affairs of someone being "considered to be at high risk". In the second example, Argument 2 is a nominalization.

Figure 7.4 Examples of Discourse relations.

Example	Relation type
She hasn't played any music <u>since</u> the earthquake hit.	(Temporal.Succession)
She was originally considered to be at high risk <u>due to</u> the familial occurrence of breast and other types of cancer.	(Cause.Reason)

The theory and methods for annotating discourse relations were developed by researchers at the University of Pennsylvania, who have annotated hundreds of texts into two discourse-level treebanks. The annotation is described in a written guideline document[16]. Discourse relations can be *Temporal, Contingency, Comparison,* or *Elaboration* relations, the last of which corresponds to just saying more about the same topic. There are dozens of discourse relations and hundreds of discourse connectives, as sometimes each relation can be expressed by several different connectives.

7.2.2 Rhetorical Relations

Rhetorical relations are binary relations that hold between linguistic expressions but they are not limited to the semantics of the expressions themselves. Rhetoric, as a discipline, pertains to strategies for making discourse effective or persuasive in achieving the goals of the author or speaker. Effective communication has a well-defined goal, and each element contributes in some way, such as providing background, evidence, comparison, or contrast. The related expressions can be clauses, groups of clauses, or phrases used as titles or subheadings. Rhetorical Structure Theory (RST)[17] defines a set of relations by giving a set of conditions to be satisfied, without providing a specific syntax, such as discourse connectives. The types of relations include informational relations, like elaboration, which, like discourse relations, pertain to the semantics of text, and also presentational relations, which pertain to the purpose or intention of the author. For example, a writer may want to *motivate* the reader to do something, and so they may describe a state of affairs along with some reason that the reader might find the state beneficial. As with discourse relations, the relations are asymmetric. In RST, this is handled by designating one of the elements as the *nucleus* and the other as a *satellite*, where the nucleus corresponds the main assertion and the satellite is the segment that modifies it. Every relation is given a definition that includes semantic constraints on both the nucleus and the satellite. These definitions can be used to select among alternative relation types, or to add implicit information to a representation of discourse meaning.

Figure 7.5 Rhetorical relations: Evidence vs. Justify

Definition of relation	Example
Relation name: EVIDENCE Constraints on N: R might not believe N to a degree satisfactory to W(riter) Constraints on S: The reader believes S or will find it credible Constraints on the N+S combination: R's comprehending S increases R's belief of N The effect: R's belief of N is increased Locus of the effect: N	1.The program as published for calendar year 1980 really works. 2.In only a few minutes, I entered all the figures from my 1980 tax return 3.And got a result which agreed with my hand calculations to the penny. 2-3 EVIDENCE for 1
Relation name: JUSTIFY Constraints on N: none Constraints on S: none Constraints on N+S combination: R's comprehending S increases R's readiness to accept W's right to present N The effect: R's readiness to accept W's right to present N is increased Locus of the effect: N	1. No matter how much one wants to stay a nonsmoker, 2. the truth is that the pressure to smoke in junior high is greater than it will be in any other time of one's life. 3. We know that 3,000 teens start smoking each day. 3 is EVIDENCE for 2 1 is JUSTIFICATION for believing 2

Use of RST has included the creation of discourse-level parsers and several datasets annotated with RST relations. One example is the Potsdam Commentary Corpus[18], which is a large dataset created at the University of Potsdam in Germany[19] that has been annotated with several types of linguistic information, including sentence syntax, coreference, discourse Structure (RST & PDTB), and "aboutness topics". Rhetorical relations have also been included in other models of discourse, including Segmented Discourse Representation Theory[20] and in the Dialog Annotation Markup Language (DiAML), as part of the ISO standard for annotating semantic information in discourse[21, 22].

7.2.3 Discourse Representation Theory

Discourse Representation Theory (DRT)[23, 24] is an extension of predicate logic, covering the representation of entities, relations, and propositions as they arise in discourse. DRT structures have two main parts, a set of discourse referents representing entities that are under discussion and a set of propositions capturing information that has been given about discourse referents, including their type, their properties, and any events or states that would be true of them. Past work involved writing parsers to map sentences onto DRT using logic programming, so that they could be used to answer general queries about the content[25]. DRT has been used more recently for creating new datasets[26]. DRT is similar in expressiveness to frameworks based on semantic networks, such as SNePS[27, 28], or modern ontology languages such as the Web Ontology Language (OWL)[29]. While logic-based representations have a well-defined semantics, inference as theorem proving is generally less efficient than reasoning with graph-based representations, because graphs represent each entity as a single node, shared across all mentions within a text and use graph traversal, instead of exhaustive search, to perform inference.

7.2.4 Referring Expressions

In communication, topics and entities can be introduced into the context using a proper name or a complex description with sufficient detail for the hearer or reader to identify the concept that the speaker or author intended. Subsequent mentions will be shorter, either by eliminating some detail, or by using a pronoun.

The fact that different mentions of a discourse entity can refer the same entity contributes to structure, meaning, and coherence, as repeated reference to the same entity is evidence that the enclosing units are part of a common structure (such as a discourse relation or rhetorical relation). Figure 7.6 includes the pseudocode for a search-based algorithm for finding the referent of a referring expression in either the current clause or the preceding one, an approach known as "centering"[30]. The algorithm keeps track of the mentions of entities for each clause and for the preceding one. (For the first clause, the preceding one is empty.) The algorithm iterates through each referring expression in the current clause, comparing it to ones seen so far, looking first within the current sentence and then to the previous ones. It also checks whether features of the pronoun and candidate referent, such as gender and number, are compatible.

Figure 7.6 Algorithm to resolve referring expressions

1. From preceding clause, get all mentions of objects
2. From the current sentence, get all references to discourse entities
3. For each pronoun in the set of forward references do
   a) Try to find a referent within the current sentence (either nearest or nearest the subject).
   b) Otherwise, look for an antecedent from the set mentions from the preceding utterance that also meet feature and binding constraints.

More recent approaches use statistical modelling[31] and classification[32]. There is a huge literature in this area; one useful resource is the book by Van Deemter[33].

7.2.5 Entailments of Discourse

The semantics of discourse includes both explicit meaning and implicit inferences. Explicit meaning corresponds to what is literally expressed by the sentences that comprise the discourse, such as an assertion about an event related to the main verb and its arguments. Implicit meaning is much more complex, as it relies on the physical, social, and cognitive context that each reader or listener uses to understand a discourse. Implicit meaning derives from presumptions that people who communicate are aware of their context, understand how language and objects in the world interact, and are generally rational and cooperative beings. Not all people are uniform in these capabilities, so we will describe what is considered implicitly known among people who are fluent and neurotypical (not having a communication disorder[34]).

Knowing how language works and being rational results in three types of inferences that we call entailments or implicatures: 1) inferences made because we assume that speakers want us to understand them, known as conversational implicatures; 2) inferences made because of the meanings of words, known as conventional implicatures; and 3) inferences made because they are necessary to make sentences appropriate, known as presuppositions. Conversational implicatures arise because we expect that speakers and hearers cooperate to allow each other to be understood with minimal effort. Grice, a philosopher of language, expressed this expectation as a general Cooperative Principle, along with a set of four maxims of quality, quantity, relevance, and manner[35]. These maxims can be paraphrased as: speak the truth, say what you mean, pay attention to others, and be clear in how you say something – reducing the effort needed to understand you. The division of the Cooperative Principle into separate maxims is helpful, because the separate maxims can be associated with different types of expressions and mechanisms for drawing inferences. For example, quantity often relates to a noun phrase, relevance relates to a discourse or rhetorical relation, and manner presumes that if a word is ambiguous, the word sense that is most likely given the context is the one that was intended, unless there is some indication otherwise.

Conventional implicatures occur because the definitions of some words specify that certain attributes necessarily hold. For example, the meaning of the word "and" as a clause-level conjunction includes that the two asserted propositions being conjoined are true. Presuppositions are similar, in that they arise from meanings of words or expressions, but the inferences they trigger are defeasible. By defeasible, we mean that although they be derivable as true from a certain set of facts, with additional facts they can be overridden (and no longer derivable). For example, change of state verbs like "start" and "stop" entail that the state or action described was previously in a different state. Presuppositions are used frequently in advertisements, because they make claims about the world without making explicit assertions about their truth. For example, "New Cheerios are even better than they were before." presupposes they were good in the past.

A fourth source of inference arises when we consider language as an example of rational behavior where actions have expected and intended outcomes. Actions are planned and performed to achieve a goal. For example, we wash things to make them clean; we tell people statements so they will believe those statements are true (or at least that we believed that they were true). Also, different types of actions have different conditions for their success and make different types of changes to the environment in which they occur. So, asking someone how to find a particular building will be successful (that is, I will learn where the building is) only if it has been said to someone who knows where the building is and they could understand the question. Traditional AI planning has addressed problems like this by creating formalisms, such as ontologies, to capture the necessary relationships. Before that, early AI work used a variety of ad hoc representations, such as production rules and STRIPS style operators[36], that could derive plans using search-based problem solvers. Operators for planning are most often described using a dialect of The Planning Domain Definition Language (PDDL), such as PDDL3[37]. A few recent approaches to operator-based planning use machine learning[38].

7.2.5.1 Implementations and Resources for Entailments

All types of entailments can be represented as ad hoc rules or as inference over well-formed expressions in a suitable logic. Nondefeasible inferences can be captured in first order logic. Defeasible inferences require mechanisms that allow one to "override" assertions based on new information. These frameworks are known collectively as non-monotonic logics. Examples include default logic and circumscription[39]. Recent work includes classification-based approaches that address some forms of inference. This work falls under either: Recognizing Textual Entailments (RTE) or Natural Language Inference (NLI). To enable these classification-based approaches, artificial datasets have been created, often as part of challenge tasks at a conference. The labels for the data are *entails*, *contradicts*, and *neutral*. The sentences for the datasets have been created by asking crowdsource workers (such as those who take jobs posted to Amazon Mechanical Turk) to provide a neutral, contradictory, or entailed sentence for a given one. The given sentences have been previously created by experts to capture the different types of implicatures we discussed previously. More information, including examples, is included in Chapter 6, as RTE and NLI are among the current benchmark tasks for NLP.

7.3 MODELS OF DIALOG

In dialog, there multiple presumed speakers or participants, who interact with each other by making contributions to the interaction that we refer to as turns. For each pair of turns, there is a primary turn and a dependent, although a complex turn can be both a dependent of the preceding one and primary to the one that follows. The primary turn creates a context in which the dependent turn must fit. Another way of describing this dependency is that the speaker who makes the primary turn has control or initiative. During an interaction, turns shift among the participants, as determined by the conventions of communication and the expectations they create. In some types of dialog, control may also shift.

Dialog has several aspects that make it more challenging than a narrative created by a single author. The first challenge is that it unfolds in real time, which limits the amount of inference that participants can be expected to do. Also, since participants do not share a common representation of discourse meaning, participants must include mechanisms (or rely on accepted defaults) for managing dialog control and for addressing possible mishearing or misunderstanding[40]. As turns shift, the respondent will indicate whether they understood or agreed with the prior turn, either explicitly or implicitly. The process of exchanging evidence of the success of dialog is called **grounding**.

There are subtypes of dialog that differ based on whether control is fixed with one participant or may be relinquished and claimed[41]. In natural conversation, any of the participants may have control. The first speaker makes his contribution and either implicitly selects the next speaker (while maintaining control) or explicitly gives up control, for example by pausing for more than the "usual" amount of time between clauses. However, in most human-machine interaction, usually only one participant has control. In a command system, the user has all control; a typical example is a question-answering system or an information retrieval system. In a single-initiative system, the system has control; a typical example would be a system for automated customer support or other automated telephony.

7.3.1 Turn taking and Grounding

Turn taking is how participants in a multi-party spoken interaction control whose turn it is, which they accomplish through a combination of content (what they say) and timing (how long they pause after speaking). Conventions from spoken interaction also sometimes carryover into other modalities such as text messaging. Many utterances occur in well-defined pairs of contribution and acceptance, sometimes called adjacency pairs[42], including: question-answer, greeting-greeting, and request-grant. Then, whenever a speaker says the first part of a pair, they are indicating both who will speak next for the second part and what type of response is expected. Speakers use pauses after their utterances to indicate where turns end or a new one should begin. For example, a long pause gives away control – and if someone waits too long to answer, it implies there is a problem (e.g., they did not hear something).

Respondents continuously verify to speakers that they have heard and understood by including explicit markers or following conventional strategies, to provide evidence of grounding[43, 44]. In face-to-face interaction, these cues can be silent and implicit, such as just appearing to pay attention. However, as the possibility of breakdown increases, the cues become increasingly explicit. The second-most implicit cue is to provide the most relevant next contribution. For example, given a yes-no question, the respondent will provide one of the expected types of answers (a yes or a no). The next step up, a minimal explicit cue, would be to provide an acknowledgement. This feedback might be given by a nod, an audible backchannel device ("uh-huh"), a simple continuer ("and") or a non-specific assessment ("Great" or "No kidding"). Then, as uncertainty increases, a more disruptive explicit cue would be demonstration, which involves paraphrasing the original contribution or collaboratively completing it. For example, a response to a possibly ambiguous request such as "Sandwich, please." might be a question – "So you want me to make you the sandwich?" Paraphrases like this are good for noisy situations, even though it takes extra time, because it confirms precisely which parts of the prior turn were heard and understood (and possibly reduces the amount of repetition overall). The last, and most highly explicit cue, called a verbatim display, is for the hearer to repeat word-for-word everything the speaker said. The problem with this approach, from the speaker's point of view, is that it confirms "hearing" without conveying understanding or agreement. Thus, a verbatim display may be accompanied by a paraphrase demonstration too. Figure 7.7 provides an example for each type of grounding device.

Figure 7.7 Examples of Grounding Acts in Dialog
(as specified by Clark and Schaefer 1989)

Grounding type	Example of a turn (A) and a reply (B) with grounding
Continued attention	 *(illustration: A says "Hi" to B)*
Relevant next contribution	A: How are you? **B: I am fine thank you.**
Acknowledgement	A: I'd like a small burger. **B: Okay. Would you like fries with that?**
Demonstration	A I'd like a small burger. **B: You want to order a hamburger. Anything else?**
Display	A. I'd like a small burger. **B: a small burger...**
Display+Demonstration	A. I'd like a small burger. **B: a small burger, and besides the burger, anything else in your order today?**

Speakers specify the relevant next contribution through a combination of the surface form (the syntax) and a shared expectation that respondents will do something or draw inferences, as needed, about why something was said, if the surface form does not directly correspond to something that would be perceived as useful for the speaker. There are five surface forms used in English. The five types are shown in Figure 7.8. Assertives state something as a fact. Directives tell someone to do something. Commissives tell someone that the the speaker agrees to do something. Expressives state an opinion or feeling (which must be accepted at face value). Declaratives make something true by virtue of saying it, such as offering thanks, making promises, expressing congratulations, etc.

Figure 7.8 Examples of Surface Forms for Dialog Acts

Type	Example	Possible intended responses
Assertive	That is a cat.	Hearer will be able to identify a cat.
Directive	Let the cat out.	Hearer will let the cat out.
Commissive	I will let the cat out.	Hearer will know that the cat will be let out.
Expressive	Cats are great pets.	Hearer will know that the speaker likes cats.
Declaratives	I compliment your good manners.	Hearer will feel their behavior was accepted or appreciated by the speaker.

When the type of action matches the surface form, we say that the expression is direct or literal, otherwise it is indirect or non-literal. For example, the expression *"Can you pass the salt?"* is a direct yes-no question, but an indirect request (to pass the salt), which can be further clarified by adding other request features, such as *"please"*[45]. The acceptable use of indirect language is specific to particular language groups. For example, in some cultures (or family subcultures) it is considered impolite to request or order something directly (e.g., "Close the window."), so speakers will put their request in another form that is related, and rely on the listener to infer the request (e.g., "Can you close the window?" or "I'm feeling cold with that window open."). These forms are not universal, and thus others may find such indirect requests impolite or confusing[46].

7.3.2 Mixed-Initiative Dialog and the Turing Test

In natural dialog, control may begin with one participant, for example by introducing a topic, but may shift to others, who can introduce subtopics or ask questions. These dialogs are called mixed initiative to distinguish them from the more typical systems that are either command systems or single-initiative[47]. Mixed-initiative has been the ideal for human-machine interaction, however, no system yet achieves this standard. Telephony systems come close to mixed initiative (and they call it that) by allowing users to specify more than one field value per prompt, rather than requiring them to explicitly follow one prompt per field. Attempts to drive progress have taken various forms, including the Loebner prize, which is based on the Turing Test. The Turing Test, first proposed by Alan Turing 1950 as a parlor game – as computers didn't exist – has long been used as a benchmark for AI. The AI Turing Test for AI is such that, if you cannot tell whether you are talking to a person or machine, then the AI is "successful". For many years, the Turing Test was just a thought experiment, but starting around 1990 it became the focus of an annual challenge, called the Loebner prize. This competition offers a large financial prize (equivalent to a million U.S. dollars) for creating a system that provides the most convincingly natural dialog. Most recently, this competition has been sponsored by the Society for the Study of Artificial Intelligence and Simulation of Behaviour, the largest and most longstanding AI society in the UK, active since 1964[48]. You can find a video online by Data Skeptic that describes the Loebner Prize[49].

7.3.3 Frameworks for Implementing Dialog Systems

Superficial general-purpose dialog systems (also called dialog agents) can now be built with relatively little programming effort. These systems can be created either using rule-based chatbot libraries, interpreters for a subdialect of XML called VoiceXML, or commercial Machine Learning-based toolkits that rely on datasets of turns labeled with the desired type of response, such as the Alexa Skills Kit. To support more complex machine learning approaches in the future, there is also an annotation framework called the Dialog Act Markup Language (DiAML), which is covered by an ISO Standard[50]. DiAML provides a framework for labelling dialog turns in a task independent way. Here we will provide a brief overview of these methods.

7.3.3.1 Rule-based chatbot libraries

Rule-based chat systems, such as found in the NLTK chat package, "perform simple pattern matching on sentences typed by users, and respond with automatically generated sentences"[51]. This approach is similar to the one used for first chatbots, such as ELIZA[52]. Patterns are specified using ad hoc code or regular expressions, and they may bind a variable to parts of what was said to provide more tailored responses. Associated with each pattern is a list of replies, from which the system selects randomly. To build more complex behavior that addresses more than just the contents of the current utterance, one must do some programming to keep track of past exchanges. For example, to use the NLTK one must alter the chat.converse() function to do the necessary data storage and lookup.

7.3.3.2 VoiceXML-based frameworks

VoiceXML is a markup language for designing speech dialog systems. It is a subdialect of XML that resulted from a collaborative effort begun in 1999 with input from major U.S. computer companies of the time, AT&T, IBM, Lucent, and Motorola. Other companies participated in subsequent forums and revisions and the most recent version (3.0) was released by W3C in 2010 as a "Working Draft". Along with the specified syntax, there are numerous providers of interpreters for VoiceXML that link directly to the international telephone network through standard phone numbers. These interpreters provide automated speech recognition (ASR) and text-to-speech (TTS) for a variety of languages, so that the utterances of the system will be heard as a natural voice, when a person (or another system) interacts with a deployed system. Using VoiceXML allows individuals and companies to quickly build task-specific dialog systems that follow a simple, frame-based model of mixed initiative interaction, where the user's range of replies can be specified as a set of predefined slots. Figure 7.9 is an example of how VoiceXML could be used for choosing among different services, which might be part of a longer dialog for booking travel.

Figure 7.9 Sample VoiceXML Form

```
<form>
  <field name="transporttype">
    <prompt>
      Please choose airline, hotel, or rental car.
    </prompt>
    <grammar type="application/x=nuance-gsl">
    [airline hotel "rental car"]
    </grammar>
  </field>
  <block>
    <prompt>
    You have chosen <value expr="transporttype">.
    </prompt>
  </block>
</form>
```

In VoiceXML, each dialog is specified either as a form or a "menu" which gives the user a choice of options and then transitions to another dialog based on their choice (like a phone tree). Figure 7.9 shows a simple form. Forms consist of a sequence of fields along with some other commands. For example, "prompt" is a command for the system to say something. (As in all html/xml type frameworks, labels are enclosed in left and right angle brackets, where boundaries of a data object are marked by matching opening <label> and closing </label> tags. The example defines a single slot (called a field) called "transporttype", and provides a prompt and a grammar for analyzing the response. The final prompt at the bottom confirms the inputs values. Commands are specifications that identify significant events (like getting no input or no match) and map the event to the action the system should take, such as repeating the prompt. Simple mixed initiative dialogs can be approximated by defining multiple slots, which the interpreters will fill in any order, including matching multiple slots from a single utterance. Figure 7.10 shows a fragment of a form that specifies multiple slots related to booking an airline ticket.

Figure 7.10 Example of multiple VoiceXML fields

```
<field name="destination">
    <prompt>
        And which city do you want to go to?
    </prompt>
    <grammar type="application/x=nuance-gsl">
     [(san francisco) denver (new york)  barcelona]
    </grammar>
    <filled>
      <prompt>
         OK, to <value expr="destination">
      </prompt>
    </filled>
</field>
<field name="departdate" type="date">
    <prompt>
        And what date do you want to leave?
    </prompt>
    <filled>
      <prompt>
         OK, on <value expr="departdate">
      </prompt>
    </filled>
</field>
```

7.3.3.3 Commercial ML based chatbot toolkits

Both software libraries and VoiceXML lack flexibility desired by modern users. To address this limitation, a number of commercial software service providers, including Google, Amazon,

Cisco, and Facebook provide tools for implementing chatbots. These chatbots are platform specific, as the companies intend that they be deployed on their proprietary smart speakers and devices (e.g., Siri, Amazon Alexa, Facebook Dialogflow, etc.). To use these toolkits, a developer specifies a set of "intents" which are labels for each type of response. Developers also provide labelled training data and the response to be associated with each label. These responses can use of any of the functions supported by the platform, e.g., anything in Amazon Web Services (AWS). The training data for each intent will be a set of verbatim alternative sentences with patterns that include predefined types, such as days of the week, names of cities, numbers, etc. These platforms also include a few predefined intents (such as for indicating Yes or No or for restarting the dialog). Figure 7.11 shows the definition of a simple intent[53], using Amazon's specification language; it presumes that "course_name" has been predefined (as a developer-specified category).

Figure 7.11 An intent for Amazon Alexa

```
intents:
  enroll_for_course:
    - 'enroll me for the course {course_name}'
    - 'enrollment for {course_name}'
    - '{course_name} enrollment start'
```

7.3.4 The Dialog Action Markup Language

The development of classifier-based systems for dialog is limited by lack of availability of high quality datasets. The datasets collected by commercial systems are not generally available. Creating large, task-independent datasets will require significant resources. As a step toward this goal, researchers have specified a general framework for annotating semantics (now covered by an ISO standard) that includes a specification for annotating dialog data[54]. The specified labels cover both semantic content and communicative function. In the framework, semantic content includes semantic roles and entities and the communicative function is akin to the utterance types shown in Figure 7.2, such as assertive or directive. There are also nine semantic dimensions which correspond to the overall purpose of an act, which include information exchange, social functions, and dialog management. The most commonly occurring semantic dimensions are tasks (such as to exchange information), social obligations (such as to apologize), feedback (to indicate what was heard/understood/ agreed upon about a prior behavior), discourse structuring (to introduce new topics or correct errors in what was said earlier), and own-communication management (such as to correct prior speech errors). Communicative functions include actions that manage the interaction itself, such as pause, apology, take-turn, question, answer, offer, and instruct. The DiAML standard also specifies functional qualifiers, such as, conditionality, certainty, and sentiment and dependence relations, such as the use of pronouns.

7.3.4.1 DiAML Syntax

The DiAML dialog annotation standard defines a functional segment as the smallest span of behavior having at least one complete communicative function. These segments are the units that are to be annotated, where each segment can have several (possibly overlapping) semantic dimensions. For example, a segment with a feedback function can overlap a segment that has a semantic function, since typically only the first few words provide feedback, but the entire utterances is considered to perform the task-related function. The syntax for annotating segments is expressed using XML. It has elements corresponding to dialog acts (labelled as dialogueAct) and rhetorical relations (labelled as rhetoricalLink), which are semantic relations between two acts, such as Justify or Motivate. In the markup, each segment provides a label for the span of text, the sender, the addressee, the communicative function, and the semantic dimension. The specification for a segment can also include dependence relations, if those relations exist. Rhetorical links specify the two segments being linked and the name of the linking relation, where the names of the rhetorical relations (such as Motivate or Justify) are left to the individual project guidelines to determine, and are not part of the ISO standard.

7.3.4.2 Resources for DiAML

Resources for using DiAML are limited. There is a tool for annotating multimodal dialog in video data, called "ANVIL"[55, 56, 57]. The creators of ANVIL provide small samples of annotated data to help illustrate the use of the tool.

One older, but still useful dataset, is a version of the Switchboard Corpus[58] that has been annotated with general types of dialog actions, including yes-no questions, statements, expressions of appreciation, etc, comprising 42 distinct types overall[59]. The corpus contains 1,155 five-minute telephone conversations between two participants, where callers discuss one of a fixed set of pre-defined topics, including child care, recycling, and news media. Overall, about 440 different speakers participated, producing 221,616 utterances (or 122,646 utterances, if consecutive utterances by the same person are combined). The corpus is now openly distributed by researchers at the University of Colorado at Boulder[60].

7.4 SUMMARY

Discourse, like sentences, has identifiable components and semantic relations that hold between these components. The overall structure is treelike (although some referring expressions may require a graph to capture all the dependencies). The leaves of these structures are the simplest clause-level segments. Coherence is what determines the boundaries of units. Boundaries between segments can often also be detected statistically, as there tends to be more correlation among words and concepts within a unit than across them. Meaning derives both from what is explicitly mentioned and also the implicit inferences that follow from the knowledge of the people who produce and interpret linguistic expressions. Today, some of these inferences can be captured via classification-based approaches, such for classifying textual entailments, but a deeper analysis requires more specialized data or methods, yet to be developed. Dialog is a special case of discourse where the meaning and structure are managed through the interaction and cooperation of the participants, using devices such as grounding. They also rely on expected patterns among pairs of turns, such as question and answer, to reduce the need for explicit grounding.

Notes

1. Fitzpatrick, K. K., Darcy, A., and Vierhile, M. (2017). Delivering Cognitive Behavior Therapy to Young Adults with Symptoms of Depression and Anxiety using a Fully Automated Conversational Agent (Woebot): A Randomized Controlled Trial. *JMIR Mental Health*, 4(2), e7785.
2. Charniak, E. (1972). Towards a Model of Children's Story Comprehension (AI TR-266). *Cambridge, Mass.: Massachusetts Institute of Technology*. Available online at: https://dspace.mit.edu/bitstream/handle/1721.1/13796/24499247-MIT.pdf
3. Dunietz, J. (2020) "The Field of Natural Language Processing is Chasing the Wrong Goal". *MIT Technology Review*, July 31, 2020. https://www.technologyreview.com/2020/07/31/1005876/natural-language-processing-evaluation-ai-opinion/ Accessed August 2020.
4. For example, apparently the thesis advisors of Charniak were so disappointed in the work at the time that neither Marvin Minsky nor Seymour Papert bothered to attend the defense of his dissertation. (Personal communication, 1992).
5. Glass, M. (2001). Processing Language Input in the CIRCSIM-Tutor Intelligent Tutoring System. *Artificial Intelligence in Education* pp. 210-221.
6. Williams, J. D., Henderson, M., Raux, A., Thomson, B., Black, A., & Ramachandran, D. (2014). The Dialog State Tracking Challenge Series. *AI Magazine*, 35(4), 121-124.
7. Gunasekara, C., Kim, S., D'Haro, L. F., Rastogi, A., Chen, Y. N., Eric, M., ... & Subba, R. (2020). Overview of the Ninth Dialog System Technology Challenge: DSTC-9. arXiv preprint arXiv:2011.06486.

8. Chinchor, N., Lewis, D. D., & Hirschman, L. (1993). Evaluating Message Understanding Systems: An Analysis of the Third Message Understanding Conference (MUC-3). SCIENCE APPLICATIONS INTERNATIONAL CORP SAN DIEGO CA.

9. Gupta, I., Di Eugenio, B., Ziebart, B., Liu, B., Gerber, B., and Sharp, L. (2019) Modeling Health Coaching Dialogues for Behavioral Goal Extraction, Proceedings of the IEEE International Conference on Bioinformatics and Biomedicine (BIBM), San Diego, CA, USA, pp. 1188-1190.

10. Gupta, I., Di Eugenio, B., Ziebart, B., Baiju, A., Liu, B., Gerber, B., Sharp, L., Nabulsi, N., Smart, M. (2020) Human-Human Health Coaching via Text Messages: Corpus, Annotation, and Analysis. In *Proceedings of the 21th Annual Meeting of the Special Interest Group on Discourse and Dialogue*, pp. 246-256.

11. Halliday, M.A.K., Hasan, R. (1976). *Cohesion in English*. London: Longman.

12. McRoy, S. W., Ali, S. S., and Haller, S. M. (1998). Mixed Depth Representations for Dialog Processing. Proceedings of Cognitive Science, 98, 687-692.

13. McRoy, S. W., and Ali, S. S. (1999). A Practical, Declarative Theory of dialog. Electron. Trans. Artif. Intell., 3(D), 153-176.

14. McRoy, S. W., Ali, S. S., Restificar, A., and Channarukul, S. (1999). Building Intelligent Dialog Systems. *intelligence*, 10(1), 14-23.

15. Prasad, R., Dinesh, N., Lee, A., Miltsakaki, E., Robaldo, L., Joshi, A.K. and Webber, B.L. (2008). The Penn Discourse TreeBank 2.0. In *Proceedings of the International Conference on Language Resources and Evaluation*, LREC 2008, pp. 2961-2968.

16. Webber et al (2019). PDTB 3.0 Annotation Manual. Available online at: https://catalog.ldc.upenn.edu/docs/LDC2019T05/PDTB3-Annotation-Manual.pdf

17. Mann, W.C. and Thompson, S.A. (1988). Rhetorical Structure Theory: Toward a Functional Theory of Text Organization. *Text*, 8(3), pp.243-281.

18. Potsdam Commentary Corpus website URL: http://angcl.ling.uni-potsdam.de/resources/pcc.html

19. Link to annotation guideline used in Stede and Das (2018): http://angcl.ling.uni-potsdam.de/pdfs/Bangla-RST-DT-Annotation-Guidelines.pdf

20. Asher, N. (1993). *Reference to Abstract Objects in Discourse*. Kluwer Academic Publishers.

21. Bunt, H., & Prasad, R. (2016). ISO DR-Core (ISO 24617-8): Core

concepts for the annotation of discourse relations. In Proceedings 12th Joint ACL-ISO Workshop on Interoperable Semantic Annotation (ISA-12) (pp. 45-54).

22. Bunt, H., Petukhova, V., & Fang, A. C. (2017). Revisiting the ISO standard for dialogue act annotation. In Proceedings of the 13th Joint ISO-ACL Workshop on Interoperable Semantic Annotation (ISA-13).

23. Kamp, H. (1981). A Theory of Truth and Semantic Representation, In *Formal Methods of the Study of Language*. Groenendijk, J., Janssen, T., and Stokhof, M (eds). pp. 277-322.

24. Kamp, H., Van Genabith, J. and Reyle, U. (2011). Discourse Representation Theory. In *Handbook of Philosophical Logic* Springer, Dordrecht, pp. 125-394.

25. Covington, M.; Nute, D.; Schmitz, N.; and Goodman, D. (1988). *From English to Prolog via Discourse Representation Theory.* ACMC Research Report 01–0024, University of Georgia

26. Basile, V., Bos, J., Evang, K. and Venhuizen, N. (2012). Developing a Large Semantically Annotated Corpus. In *Proceedings of the Eighth International Conference on Language Resources and Evaluation* pp. 3196-3200.

27. Shapiro, S.C. and Rapaport, W.J. (1987). SNePS Considered as a Fully Intensional Propositional Semantic Network. In *The Knowledge Frontier* Springer, New York, NY, pp. 262-315.

28. McRoy, S. W., & Ali, S. S. (2000). A Declarative Model of Dialog. In in Carolyn Penstein Ros & Reva Freedman (eds.), *Building Dialog Systems for Tutorial Applications: Papers from the 2000 Fall Symposium* (Menlo Park, CA: AAAI Press Technical Report FS-00-01): 28–36; https://www. aaai. org/Papers/Symposia/Fall/2000/FS-00-01/F.

29. Antoniou, G., and Van Harmelen, F. (2004). Web Ontology Language: OWL. In *Handbook on Ontologies* (pp. 67-92). Springer, Berlin, Heidelberg.

30. Tetreault, J.R. (1999). Analysis of Syntax-Based Pronoun Resolution Methods. In *Proceedings of the 37th Annual Meeting of the Association for Computational Linguistics on Computational Linguistics* (ACL '99). Association for Computational Linguistics, USA, pp. 602–605. DOI:https://doi.org/10.3115/1034678.1034688

31. Engonopoulos, N., Villalba, M., Titov, I., and Koller, A. (2013, October). Predicting the resolution of referring expressions from user behavior. In *Proceedings of The 2013 Conference on Empirical Methods in Natural Language Processing* (pp. 1354-1359).

32. Celikyilmaz, A., Feizollahi, Z., Hakkani-Tur, D., & Sarikaya, R.

(2014, October). Resolving referring expressions in conversational dialogs for natural user interfaces. In Proceedings of the 2014 Conference on Empirical Methods in Natural Language Processing (EMNLP) (pp. 2094-2104).

33. Van Deemter, K. (2016). Computational Models of Referring: A Study in Cognitive Science. MIT Press.

34. Indeed, an inability to "understand what is not explicitly stated" is part of the diagnostic criteria for "Social (Pragmatic) Communication Disorder" as detailed in the Diagnostic and Statistical Manual of Mental Disorders, 5th Edition (DSM-5; American Psychiatric Association [APA], 2013).

35. Grice, H.P. (1975). *Logic and Conversation*. In Cole, P. & Morgan, J. (eds.) *Syntax and Semantics*, Volume 3. New York: Academic Press. pp. 41-58.

36. Fikes, R. E., & Nilsson, N. J. (1971). STRIPS: A new approach to the application of theorem proving to problem solving. Artificial intelligence, 2(3-4), 189-208.

37. Gerevini, A., & Long, D. (2005). Plan constraints and preferences in PDDL3. Technical Report 2005-08-07, Department of Electronics for Automation, University of Brescia, Brescia, Italy.

38. Sarathy, V., Kasenberg, D., Goel, S., Sinapov, J., & Scheutz, M. (2021, May). SPOTTER: Extending Symbolic Planning Operators through Targeted Reinforcement Learning. In Proceedings of the 20th International Conference on Autonomous Agents and MultiAgent Systems (pp. 1118-1126).

39. Etherington, D.W. (1987). Relating Default Logic and Circumscription. In *Proceedings of the Tenth Joint Conference on Artificial Intelligence* IJCAI.

40. Cahn, J.E. and Brennan, S.E. (1999). A Psychological Model of Grounding and Repair in Dialog. In *Proceedings of the Fall 1999 AAAI Symposium on Psychological Models of Communication in Collaborative Systems*.

41. Rosset, S., Bennacef, S. and Lamel, L., 1999. Design Strategies for Spoken Language Dialog Systems. In the *Proceedings of the Sixth European Conference on Speech Communication and Technology*.

42. Sacks, H., Schegloff, E.A. and Jefferson, G. (1974). A Simplest Systematics for the Organization of Turn-Taking for Conversation. *Language* 50(4), 696-735; reprinted in Schenkein, J. (ed.), (1978) *Studies in the Organization of Conversational Interaction*, Academic Press, pp. 7-55.

43. Clark, H. H., and Schaefer, E. F. (1987). Collaborating on Contribu-

tions to Conversations. *Language and Cognitive Processes*, 2(1), 19-41.

44. Clark, H. H., and Schaefer, E. F. (1989). Contributing to Discourse. *Cognitive Science*, 13:259-294.

45. Hinkelman, E. and Allen, J. (1989). Two Constraints on Speech Act Ambiguity. (Tech Report UR CSD / TR271) Available online at: http://hdl.handle.net/1802/5803

46. YU, K. A. (2011). Culture-specific concepts of politeness: Indirectness and politeness in English, Hebrew, and Korean Requests. *Intercultural Pragmatics*, 8(3), 385-409.

47. Haller, S., McRoy, S. and Kobsa, A. eds. (1999). *Computational Models of Mixed-Initiative Interaction*. Springer Science & Business Media.

48. Society for the Study of Artificial Intelligence and Simulation of Behavior. Homepage: https://aisb.org.uk/ Accessed August 2020.

49. Data Skeptic (2018). "The Loebner Prize" URL: https://www.youtube.com/watch?v=ruueEq_ShFs.

50. ISO 24617-2:2012 Language resource management — Semantic annotation framework (SemAF) — Part 2: Dialogue acts. URL: https://www.iso.org/standard/51967.html Accessed August 2020.

51. Bird, S., Klein, E. and Loper, E. (2009). *Natural Language Processing with Python: Analyzing Text with the Natural Language Toolkit.* O'Reilly Media, Inc.".

52. Weizenbaum, J. (1966). ELIZA — A Computer Program for the Study of Natural Language Communication between Man and Machine, *Communications of the Association for Computing Machinery* 9: 36-45.

53. Documentation for defining Amazon intents: https://developer.amazon.com/en-US/docs/alexa/custom-skills/standard-built-in-intents.html Accessed August 2020.

54. Bunt, H., J. Alexandersson, J. Carletta, J.-W. Chae, A. Fang, K. Hasida, K. Lee, V. Petukhova, A. Popescu-Belis, L. Romary, C. Soria, and D. Traum (2010). Towards an ISO Standard for Dialogue Act Annotation. In *Proceedings of the International Conference on Language Resources and Evaluation,* LREC 2010, Malta, pp. 2548–2555.

55. Kipp, M. (2012) Multimedia Annotation, Querying and Analysis in ANVIL. In: M. Maybury (ed.) *Multimedia Information Extraction*, Chapter 21, John Wiley & Sons, pp: 351-368.

56. Kipp, M. (2014) ANVIL: A Universal Video Research Tool. In: J. Durand, U. Gut, G. Kristofferson (Eds.) *Handbook of Corpus Phonology*, Oxford University Press, Chapter 21, pp. 420-436

57. Main ANVIL webpage: www.anvil-software.org Accessed August 2020

58. Godfrey, J.J., Holliman, E.C. and McDaniel, J. (1992). SWITCHBOARD: Telephone Speech Corpus for Research and Development, In the Proceedings of the 1992 IEEE International Conference on Acoustics, Speech, and Signal Processing ICASSP, 517-520.

59. Stolcke, A., Ries, K., Coccaro, N., Shriberg, E., Bates, R., Jurafsky, D., Taylor, P., Martin, R., Ess-Dykema, C.V. and Meteer, M. (2000). Dialogue Act Modeling for Automatic Tagging and Recognition of Conversational Speech. *Computational Linguistics*, 26(3), pp.339-373.

60. The Switchboard Dialog Act Corpus website. http://comp-prag.christopherpotts.net/swda.html Accessed August 2020.

CHAPTER 8.

QUESTION ANSWERING, TEXT RETRIEVAL, INFORMATION EXTRACTION, & ARGUMENTATION MINING

This chapter considers two special cases of discourse: questions and arguments; and methods that support them: question-anwering, text retrieval, information extraction, and argumentation mining. In the traditional account of language, we distinguish three types of sentences: statements (declaratives), questions (interrogatives), and commands (imperatives). During an interaction among multiple people or people and a computer system, these types of sentences occur together to address the goals of information seeking (e.g., via question answering) or persuasion (e.g., argumentation). An overview each of these topics follows:

- Question Answering (QA), also known as information-seeking dialog, is a type of two-way interaction where the user controls the primary turns and the system responds. Such a system must first interpret the question and then create and deliver the response. Creating the response may be a relatively simple matter of finding an answer within a table (e.g., within a FAQ), or initiating a pipeline of processes to find the most relevant document and extract a response from the document.

- Text retrieval returns ranked lists of documents, but not an "answer". For real-time QA, one needs a separate system to preprocess the documents to support search for a wide range of information needs, a task called information retrieval. When the documents are mostly unstructured text, we call it text retrieval.

- Information extraction finds a specific answer to address the focus of a question. Information extraction methods can also be applied to find all possible properties or relations mentioned in a text, either based on the main verb, or on predefined entity types, such as person, location, and time.

- Argumentation mining is a special case of information extraction where the extracted components have been defined to model the legal notion of an argument, such as claim, attack, and rebuttal.

We will consider both the characteristics of these types of discourse and the computational methods for achieving them in greater detail. However, first we will consider some interesting real-world examples.

8.1 EXAMPLES OF QUESTION ANSWERING

Suppose that you wish to create a chatbot style front end to a general purpose search engine, such as provided by many smart speakers like Amazon's Alexa or Apple's Siri as well as the search boxes of modern browsers, such as Chrome. You would like it to process questions in context – which includes the time and place of the question. Sometimes it can answer with information drawn from static stored sources, like Wikipedia, but sometimes it must be able to access sources that change.

Figure 8.1 shows some examples of questions and replies from Chrome, on a Sunday in January, 2021 in Milwaukee, Wisconsin.

Figure 8.1 Examples of Question Answering by Chrome (2021)

Question	Response
When do the Bucks play?	Untailored table of the dates, times and opponent of four Milwaukee Bucks basketball games in the second half February, but none for the up coming week
Where is Milwaukee playing this week?	A tailored display (with team logo) of 4 games between Feb 3 and Feb 6
Who beat the Bucks?	A tailored display of the score from yesterday's game and a link to the entire schedule, with scores of past games.
Who beat Milwaukee this year?	The same display as above
Who owns the Bucks?	Untailored table of the coach, the ownership, the affiliations, etc, and a link to the Wikipedia page

Now suppose that one wishes to create a tool to help the moderator of an online forum answer questions from cancer survivors. People can post their stories to a forum, including requests for information or advice, and forum members can also respond to each other. The moderator may chime in with the answer to a question if it has gone unanswered for too long or the best answer is missing. Sometimes the questions are answerable without more information; sometimes the best thing to do is to refer them to a healthcare provider. The challenges include: identifying requests for information,identifying whether the responses have adequately answered the question, and if necessary, finding and providing either a direct answer (if it is brief) or reference to a longer document that would contain the answer. One recent approach tested the idea of training a classifier to identify sentences that express an information need, extracting keywords from those sentences to form a query to a search engine to extract passages from the provider's existing educational materials for patient. They study found that very few questions would be answerable from the educational documents, because they contained concepts outside the scope of the materials[1]. (For example, the patient might have already read the materials and found they did not address their concerns, e.g., how to cope with hair loss, or were too generic, and that is what motivated them to seek help from peers.)

8.2 QUESTION ANSWERING

In a general dialog system, handling questions requires identifying that a clause in the dialog expresses a question, identifying the semantics of the question, such as the topic and any constraints, and identifying the expected answer type (EAT) of the question, such as a person, location, or description. The identified information is then used to decide how to address the question, which might be a direct answer, or an explanation of why the EAT is not provided. Sometimes frequently asked questions (FAQ) are known and their answers can be precomputed and stored so that they can be delivered quickly. Less frequent, but predictable, questions are often anticipated by document authors and included in the metadata stored with a document. The types of information typically found in metadata include the names of authors, the title, the date of publication, and several subject headings, which are terms from a controlled vocabulary. To answer a question, selected information from the metadata can be aggregated and used as input to a natural language generation system (see Chapter 9). Otherwise, novel or unexpected questions, which are sometimes referred to as "open domain" questions, can be answered by applying a pipeline of processes to extract an answer from a set of previously processed passages (paragraphs) created from a collection of documents or from a call to a general web search engine[2]. Figure 8.2 shows an example of a pipeline for complex question answering[3].

The QA pipeline shown in Figure 8.2 begins with classification to determine the question and answer types, which may require subtasks of "feature engineering" to identify important noun phrases (using named entity recognition), important relations between verbs and nouns (using semantic role labelling, or relation extraction) or to build vector representations (of the words or the whole question). These inputs are used for querying a search engine and for extracting information from retrieved texts. A search engine is a general purpose system for finding relevant text units. Information extraction is a complex task that maps unstructured text into a variable or a structure with multiple slots and fillers.

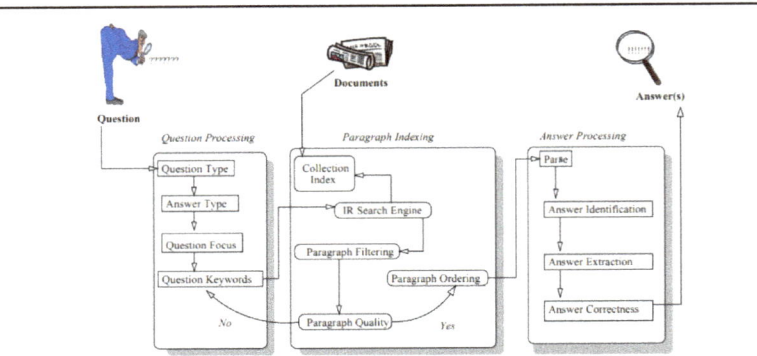

8.2 Example of pipeline for question answering from documents (Image: Moldavan et al 2000)

8.2.1 Characterization of Questions

Questions are distinct from statements at every level. Question syntax often uses distinct words, such as who, what, when, where, why, and how (called "wh-words"). They also have different linear order, such as putting the auxiliary verb before the main verb: "Is that a duck?", or moving a wh-expression to the front as in "What food does a duck eat?" or "In what drawer did you put my socks?" Recognizing the expected answer type (EAT) depends on the syntax and semantics of the question. For example, a "who" question expects the name of a person, or a very specific description of an individual or group of people (e.g., "the Congress of the United States"); a "what" question expects a (nonhuman) object or idea; a "when" question expects a time (or a description of temporal constraints); a "where" question expects a name or description of a location; a "why" question expects an explanation. Representations of the meanings of questions may involve operators that indicate the type of question (Y/N vs WH), or designated quantified variables in a logical expression or, in a procedural semantics, the specification of a function that will retrieve or display information rather than store it. (For example, in an SQL representation, we would use SELECT to retrieve infromation and INSERT INTO to store it.) Question answering, like other forms of discourse, may also involve making inferences from background beliefs (such as what is already known or possessed) and forward-looking inferences about the intended goal of having an answer. An example of an inference would be when people are in a cooperative conversation with a travel agent, they can expect that a "I need the price of a train from Milwaukee to Chicago" will be treated as a wh-type question, like "What is the price of a ticket to Chicago?"

8.2.2 Characterization of Answers

Answers are distinct from statements in isolation. The form of an answer may be a single word, a short phrase, or a complete sentence. The abbreviated forms are possible because dialog participants can expect that an answer will be understood in the context of the question, and that answer semantics "inherit" the semantics of the question that prompted it. For example, a question that asks "What does a duck say?" can be answered with just "Quack", which should be interpreted as "A duck says quack". Answers also have implicit meaning, corresponding to the normal entailments derivable from discourse, based on cooperativeness, word meanings, and the fact that language use is a form of rational behavior (see Chapter 7). In cooperative interaction, it is the responsibility of the answer provider to assure that any obvious false inferences are not derivable from the answer [4]; for all other interactions, it is up to the questioner to decide if the respondent is being misleading.

8.3 TEXT RETRIEVAL

Text retrieval systems, such as search engines, map an information need to a written document or list of documents sorted by a measure specific to the goals of the system. This measure is typically a combination of relevance to a need, information quality, and business goals (e.g., driving sales). The earliest models of text retrieval followed the organization of libraries and search methods of expert librarians. Automated methods were first introduced to handle large domain-specific collections, especially for law and medicine. The massive scale of these collections relative to the computing power of the time created a need for shallow methods capable of filtering and sorting through large collections in a relatively short amount of time[5]. These shallow methods include counting words, or short sequences of words, that occur in each document and across a collection as a whole. The methods did not include syntactic or semantic processing of the documents, and except for small sets of a few adjacent words, the order of words generally was ignored. The scale also necessitated a division of labor between tasks that are done offline, such as creating data structures that facilitate document access and tasks that are done online, such as accessing stored data structures and presenting the results as a ranked list.

Figure 8.3 illustrates the architecture of a typical text retrieval system[6]. The main components are indexing, query processing, search, ranking, and display of results. We will consider each of these in turn, moving top to bottom and then left to right across the figure.

Indexing processes a collection of documents and builds a table that associates each term (word) in a vocabulary with the set of items from the collection in which it occurs. This type of table is called a postings file, or an "inverted" index, because the normal way people think of an index is to map from a document or chapter to the words. In the process of indexing, the system will also score the importance of each term for each of the documents in which it occurs.

8.3 Architecture of a text retrieval system (Image: Jurafsky and Martin 2008)

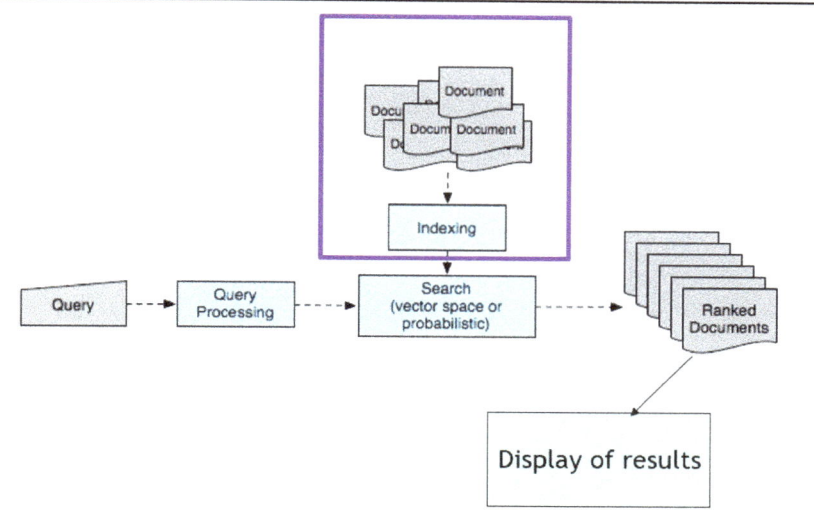

Query processing takes the input from the user (which we call a query) and performs standardization and generalization steps to improve the likelihood of a finding a match between the inferred intent and the documents that are retrieved. Terms in a query may be removed if they are too general (based on a hand-created "stoplist") or terms may be added, such as synonyms from a thesaurus ("query expansion"). Sometimes unrelated terms are added on the basis that they were frequent in the top-ranked matched documents of the original query ("pseudo-relevance feedback"), which is one method of biasing the search towards one sense of an ambiguous term. Terms may also be reordered for efficiency. For example, when the results of queries with multiple terms conjoined by "and" are merged via an intersection operation, the smallest sets of results are merged first, decreasing the number of steps.

Search, also called matching, uses the processed query to find (partially) matching documents within the index and assigns them a score, typically based on the number of terms matched and their importance.

Ranking sorts the matched items according to a function that combines the search score with other proprietary factors. Ranking is a critical component, as it has been shown that many users never look beyond the first page results and instead will try a different query when the results do not appear to match their need[7]. Thus, many methods focus solely on the task of *reranking* the results of a less complex retrieval method.

A display of results presents the ranked results, along with other information about them. The information to be displayed is selected and formatted to help the user understand the result, such as what the document might contain and why it was ranked highly. For example, search terms may be highlighted using bold font, and spans of text that contain the terms may be extracted and concatenated so that more of them can be shown on a single page. Another type of display, called facetted, arranges the search results into categories, using terms from the retrieved documents. For example, a search for t-shirts might return a page with tabs to filter products by price, style (e.g., short-sleeve or v-neck), or sale items.

The role of natural language processing in the typical IR architecture is very limited. Morphological analysis and part of speech tagging are sometimes used in the standardization and generalization steps when creating an index and when processing the query. Natural language generation is sometimes used as a step in displaying the results. A stronger influence has been from IR to NLP, as now NLP uses much more statistical analysis of text and models text with vectors, both of which originated as ways to model documents efficiently (discussed below). However, today, the concept of using vectors as a representation has been extended to the word and sentence level, and the values of the vector elements are learned as a parameter in an optimization process, rather than direct counting of terms, as typical of text retrieval approaches.

8.3.1 Vector Spaces for Text Retrieval

In the Vector Space Model (VSM)[8] of text retrieval, both documents in the collection and queries from users are represented as vectors. Each vector has N elements (dimensions), where each dimension corresponds to a distinct word type. A word type might be a syntactic root, or a stem, which is substring of the original word that need not be an actual word. They are derived during a linear traversal of all documents in the collection. For each dimension, for each document, the value will be zero when the word type does not occur in the document; otherwise it will be a weight corresponding to the importance of the word type for discriminating among different documents that might match the inferred intent of the query. Weights for document and query vectors are computed as a combination of measures that are derived from two types of counts: a count of the number of times that a term occurs in a document, called term frequency, and a count of the number of times that a term occurs across a collection of documents, called document frequency[9]. Having higher term frequency generally corresponds to higher importance; having higher document frequency corresponds to lower importance (for discriminating between documents). The actual measure used as a weight is called tf-idf, which is calculated as the product of the term frequency and the log of the inverse document frequency. The log is used as otherwise the numbers would be too small to represent accurately by current computers for large document collections. Sometimes small numbers are added to the numerator and denominator of the fraction used to compute inverse document frequency, to reduce the impacts of documents that vary significantly in overall length across the collection, or when there are documents where a term never occurs.

Scoring the relevance of a document to the inferred intent can be calculated as the difference between the weight vectors, such as the "cosine distance" (discussed in Chapter 2), or a variant that tries to normalize for various factors that can skew the results, such as differences between the overall lengths of documents or terms that do not occur in some documents. Current search engine libraries, such as Lucene, and tools based on it, such as ElasticSearch, now use a complex measure, derived from tf-idf, known as *Okapi BM25* (for "Best Match 25") as the default function for scoring the match between queries and documents[10]. It has additional parameters to account for the average length of documents across a collection and to allow adjustments to the balance between term frequency and document frequency.

8.3.2 Evaluation of Text Retrieval Systems

Query processing and ranking methods are optimized by developers to enhance their performance. Standard measures of performance for text retrieval combine two primary measures: recall, and precision. Recall is the fraction of the total number of documents that should have matched that were actually retrieved, so the denominator is the total number of positives in the data set. Precision is the fraction of the set of retrieved results that are actually true examples, so the denominator is the total number of documents returned. In both precision and recall, the numerator is the number of relevant items returned, called the true positives. Accuracy is the sum of the proportion of the relevant things returned and the proportion of irrelevant things not returned. (Accuracy alone is rarely useful however, because typically the number of irrelevant items is many orders of magnitude greater than the number of relevant items and thus a system could just return false all the time and achieve high accuracy.) Another derived measure is called the F1 measure. F1 is the harmonic mean of the precision and recall, which, when simplified, is equivalent to two times the product of precision and recall divided by their sum. For most evaluations, F1 is used because it balances precision and recall and stays in the range 0 to 1, in a way that works better for most text retrieval than a simple average of the two values.

Other measures are sometimes used when trying to compare systems with different recall results or to better predict the experience of users, who typically make multiple queries. These other measures include Mean Average Precision (MAP) and precision and recall at rank. MAP measures the precision averaged over all levels of recall. MAP is used in many shared task challenges, where recall is determined using results pooled from all the participants. The precision and recall at rank measures are useful for comparing ranking methods, where only the top ranked items are compared. If precision and recall are measured for just the top N ranked subsets of items, this is called "precision at rank N" and "recall at rank N", respectively. These values are useful from a practical point of view, because many people never look beyond elements that rank 10 or less when using a search engine; instead they prefer to try a new query.[11]

Precision and recall both depend on some external measure of relevance to use as a "gold standard". Relevance judgement is a type of binary classification problem: sometimes the class can be derived from part of the data itself, but sometimes it is added manually by asking people to follow an annotation guideline. Kappa, Krippendorff's alpha, and confusion matrices are all methods of assessing agreement for hand-labelled data. For example, Kappa is used for binary judgements involving two judges, and is computed as shown in Figure 8.4, where relevance corresponds to the label "Y" and irrelevant corresponds to the label "N". Software libraries for training classification models, such as scikit-learn, include functions for computing precision, recall, F1, Kappa, and a variety of alternative measures for special circumstances.[12]

Figure 8.4 Calculation of agreement using "Kappa"

Observed agreement	[(# both Judges said Y) + (# both Judges said N)] ÷ (# of samples)
Expected agreement	square(Estimated Probability_Y) + square(Estimated Probability_N)
Estimated Probability_Y	[(# Judge 1 said Y) + (# Judge 2 said Y)] ÷ [2* (# of samples)]
Estimated Probabillty_N	[(# Judge 1 said N) + (# Judge 2 said N)] ÷ [2* (# of samples)]
Kappa	[ObservedAgreement−ExpectedAgreement] ÷ (1−ExpectedAgreement)

8.3.3 Software for Information Retrieval

The most widely used software library for creating IR systems is Lucene,[13, 14] which is open source. Lucene provides everything needed to create an IR system except a user interface. A related tool, SOLR[15], is a complete search engine based on Lucene. Lucene has also been used to create a commercial system, ElasticSearch[16]. These two systems offer many similar features (such as flexible query languages, control over ranking, and a backend NoSQL distributed database), but also have some important differences. SOLR is considered lightweight because compressed it is less than 200 MB, whereas ElasticSearch is about 315 MB compressed. SOLR offers an HTTP based API and supports a wide range of rich-text input formats. Its display options include highlighting and facetting. ElasticSearch uses a RESTful (a web standard) API and supports both text and non-text queries, including geospatial queries (which return documents associated with specific latitude and longitude coordinates for mapping) and time-series queries (which return time-stamped documents that ranked highly for dates associated with a given time-series, such as stock prices, weather, or political events). It also provides log analytics. Overall, SOLR might be favored for large, static collections of text; ElasticSearch might be better for dynamic web-based collections.

8.4 INFORMATION EXTRACTION

Information extraction (IE) involves identifying entities within unstructured text and organizing them into (predefined) structures that can be used as input to downstream tasks, such as QA or summarization. IE may extract a single entity or it may extract several to fill multiple roles in a structure at once. Single entities or "factoids" include simple attributes of objects (such as its proper name, its size, or its superordinate type in an abstraction hierarchy). Examples of composite structured descriptions include specifications of events, which might include the agent, the object, and various attributes. We will consider two cases of information extraction: task-dependent information extraction and open information extraction.

8.4.1 Task-Dependent Information Extraction

In traditional, task-dependent information extraction, structures are defined by the knowledge engineer or software developer, for example to populate a database with a fixed schema. An example of a complex event would be when one company merges with another (a "merger event") or one executive of a company is replaced by another (a "succession" event). A structure for describing a succession event might be as shown in Figure 8.5, where an empty template is shown on the left, and a filled one on the right. The candidates for the different slots would be determined using a combination of named entity recognition and some rule-based filtering. Systems that use named entity recognition can use either predefined types, or can retrain an existing model to recognize new types of entities. Formats for retraining data is often the BIO encoding of individual words, to indicate the start and continuation of each entity type. Training data for retraining the spaCy NER model is given a list where each training example is a tuple of the text and a dictionary that provides a list of entities comprising the start and end indices of the enity in that text, and the category for the named entity, e.g., (`"Cats sleep a lot", {"entities": [(0, 3, "PET")]}`).

Figure 8.5 Example of a template for information extraction

Example text	Filled template

New York Times Co. named Russell T. Lewis, 45, president and general manager of its flagship New York Times newspaper, responsible for all business-side activities.	`<SUCCESSION-1>`
	`ORGANIZATION : New York Times Co.`
	`POST :  president`
	`WHO_IS_IN : Russell T. Lewis`
	`WHO_IS_OUT :`
	`</SUCCESSION>`

8.4.2 Open Information Extraction

Open information extraction (also called relation extraction or script inference) aims to convert text into simple triples of a relation and its two arguments based simply on the semantics and proximity of the words. The goal is to enable the prediction of a missing argument, when given a relation and either one of the arguments (as a query). The relation is usually taken to be the verb itself. Figure 8.6 shows example output from the online versions of the Open IE software from AllenNLP[17], which is a reimplementation of a system by Stanovsky et al[18], at the top, and shown at the bottom, from Stanford CoreNLP[19].

Figure 8.6 Examples of output from Open IE online software from AllenNLP and Stanford CoreNLP

Sentence	Extreme weather is battering the Western United States, with fires raging along the Pacific Coast and snow falling in Colorado.

AllenNLP	**battering**: [ARGM-TMP: Extreme] [ARG0: weather] is [V: battering] [ARG1: the Western United States] , [ARGM-MNR: with fires raging along the Pacific Coast and snow falling in Colorado]
	raging: Extreme weather is battering the Western United States , with [ARG1: fires] [V: raging] [ARGM-LOC: along the Pacific Coast] and snow falling in Colorado
	falling: Extreme weather is battering the Western United States , with [ARG1: fires raging along the Pacific Coast and] [ARG1: snow] [V: falling] [ARGM-LOC: in Colorado]

Stanford CoreNLP	[relation: is_battering, subject: extreme weather, object: Western United States, object: fires raging along the Pacific Coast]
	[relation: raging_along, subject: fires, object: Pacific Coast]
	[relation: falling_in, subject: snow, object: Colorado]

Identification of the arguments can be performed as a chunking task, using either search-based matching with regular expressions or a classification-based approach that classifies the starting point and continuations, based on similarly labelled training data. Alternatively, some implementations use structured classification and train on data that includes syntactic dependency structures. Examples of structured classification for OIE include the work of Chambers and Jurafsky[20], Jans et al.[21] and Pichotta and Mooney[22,23] and Osterman et al.[24]. The most recent versions use Deep Learning approaches, such as LSTM language modelling.

8.5 ARGUMENTATION MINING

Argumentation mining (AM) is an extraction task specialized for multi-sentence texts that present a particular claim or point of view along with statements that are intended to increase or decrease the acceptability of that claim for the intended audience. A canonical example would be a legal argument, where the statements brought to bear might describe relevant legal statutes, physical evidence collected at the scene, or reported observations of witnesses. In legal terms, the primary statement being asserted is the "claim" and the other statements are known as "premises". The relevant statutes would be the "warrant". The structure of such arguments is similar to the type of discourse-level analysis provide by Rhetorical Structure Theory[25]. In particular graphs are used to represent the supporting and attacking relationships between statements of an argument. Potential applications of AM are still emerging, such as to gain a deeper understanding of reviews of products and services or to better understand how the general public perceives important issues of the day and what arguments would be most persuasive to changing damaging behavior. One recent example involves detecting false claims by politicians[26, 27].

Classification tasks for argumentation include identifying the boundaries of constituent elements and the argumentative relationships that hold among elements[28]. There are many common forms of argument that might be recognized, such as argument from analogy. Two markup languages have been developed for creating datasets, the Argument Markup Language[29,30] and Argdown[31], a variant of Markdown.

Argumentation Mining is considered a much harder task than generic information extraction or event mining, because argumentation structures can be nested recursively. That is, a complete argumentation structure (claim and premises) might function as the premise of some more general claim, and so on. Recognizing the relationships among components of an argument also requires real-world knowledge, including knowing when one thing is a subtype of another. In the example shown in Figure 8.7, from Moens (2018)[32], the second sentence provides evidence for the claim which appears first, but requires real-world knowledge that a cellphone is a type of communication device.

Figure 8.7 Example of an argument including claim and premise from Moens (2018)

[CLAIM Technology negatively influences how people communicate.] [PREMISE Some people use their cellphone constantly and do not even notice their environment.]

8.6 SUMMARY

In this chapter, we considered four higher-level tasks: Question Answering, Text Retrieval, and Information Extraction, along with subtypes such as Argumentation Mining. The first two (QA, TR) are interactive tasks that involve a system trying to meet the information needs of the user. Information Extraction and Argumentation Mining are both forms of knowledge acquisition, which can be done offline, and thus better exploit data intensive methods, such as Deep Learning. Both use NLP methods to map unstructured text onto graph-like structures or databases. The resulting information is easier to analyze for a variety of tasks, such as learning about social or political views, advising people about how to weigh the evidence for or against some choice, or helping companies to market products or perform quality assurance. Most of these tasks use hand-built templates that have been specified to fit a particular task or observed style of communication. Open Information Extraction is a subtype that attempts to build structures automatically, based on the proximity of words and the structure of phrases.

Notes

1. McRoy, S., Rastegar-Mojarad, M., Wang, Y., Ruddy, K. J., Haddad, T. C., and Liu, H. (2018). Assessing Unmet Information Needs of Breast Cancer Survivors: Exploratory Study of Online Health Forums using Text Classification and Retrieval. *JMIR Cancer*, 4(1), e10.
2. See for example, Purkayastha, S. (2019) Top 10 Best Search API's.

Web article. URL: https://blog.api.rakuten.net/top-10-best-search-apis/ Accessed August 2020.

3. Moldovan, D., Harabagiu, S., Pasca, M., Mihalcea, R., Girju, R., Goodrum, R. and Rus, V. (2000). The Structure and Performance of an Open-Domain Question Answering System. In *Proceedings of the 38th Annual Meeting of the Association for Computational Linguistics*, pp. 563-570.

4. Joshi, A., Webber, B. and Weischedel, R. (1984). Preventing False Inferences. In *Proceedings of the 10th International Conference on Computational Linguistics and 22nd Annual Meeting of the Association for Computational Linguistics*, pp. 134-138.

5. Greenberg, S. J., & Gallagher, P. E. (2009). The Great Contribution: Index Medicus, Index-Catalogue, and IndexCat. *Journal of the Medical Library Association* 97(2), 108–113. https://doi.org/10.3163/1536-5050.97.2.007

6. Jurafsky, D., & Martin, J. H. (2008). Speech and Language Processing: An introduction to speech recognition, computational linguistics and natural language processing. Upper Saddle River, NJ: Prentice Hall.

7. Spink, A., Wolfram, D., Jansen, M.B. and Saracevic, T. (2001). Searching the Web: The Public and Their Queries. *Journal of the American Society for Information Science and Technology*, 52(3), pp. 226-234.

8. Salton, G., Wong, A. and Yang, C.S. (1975). A Vector Space Model for Automatic Indexing. *Communications of the Association for Computational Machinery*, 18(11), pp.613-620.

9. Jones, K.S. (1973). Index Term Weighting. *Information Storage and Retrieval*, 9(11), pp.619-633.

10. Pérez-Iglesias, J., Pérez-Agüera, J.R., Fresno, V. and Feinstein, Y.Z. (2009). Integrating the Probabilistic Models BM25/BM25F into Lucene. ArXiv preprint arXiv:0911.5046.

11. Jansen, B.J. and Spink, A. (2006). How are We Searching the World Wide Web? A Comparison of Nine Search Engine Transaction Logs. *Information Processing & Management*, 42(1), pp.248-263.

12. Scikit-learn Developers. (2020). Metrics and Scoring: Quantifying the Quality of Predictions, Web Page, URL https://scikit-learn.org/stable/modules/model_evaluation.html Accessed August 2020.

13. Białecki, A., Muir, R., Ingersoll, G., and Imagination, L. (2012). Apache Lucene 4. In SIGIR 2012 Workshop on Open Source Information Retrieval (p. 17).

14. Apache Lucene (2021) website URL https://lucene.apache.org/

15. Apache SOLR (2021) website URL https://solr.apache.org/
16. Elasticsearch B.V. (2021) website URL https://www.elastic.co/ Accessed July 2021
17. AllenNLP 2020, Open Information Extraction, URL: https://demo.allennlp.org/open-information-extraction Accessed September 2020.
18. Stanovsky, G., Michael, J., Zettlemoyer, L., and Dagan, I. (2018). Supervised Open Information Extraction. In *Proceedings of the 16th Annual Conference of the North American Chapter of the Association for Computational Linguistics: Human Language Technologies,* .
19. Angeli, G., Premkumar, M.J.J. and Manning, C.D. (2015). Leveraging Linguistic Structure for Open Domain Information Extraction. In *Proceedings of the 53rd Annual Meeting of the Association for Computational Linguistics and the 7th International Joint Conference on Natural Language Processing* (Volume 1: Long Papers), pp. 344-354.
20. Chambers, N. and Jurafsky, D., (2008). Unsupervised Learning of Narrative Event Chains. In Proceedings of ACL/HLT 2008, pp. 789-797.
21. Jans, B., Bethard, S., Vulić, I. and Moens, M.F. (2012). Skip N-grams and Ranking Functions for Predicting Script Events. In *Proceedings of the 13th Conference of the European Chapter of the Association for Computational Linguistics,* pp. 336-344.
22. Pichotta, K. and Mooney, R. (2014). Statistical Script Learning with Multi-Argument Events. In *Proceedings of the 14th Conference of the European Chapter of the Association for Computational Linguistics,* pp. 220-229.
23. Pichotta, K. and Mooney, R. J. (2016). Using Sentence Level LSTM Language Models for Script Inference. In *Proceedings of the 54th Annual Meeting of the Association for Computational Linguistics* (ACL-16), Berlin, Germany.
24. Ostermann, S., Roth, M., Thater, S. and Pinkal, M. (2017). Aligning Script Events with Narrative Texts. In *Proceedings of the 6th Joint Conference on Lexical and Computational Semantics* (SEM 2017) pp. 128-134.
25. Peldszus, A. and Stede, M. (2013). From Argument Diagrams to Argumentation Mining in Texts: A Survey. *International Journal of Cognitive Informatics and Natural Intelligence,* 7(1), pp.1-31.
26. Naderi, N. and Hirst, G. (2018). Automated Fact-Checking of Claims in Argumentative Parliamentary Debates. In *Proceedings of the First Workshop on Fact Extraction and Verification* (FEVER), Brussels, pp. 60–65.

27. Naderi, N. (2020) Computational Analysis of Arguments and Persuasive Strategies in Political Discourse (PhD thesis). Available online URL: https://tspace.library.utoronto.ca/bitstream/1807/101043/4/Naderi_Nona_%20_202006_PhD_thesis.pdf
28. Walton, D. and Macagno, F. (2016). A Classification System for Argumentation Schemes, *Argument & Computation*, DOI: 10.1080/19462166.2015.1123772
29. Reed, C. and Rowe, G. (2001). Araucaria: Software for Puzzles in Argument Diagramming and XML. Technical Report, Department of Applied Computing, University of Dundee.
30. Reed, C., Mochales Palau, R., Rowe, G. and Moens, M.F. (2008). Language Resources for Studying Argument. In *Proceedings of the 6th Conference on Language Resources and Evaluation* LREC 2008, pp. 2613-2618.
31. Voigt, C. (2014). Argdown and the Stacked Masonry Layout: Two User Interfaces for Non-Expert Users. Computational Models of Argument In *Proceedings of COMMA 2014*, 266, p.483.
32. Moens, M.F. (2018). Argumentation Mining: How can a Machine Acquire Common Sense and World Knowledge?. *Argument & Computation*, 9(1), pp.1-14.

CHAPTER 9.

NATURAL LANGUAGE GENERATION, SUMMARIZATION, & TRANSLATION

In this chapter, we overview three tasks that involve the production of well-formed natural language: text generation, text summarization, and automated translation of natural language. These three tasks all focus on the synthesis of language from either structured or unstructured content, rather than the analysis of language, which we considered in prior chapters. Some applications that use generation are: creating reports and letters, presenting information retrieval results as snippets, and writing captions for tables or images. (An example of report generation would be describing the results of a database query when the number of results is large. For example, one might present the results of a query of "cats" on the online database Wikidata as "There are between 140 and 150 different cats mentioned in Wikidata; a few examples are Meuzza, Orangey, and Mrs. Chippy.") Summarization and translation both involve sequence to sequence transduction, which means that the input and output are both sequences. Text summarization starts with a long sequence of words and produces a shorter one; machine translation starts with sequences of words in one language and creates sequences with the same general meaning in another language. We will consider each of these three tasks, after we first consider a more detailed example of a real-world application of natural language generation.

9.1 AN APPLICATION OF NATURAL LANGUAGE GENERATION

Recommender systems are programs that help people decide among several choices (e.g., different models or brands of an unfamiliar product)[1]. Suppose that we wish to create a system that will provide a summary of comments from a range of customers, rather than the results of our own testing. To get the comments, we could extract product reviews from an online marketplace, which typically include text, an overall rating, and sometimes a rating of "usefulness" provided by other shoppers. The output might include a well-formed paragraph describing what features purchasers liked or disliked. The objective would be that these automatically written reviews be as informative and fluid as reviews published in professional publications, such as "Tom's Guide" or "Consumer Reports".

To see what professionals write, consider the example in Figure 9.1, which includes sentences from the opening paragraphs of a review written for "Tom's Guide"[2] based on the author's personal opinion and testing of the "Roborock S4 Max", an autonomous vacuum that entered the market in late 2020. The review starts with engaging generalities, mentions some specific features, and then continues afterwards with several labelled subsections on: price and availability; design; cleaning performance; setup, map, app, and mapping; and verdict. These subsections include both text and tables.

Figure 9.1 Sentences from McDonough (2020) review of Roborock S4 Max

While there are plenty of budget-busting robot vacuums ready to do your bidding, finding one like the Roborock S4 Max, which combines performance and affordability, is rare. It gets the job down smartly and efficiently– without cleaning out your wallet. ...
In our Roborock S4 Max review, we found a vacuum that works well and has useful, modern features. With fast mapping, single room cleaning, and automatic carpet detection, the $429 S4 Max strikes the right balance of performance, features, and cost. All of that has earned a spot at the top of our best robot vacuums list.

At the same time, if you had searched online, you would have found customer reviews as shown in Figure 9.2. In the positive review, the features mentioned were: mopping, camera based object avoidance, (quality of) cleaning, WiFi setup, laser navigation, battery life, (degree of) quiet, (speed of) mopping, (accuracy of) map, virtual walls, no-go function. In the negative review, the features mentioned were: (accuracy of) map, (quality of) cleaning (expressed as "There was a lot of debris left after two cycles on max mode"), (quality of) suction, (accuracy of) mapping, expressed as "It is currently in my master bathroom running into the cabinet although it was set to clean the kitchen"; and (quality of) object avoidance (expressed as "running into walls" and "stuck under the dishwasher").

Figure 9.2 Sample reviews from Amazon.com

Negative review (1 star)	Let me start by saying this is my first robot vacuum. I read a million reviews and did my research. I am less than impressed! The first day it didn't map my house correctly so I mapped it again no biggie. It worked great on my tile floor the first couple of days but not so much on my large area rug. There was a lot of debris left after two cycles on max mode. The suction is awful on rugs we are about a week in and it's the same with my tile. I would like to mention I have cleaned the dust bun and untangled hair from the rollers after every cycle. Now it doesn't even clean the rooms I set for it to clean. It is currently in my master bathroom running into the cabinet although it was set to clean the kitchen. I also had issues with it going in circles running into walls. It literally runs into EVERYTHING it is constantly stuck under the dishwasher. Even after I set it as a no go zone! I tried to contact support but they haven't responded. Highly disappointed as I have heard good things about roborock. I would look elsewhere save your money!
Positive review (5 star)	If you don't need mopping, get the S4 Max vs the S5 Max. If you don't need camera based object avoidance, and most people don't (or don't want vacuum cameras in your house) get the S4 Max vs the S6 Max. Great cleaning, easy WiFi setup, laser navigation, ~150 minutes of battery life, surprisingly quiet especially on the lowest power setting, and you can now know the precise square footage of every room you have! Better cleanup performance than the Roomba s9 and the same as the S6 Max. I like that it doesn't include a mopping function as I didn't need this, saving extra costs. The Roborock S4 Max uses LiDAR navigation enabling super fast mapping. Same capability as the Roborock S5 Max. I was amazed how quickly you can see on the app the map being generated; it created an accurate map on its first run. I found the virtual walls and no-go function to fit my needs perfectly.

A general approach to creating a summary, similar to past approaches[3,4,5], would be to first extract information about the features of the product and the value of that feature provided, which might be yes-no, or qualitative (fast, quiet), or quantitative (150 minutes). Then, the system could collect information for each feature across the set of reviews and either generate a sentence for each feature or create sentences for all the liked features and for all the disliked features.

Recent automated approaches to creating aggregated reviews do not produce actual text, that is, they do not summarize or generate text, because they treat it as more of a classification problem. For example, one approach, called Abstractive Opinion Tagging[6] used analyzed reviews of Hot-Pot restaurants to produce a ranked list of the top five items as: [hospitable service (223), delicious food (165), value for money (104), comfortable environment (65), served quickly (14)]. The tag "delicious food" would apply to sentences with phrases like "I was pleasantly surprised about how yummy the dish and the lamb were", "The shrimp was fresh and the pork mixture was tasty", and "Food is delicious". While tagging features is useful for supporting certain kinds of searches, it does not address natural language generation or summarization.

9.2 NATURAL LANGUAGE GENERATION

The task of a natural language generation (NLG) system is to create a text that will achieve a specified communicative goal. There are three steps to this: first, deciding what to say at the conceptual level (which maps a broad goal, like "respond" onto specific subgoals); second, deciding how to organize the information into sentences; and third, creating output as a sequence of words. These tasks are known as content selection, sentence planning, and realization, respectively. Some natural language generation tasks do not require planning or realization, because the target output is mostly fixed, and thus selecting the output form can be handled as a classification task. The goal of separating sentence planning and realization as a general service is to minimize the amount of linguistic knowledge that systems must encapsulate, so that they can focus on manipulating information at the task level.

Content selection involves creating a description of the content to be expressed, and possibly also the reason for expressing it, such as "to support quantitative comparison" (e.g., to allow one to compare the size or cost of two alternatives)[7,8]. Selecting content is normally a function within an application. To make it easier to use standardized components for the other steps however, applications might represent the selected content in a standardized form, such as a set of relational triples, as a record structure with multiple slots, or as a table, with labelled columns.

Sentence planning involves grouping content into a non-redundant set of sentences that will be easy to understand. (It is not a good idea to put every concept in a separate sentence because it becomes unnaturally repetitive.) Thus, in sentence planning, a system should keep track of what has already been conveyed and select appropriate referring expressions, including pronouns and shortened descriptions. Coherence is improved by adding cue phrases and discourse markers to indicate discourse relations or rhetorical structure (as discussed in Chapter 7). Cue phrases are expressions like "for example" or "The second phase". Sentence planning might also determine that entire clauses should be excluded because they are already part of the context of the interaction. To leave them in would create the mistaken inference that it was new information or that the speaker believes that the hearer has some defect in their hearing or understanding.

Sentence realization produces well-formed sequences of words in a target language. The input will be a sentence plan, which might be a semantic representation or a list of slot-filler pairs. There are several ways the plan might be mapped onto text. The simplest approach is to use canned text, which is any text that has been entirely pre-written, and to provide the mapping explicitly, using a form or table. This approach is how most chatbots and IVR systems produce their output. (Canned text can supply a broader range of outputs, but only by hand-coding collections of alternative sentences that achieve the same intent.) Rule-based approaches can specify patterns that include designated variables that are instantiated from a database or discourse context. A few dialog frameworks support these outputs, and automated form letter generators have always worked this way. When these patterns are more sophisticated, they are called templates, and may include functions for assuring that the sentences are all grammatical without forcing the application to know all derivations of a root form[9,10]. The most flexible approach to realization uses a fine-grained grammar to do realization, similar to reversing the action of a rule-based parser, typically one that relies on feature unification. Unification, with a grammar that includes precise specification of grammatical features, would be best for offline applications where output quality is more important than speed, such as professional reports[11].

9.3 TEXT SUMMARIZATION

Summarization maps an input text to a shorter one that preserves its essential meaning, where what is essential may depend on the task. For example, for information retrieval, one might want to make it clear to the user how a document uses the keywords in the query, so that they will understand the relevance. Other applications of summarization include automatically providing an abstract of a particular length for a website or providing a summary of news stories gathered across multiple documents (such as news.google.com). Summarization is most often extractive, which means that the summaries comprise selected complete sentences from the original. The alternative is abstractive summarization, which means the summaries comprise entirely new sentences that express the desired content, which would be akin to translation, where the source and target languages are the same.

Traditional methods for extractive summarization traverse the entire text and rank each sentence based on a hand-built scoring function. One popular choice involves first computing the tf-idf score for each word (as used for the Vector Space Model discussed in Chapter 8) and selecting all words with a score above a given threshold (called a "centroid") and then scoring each sentence based on similarity with the centroid, which is a vector that represents an average over all the sentences of the unit. A similar, but more sophisticated idea is to score each sentence based on its similarity to semantic vectors trained for the entire document, treated as a "sentence". These vectors are known as "universal sentence embeddings"[12]. Figure 9.3 shows the original text of a journal abstract by de Wilde et al (2018)[13], along with an extractive summaries by two systems, provided online by SMRZR.io and DeepAI.org. (The highlighting shows which sentences each summarizer selected.) The summary on the top right, by the tool SMRZR.io, reports using a technique based on the BERT deep learning architecture. BERTs for summarization are trained to create an embedding for the entire document, and then sentences are compared against this vector. The summary on the bottom right in Figure 9.3 shows a summary provided by DeepAI.org. (Unfortunately no information is provided about their approach.) The summary is reasonable. It is less readable than the other as a summary, but includes more technical content. Unsupervised approaches can also be trained to select a set of semantically related sentences (to form a more cohesive text)[14]. An alternative to such unsupervised approaches would be to train a supervised machine learning model using data where each sentence is labeled with the class INCLUDED or NOT-INCLUDED[15], but few such data sets exist.

Figure 9.3 Examples of extractive text summarization

Original text by de Wilde et al (2018)

Coronaviruses are pathogens with a serious impact on human and animal health. They mostly cause enteric or respiratory disease, which can be severe and life threatening, e.g., in the case of the zoonotic coronaviruses causing severe acute respiratory syndrome (SARS) and Middle East Respiratory Syndrome (MERS) in humans. Despite the economic and societal impact of such coronavirus infections, and the likelihood of future outbreaks of additional pathogenic coronaviruses, our options to prevent or treat coronavirus infections remain very limited. This highlights the importance of advancing our knowledge on the replication of these viruses and their interactions with the host. Compared to other +RNA viruses, coronaviruses have an exceptionally large genome and employ a complex genome expression strategy. Next to a role in basic virus replication or virus assembly, many of the coronavirus proteins expressed in the infected cell contribute to the coronavirus-host interplay. For example, by interacting with the host cell to create an optimal environment for coronavirus replication, by altering host gene expression or by counteracting the host's antiviral defenses. These coronavirus-host interactions are key to viral pathogenesis and will ultimately determine the outcome of infection. Due to the complexity of the coronavirus proteome and replication cycle, our knowledge of host factors involved in coronavirus replication is still in an early stage compared to what is known for some other +RNA viruses. This review summarizes our current understanding of coronavirus-host interactions at the level of the infected cell, with special attention for the assembly and function of the viral RNA-synthesising machinery and the evasion of cellular innate immune responses.

Extractive summary provided by SMRZR.io (September 2020)

Coronaviruses are pathogens with a serious impact on human and animal health . This review summarizes our current understanding of coronavirus-host interactions at the level of the infected cell , with special attention for the assembly and function of the viral RNA-synthesising machinery and the evasion of cellular innate immune responses .

Extractive summary provided by DeepAI.org (September 2020)

Next to a role in basic virus replication or virus assembly, many of the coronavirus proteins expressed in the infected cell contribute to the coronavirus-host interplay. Due to the complexity of the coronavirus proteome and replication cycle, our knowledge of host factors involved in coronavirus replication is still in an early stage compared to what is known for some other +RNA viruses.

An abstractive approach to summarization might identify and rank concepts rather than sentences, for example by mapping a text onto a set of relational triples) and then use a standard natural language generation pipeline. (This approach is like treating summarization akin to machine translation, where the source and target just happen to be the same language.) Of the two, extractive summarization has been the most commonly used – because it is the easiest to do. However, there has been increasing interest in abstractive summarization, especially by applying recent work on semantic textual similarity.

Other promising approaches to summarization, which could be either extractive or abstractive, make use of ranking methods developed for information retrieval, such as TextRank to select relevant sentences or concepts[16, 17].

The quality of a text summary can be evaluated in several ways[18]. The expectation is that the summary will be similar to the reference document from which it was created, so measures of general document similarity used in information retrieval (such as cosine similarity or BM25) are an option. Other methods count topics, which are sets of co-occurring words derived using clustering algorithms, such as Latent Semantic Analysis. Another method, created specifically for summarization and translation, is known as ROUGE, for "Recall-Oriented Understudy for Gisting Evaluation"[19]. The ROUGE method counts and compares surface units, such as the number of overlapping n-grams, between summaries created automatically and summaries created by human experts. It thus requires a training set that includes expert summaries. Going forward, new methods are being devised that make use of meaning representations created via machine learning to measure semantic similarity between the summary and either the reference text, or a hand-built summary[20].

9.4 MACHINE TRANSLATION

Machine Translation systems are systems that translate text from a source language into one or more target languages (or for assisting human translators in their task, known as machine-aided translation). The primary goal is to preserve the meaning of the original while observing the language conventions of the target language. Literary translation systems may have the added goal of preserving stylistic aspects of the original, including preserving the intended effects (such as amusement or suspense)[21, 22]. While the idea of machine translation is almost as old as computer science itself, it did not become practical until the development of methods based on statistical language modelling[23].

The standard current approach for developing largescale machine translation systems is to train paired language models that link syntactic structures (phrases) from a source language onto a single target, based on a collection of translated texts. These pairs of multilingual datasets form what are known as parallel corpora[24]. An example of translated sentence pairs is shown below in Figure 9.4, where translations from English to French were created using the online version of Google Translate[25]. From this collection, a model might learn to translate some words and phrases correctly, e.g. "the cat" -> "le chat", "the mat" -> "le tapis", "on" -> "sur", "under" -> "sous". It likely could not correctly learn "is sleeping", "is standing", or "stands" because of the variation in the words used for these expressions.

Figure 9.4 Examples of English-French parallel text

English	French
The cat is sleeping on the mat.	Le chat dort sur le tapis.
The cat is standing on the mat.	Le chat est debout sur le tapis.
The cat stands on the mat.	Le chat se tient sur le tapis.
On the mat, the cat is standing.	Sur le tapis, le chat est debout.
The cat is sleeping under the bed.	Le chat dort sous le lit.
Under the bed, the cat is sleeping.	Sous le lit, le chat dort.

Some of the most recent machine translation modelling approaches employ neural networks[26], although methods based on phrase-based statistical modelling still outperform them for some language pairs[27]. With a trained model associating phrases from the two languages, an efficient search algorithm or classifier can find the highest probability translation among previously seen sentences in the target language.

Earlier approaches to machine translation based on rules sometimes translated from a single source to multiple targets at once (multilingual translation) by means of an intermediate representation called an interlingua. This approach has been used in commercial settings where translation into 100's of target languages must be completed quickly and the domain is rather small (e.g., repair manuals for farm machinery). Use of an interlingua to support neural network-based multilingual translation has shown both promise and challenges[28,29].

Evaluation of Machine Translation systems most often use the same metrics for evaluating Natural Language Generation, such as ROUGE or BLEU. One metric developed specifically for Translation is called METEOR, which its orignators describe as follows:

> [It scores] "machine translation hypotheses by aligning them to one or more reference translations. Alignments are based on exact, stem, synonym, and paraphrase matches between words and phrases. Segment and system level metric scores are calculated based on the alignments between hypothesis-reference pairs. The metric includes several free parameters that are tuned to emulate various human judgment tasks" [30].

A version of the Meteor scoring metric has been implemented in NLTK V3.5[31].

Commercial providers (such as Google) provide APIs that support high-quality translation for a wide range of language pairs. For less common languages and dialects or specialized domains, open source tools, such as MOSES, are available to create machine translation systems by training them with a parallel corpus[32]. MOSES uses a statistical approach. There are several open source toolkits for creating neural network based machine translation systems, including OpenNMT[33], Sockeye[34] and MarianNMT[35].

9.5 SUMMARY

This chapter considered three related tasks, text generation, text summarization, and automated translation of natural language text, which all involve the output of well-formed natural language, rather than just the analysis of language data. The output for each of these tasks can be specified as a set of concepts using a representation of meaning, or as a sequence to sequence operation that will maximize some objective function, such as maximizing semantic similarity, while at the same time creating output in the target language and at the target length. The lack of parallel input-output data sets has led to many approaches that rely on hand-built rules. Some systems are experimenting with machine learning based methods, where datasets might already exist (e.g., because of government requirements to create documents in multiple language) or can be created using crowdsourcing.

Notes

1. Resnick, P., and Varian, H. R. (1997). Recommender Systems. *Communications of the ACM*, 40(3), 56-58.
2. McDonough, M. (2020). Roborock S4 Max robot vacuum review, November 18, 2020, Tom's Guide, Future US, Inc. URL: https://www.tomsguide.com/reviews/roborock-s4-max-robot-vacuum Accessed Jan 2021
3. Carenini, G., Ng, R., and Pauls, A. (2006). Multi-document Summarization of Evaluative Text. In *Proceedings of EACL 2006*.
4. Tata, S. and Di Eugenio, B., (2010). Generating Fine-Grained Reviews of Songs from Album Reviews. In *Proceedings of the 48th Annual Meeting of the Association for Computational Linguistics* (ACL '10). Association for Computational Linguistics, USA, pp. 1376–1385.
5. Gerani, S., Mehdad, Y., Carenini, G., Ng, R., and Nejat, B. (2014). Abstractive Summarization of Product Reviews Using Discourse Structure. In *Proceedings of EMNLP 2014*. 1602–1613.
6. Li, Q., Li, P., Li, X., Ren, Z., Chen, Z., & de Rijke, M. (2021). Abstractive Opinion Tagging. In *Proceedings of the Fourteenth ACM International Conference on Web Search and Data Mining* (WSDM '21), March 8–12, 2021, Virtual Event, Israel. ACM, New York, NY, USA, 9 pages. Link to a github site with their review data: https://github.com/qtli/AOT.
7. Mittal, V.O., Moore, J.D., Carenini, G. and Roth, S. (1998). Describ-

ing Complex Charts in Natural Language: A Caption Generation System. *Computational Linguistics*, 24(3), pp.431-467.

8. Baaj, I., Poli, J.P. and Ouerdane, W. (2019). Some Insights Towards a Unified Semantic Representation of Explanation for eXplainable Artificial Intelligence. In *Proceedings of the 1st Workshop on Interactive Natural Language Technology for Explainable Artificial Intelligence* (NL4XAI 2019), pp. 14-19.

9. McRoy, S.W., Channarukul, S. and Ali, S.S. (2000). YAG: A Template-Based Generator for Real-Time Systems. In *Proceedings of the First International Conference on Natural Language Generation.* pp. 264-267.

10. Channarukul, S., McRoy, S.W. and Ali, S.S. (2001). YAG: A Template-Based Text Realization System for Dialog. *International Journal of Uncertainty, Fuzziness and Knowledge-Based Systems*, 9(06), pp.649-659.

11. Elhadad, M. and Robin, J. (1997). SURGE: A Comprehensive Plug-in Syntactic Realization Component for Text Generation. *Computational Linguistics*, 99(4).

12. Lamsiyah, S., El Mahdaouy, A., El Alaoui, S.O. and Espinasse, B. (2019). A Supervised Method for Extractive Single Document Summarization based on Sentence Embeddings and Neural Networks. In Proceedings of the *International Conference on Advanced Intelligent Systems for Sustainable Development*, pp. 75-88. Springer, Cham.

13. de Wilde, A. H., Snijder, E. J., Kikkert, M., & van Hemert, M. J. (2018). Host Factors in Coronavirus Replication. *Current Topics in Microbiology and Immunology*, 419, 1–42. https://doi.org/10.1007/82_2017_25

14. Joshi, A., Fidalgo, E., Alegre, E. and Fernández-Robles, L. (2019). SummCoder: An Unsupervised Framework for Extractive Text Summarization based on Deep Auto-Encoders. *Expert Systems with Applications*, 129, pp.200-215.

15. Yao, J.G., Wan, X. and Xiao, J. (2017). Recent Advances in Document Summarization. *Knowledge and Information Systems*, 53(2), pp.297-336.

16. Mihalcea, R., and Tarau, P. (2004). Textrank: Bringing Order into Text. In Proceedings of the 2004 Conference on Empirical Methods in Natural Language Processing (pp. 404-411).

17. Wang, W. M., See-To, E. W. K., Lin, H. T., and Li, Z. (2018, October). Comparison of Automatic Extraction of Research Highlights and Abstracts of Journal Articles. In Proceedings of the 2nd International Conference on Computer Science and Application Engineering (pp. 1-5).

18. Steinberger, J. and Ježek, K. (2012). Evaluation Measures for Text

Summarization. *Computing and Informatics*, 28(2), pp.251-275.

19. Lin, C.Y. (2004). ROUGE: A Package for Automatic Evaluation of Summaries. In *Text Summarization Branches Out*, pp. 74-81.

20. Campr, M. and Ježek, K. (2015). Comparing Semantic Models for Evaluating Automatic Document Summarization. In *Proceedings of the International Conference on Text, Speech, and Dialogue*, pp. 252-260. Springer, Cham.

21. Toral, A., and Way, A. (2015). Machine-Assisted Translation of Literary text: A Case Study. *Translation Spaces*, 4(2), 240-267.

22. Toral, A., and Way, A. (2018). What level of quality can neural machine translation attain on literary text?. In *Translation Quality Assessment* (pp. 263-287). Springer, Cham.

23. Brown, P.F., Cocke, J., Della Pietra, S.A., Della Pietra, V.J., Jelinek, F., Lafferty, J., Mercer, R.L. and Roossin, P.S. (1990). A Statistical Approach to Machine Translation. *Computational Linguistics*, 16(2), pp.79-85.

24. Williams, P., Sennrich, R., Post, M. and Koehn, P. (2016). Syntax-Based Statistical Machine Translation. *Synthesis Lectures on Human Language Technologies*, 9(4), pp.1-208.

25. Google.com (2021) Google Translate website URL: https://translate.google.com/ Accessed July 2021.

26. Bahdanau, D., Cho, K. and Bengio, Y. (2014). Neural Machine Translation by Jointly Learning to Align and Translate. arXiv preprint arXiv:1409.0473.

27. Sánchez-Martínez, F., Pérez-Ortiz, J.A. and Carrasco, R.C. (2020). Learning Synchronous Context-Free Grammars with Multiple Specialised Non-terminals for Hierarchical Phrase-Based Translation. ArXiv preprint arXiv:2004.01422.

28. Escolano, C., Costa-jussà, M.R. and Fonollosa, J.A. (2019). Towards Interlingua Neural Machine Translation. arXiv preprint arXiv:1905.06831.

29. Arivazhagan, N., Bapna, A., Firat, O., Lepikhin, D., Johnson, M., Krikun, M., Chen, M.X., Cao, Y., Foster, G., Cherry, C., Macherey, W. Chen, Z., and Wu, Y.(2019). Massively Multilingual Neural Machine Translation in the Wild: Findings and Challenges. arXiv preprint arXiv:1907.05019.

30. Denkowski M. and Lavie, A "Meteor Universal: Language Specific Translation Evaluation for Any Target Language", *Proceedings of the EACL 2014 Workshop on Statistical Machine Translation*, 2014

31. NLTK.org (2020) NLTK 3.5 Documentation Source Code for NLTK.meteor_score, Web page URL: https://www.nltk.org/_mod-

ules/nltk/translate/meteor_score.html

32. Koehn, P., Hoang, H., Birch, A., Callison-Burch, C., Federico, M., Bertoldi, N., Cowan, B., Shen, W., Moran, C., Zens, R., Dyer, C., Bojar, O., Constantin, A., and Herbst, E. (2007). MOSES: Open Source Toolkit for Statistical Machine Translation. In *Proceedings of the 45th Annual Meeting of the Association for Computational Linguistics Companion Volume Proceedings of the Demo and Poster =Sessions*, pp. 177-180.

33. Klein, G., Kim, Y., Deng, Y., Nguyen, V., Senellart, J. and Rush, A.M. (2018). OpenNMT: Neural Machine Translation Toolkit. arXiv preprint arXiv:1805.11462. Link to OpenNMT https://opennmt.net/

34. Hieber, F., Domhan, T., Denkowski, M., Vilar, D., Sokolov, A., Clifton, A. and Post, M. (2017). Sockeye: A Toolkit for Neural Machine Translation. arXiv preprint arXiv:1712.05690.

35. Junczys-Dowmunt, M., Grundkiewicz, R., Dwojak, T., Hoang, H., Heafield, K., Neckermann, T., Seide, F., Germann, U., Aji, A.F., Bogoychev, N., Martins, A.F., and Birch, A. (2018). Marian: Fast Neural Machine Translation in C++. arXiv preprint arXiv:1804.00344. Link to MarianNMT: https://marian-nmt.github.io/

APPENDIX: TOP DOWN CHART PARSING

Top-down chart parsing methods, such as Earley's algorithm, begin with the top-most nonterminal and then expand downward by predicting rules in the grammar by considering the rightmost unseen category for each rule. Compared to other search-based parsing algorithms, top-down parsing can be more efficient, by eliminating many potential local ambiguities as it expands the tree downwards[1]. Figure A1 provides the processing rules for Earley's algorithm. Figure A.2 provides pseudocode for the algorithm, implemented as dynamic programming.

Figure A.1 Processing Rules for Earley's Algorithm

Top-down initialization: When category S is the root category of the grammar, then for every rule with S on the LHS, create an empty edge at position [0:0] with a dot leftmost on the RHS. That is, whenever S -> A B, for some A, add an edge [0:0] S -> * A B

Top-down prediction rule: When category X is expected (i.e., just to the right of a dot) then for all rules where X is on the LHS, add a new edge where the dot is leftmost on the RHS with a span of length zero at the current end point. (This rule will be repeated multiple times until no new predictions can be made). That is, whenever ([i:k] A -> W * X Y) and X -> S T, for some X, add a new edge [k:k] X -> * S T. (Note: W can be empty.)

Fundamental rule: When a new category is seen or nonterminal created, then for all active rules where the category is leftmost on the RHS of the dot, and the spans are adjacent, create a new edge with the dot moved to the left of that category and combine the spans. That is, whenever ([i:j], A -> X * Y Z and [j:k] Y -> S T * , for some j and Y, add a new edge [i:k], A -> X Y * Z (Note: X and Z can be empty.)

To illustrate a top down chart parse, we will assume the CFG shown in Figure A.3.

Figure A.3. A small CFG for parsing "the dog likes meat".

```
S  → NP VBD        NN  → dog | meat
S  → NP VP         VBD → barked
NP → DT NN         VBZ → likes
VP → VBZ NN        DT  → the
```

Figure A.4 shows a trace of a top-down chart parse of the sentence "The dog likes meat.", showing the edges created in the top-down chart parser implemented in NLTK. The parse begins with top-down predictions, based on the grammar, and then begins to process the actual input, which is shown in the third row. As each word is read, there is a top-down prediction followed by an application of the fundamental rule. After an edge is completed (such as the first NP) then new predictions are added (e.g., for an upcoming VP).

Figure A.4. Trace of a top-down chart parse of the sentence "The dog likes meat."

Chart	Edges added	Explanation

0 S →* NP VBD   the
   S →* NP VP
1
2   dog
3   likes
4   meat
   0   1   2   3   4
	[0:0] S → * NP VBD
	[0:0] S → * NP VP
		For each of the sentence rules, make a top-down prediction to create an empty, active edge.

0 S →* NP VBD   the
   S →* NP VP
   NP →* DT NN
1   dog
2   likes
3
4   meat
   0   1   2   3   4
	[0:0] S → * NP VBD
	[0:0] S → * NP VP
	[0:0] NP → * DT NN
		Make more top-down predictions to create active edges for each of the nonterminal categories just to the right of the dot.

0 S →* NP VBD
   S →* NP VP
   NP →* DT NN   NP → DT * NN
   DT →* the   DT → the*
                  the
1   dog
2   likes
3
4   meat
   0   1   2   3   4
	[0:0] S → * NP VBD
	[0:0] S → * NP VP
	[0:0] NP → * DT NN
	[0:0] DT → * the
	[0:1] DT → the *
	[0:1] NP → DT * NN
		Predict *the* and use the fundamental rule to create new edges where the dot in the DT rule and in NP rule move to the right.

0 S →* NP VBD   S → NP * VBD
   S →* NP VP   S → NP * VP
   NP →* DT NN   NP → DT * NN   NP → DT NN *
                  the
1   NN →* dog   NN → dog *
                          dog
2   VP →* VBZ NN likes
3
4   meat
   0   1   2   3   4
	[0:0] S → * NP VBD
	[0:0] S → * NP VP
	[0:0] NP → * DT NN
	[0:0] DT → * the
	[0:1] DT → the *
	[0:1] NP → DT * NN
	[1:1] NN → * dog
	[1:2] NN → dog *
	[0:2] NP → DT NN *
	[0:2] S → NP * VBD
	[0:2] S → NP * VP
	[2:2] VP → * VBZ NN
		Predict *dog*; apply fundamental rule and then make a top down prediction for a VP (using the second S rule.)

PRINCIPLES OF NATURAL LANGUAGE PROCESSING 253

Chart	Edges	Notes

0 S→* NP VBD   S→NP*VBD
    S→* NP VP   S→NP*VP
    NP→*DT NN NP→DT*NN NP→DT NN*
    the
1   NN→*dog   NN→dog*
    dog
2   VP→*VBZ   VP→VBZ*N
    VBZ→*likes VBZ→likes*
    likes
3   meat
4
    0   1   2   3   4
	[0:0] S → * NP VBD
	[0:0] S → * NP VP
	[0:0] NP → * DT NN
	[0:0] DT → * the
	[0:1] DT → the *
	[0:1] NP → DT * NN
	[1:1] NN → * dog
	[1:2] NN → dog *
	[0:2] NP → DT NN *
	[0:2] S → NP * VBD
	[0:2] S → NP * VP
	[2:2] VP → * VBZ NN
	[2:2] VBZ → * likes
	[2:3] VBZ → likes *
	[2:3] VP → VBZ * NN
		Predict *likes*; apply the fundamental rule to create VBZ-> likes *, and again, to add VP -> VBZ * NN

0 S→* NP VBD   S→NP*VBD
    S→* NP VP   S→NP*VP   S→NP VP*
    NP→*DT NN NP→DT*NN NP→DT NN*
    The
1   NN→*dog   NN→dog*
    dog
2   VP→*VBZ   VP→VBZ*   VP→VBZ NN*
    VBZ→*likes VBZ→likes*
    likes
3   NN→*meat   NN→meat*
    meat
4
    0   1   2   3   4
	[0:0] S → * NP VBD
	[0:0] S → * NP VP
	[0:0] NP → * DT NN
	[0:0] DT → * the
	[0:1] DT → the *
	[0:1] NP → DT * NN
	[1:1] NN → * dog
	[1:2] NN → dog *
	[0:2] NP → DT NN *
	[0:2] S → NP * VBD
	[0:2] S → NP * VP
	[2:2] VP → * VBZ NN
	[2:2] VBZ → * likes
	[2:3] VBZ → likes *
	[2:3] VP → VBZ * NN
	[3:3] NN → * meat
	[3:4] NN → meat *
	[2:4] VP → VBZ NN *
	[0:4] S → NP VP *
		Predict *meat* apply the fundamental rule for meat as a noun (NN) and again to extend the active VP edge, to get VP -> VBZ NN *. Finally, use the fundamental rule to extend the active S edge, which is now complete.

Notes

1. Bottom-up chart parsing algorithms, as we discussed in Chapter 4, do have some advantages. For example, bottom-up methods can use rules annotated with probabilities or semantics, and then propagate values up from the leaf to the root for each subtree.

www.ingramcontent.com/pod-product-compliance
Lightning Source LLC
Chambersburg PA
CBHW041312240426
43669CB00023B/2968